Electoral Geography

Electoral Geography

Seema Jalan

RAWAT PUBLICATIONS
Jaipur • New Delhi • Bangalore • Guwahati • Kolkata

ISBN 978-81-316-0717-6

Published by

Prem Rawat for **Rawat Publications**
Satyam Apts, Sector 3, Jawahar Nagar, Jaipur 302 004 (India)
Phone: 0141 265 1748 / 7006 Fax: 0141 265 1748
E-mail: info@rawatbooks.com
Website: www.rawatbooks.com

New Delhi Office
4858/24, Ansari Road, Daryaganj, New Delhi 110 002
Phone: 011 2326 3290

Also at *Bangalore, Guwahati* and *Kolkata*

Typeset by Rawat Computers, Jaipur
Printed at Nice Printing Press, New Delhi

Contents

Preface

Electoral geography is relatively a very lately emerging field of research in geography and this too has sprouted as a subfield of political geography. Arising out of my experience initially as a research scholar for doctoral thesis followed by readings in the field I decided that young scholars embarking upon this hitherto unexplored field should be provided with the primary knowledge of major trends in research having emerged so far alongwith an exhaustive survey of works and further point out some potential areas for research. It is out of this urge that this book is seeing the light of the day. Here I attempt to briefly explain the meaning and evolution of electoral geography and also present a succinct summary of various approaches being adopted by different scholars in the field of research. Due attention has been paid in the identification of major socio-economic determinants in the Indian federal polity.

The book comprises a case study in electoral geography pertaining to north east Rajasthan consisting of 9 Lok Sabha constituencies and 72 Assembly constituencies at the time of conducting the study in 2007. Attempt has been made to briefly introduce the young scholars as how to carry out research through 'areal approach'. Chapter 2 provides a geographical background of the study area in terms of location, size, administrative configuration, spread over of Lok Sabha and Assembly constituencies, physiographic and climatic variations. Since an elector is the central point of the electoral system, population distribution and density have also been dealt with. Physiography and size of the constituency determines the frequency of the contact between the candidates and the electors as well as polling booth accessibility. Climate particularly the weather conditions during the period of elections also affect the movement of the electors ultimately resulting into high/low level of participation of the electors in the polling.

This chapter also discusses the rationale behind the research problem, objectives of the research work, basic hypothesis and methodology to complete the work.

Chapter 3 deals with the spatial distribution of electoral units in the study area and examines the disparities existing among the constituencies, both Assembly and Lok Sabha, with respect to their geographical area, size and density of electorate. Attempt has also been made to trace the geographical factors underlying spatial variations in electorate size and density.

Chapter 4 is focused on the trends and patterns of electoral participation in the study area. A comprehensive exercise encompassing identification of spatial patterns and temporal variations of voter turnout and explanation of these patterns in relation to the selected ecological voting determinants has been accomplished.

Chapter 5 provides an elaborate account of the major contemporary issues and salient features of manifestos of Congress and BJP for each election under study.

Chapter 6 examines the spatial patterns of election results with a view to identify the patterns of spatial distribution and temporal changes in electoral support for Congress and BJP so as to delineate areas of varying nature and consistency of support for both parties and further to investigate the broad nature of socio-economic base of each party.

The last chapter presents a summary of findings and inferential conclusions drawn on the basis of this study and further examines the extent to which the electoral characteristics of the study area conform to the hypotheses.

In the end all references and additional works have been incorporated in the bibliography for further readings. I hope the book to some extent will further the academic pursuits of the young scholars in this field. Suggestions from any corner for any improvement in the contents and quality of the book will receive hearty welcome.

Seema Jalan

Acknowledgement

This book has originated, albeit with enormous additions, from my research paper published in *The Geographer*, Vol. 56 (2) and my doctoral research work. The work has further been supplemented with my subsequent experience of conducting research and guiding doctoral research scholars in the field of electoral geography.

Grateful acknowledgement is made to The Geographical Society, Aligarh Muslim University, Aligarh for permission to reproduce some part of my research paper 'Status of Electoral Geography and Potential Areas of Research in India'. I express my deep sense of gratitude to Prof. H.S. Sharma, former Professor and Head, Department of Geography, University of Rajasthan, Jaipur who as a supervisor showered his scholarly guidance in completing my doctoral research work. I express my indebtedness to my husband Dr R.D. Gurjar, Professor and former Head, Department of Geography, University of Rajasthan, Jaipur for his valuable perennial guidance and ungrudging moral support throughout the production of this book.

I am thankful to Dr P.R. Binda, Cartographer for his valuable cartographic assistance. I express my thankfulness to all my friends who have generously helped me in this academic pursuit.

In the last but not the least heartfelt thanks is due to Rawat Publications without whose support this book would not have seen the light of the day.

Seema Jalan

List of Abbreviations

AIIC(S)	All India Indira Congress (Secular)
BJP	Bhartiya Janata Party
BSP	Bahujan Samaj Party
CPI	Communist Party of India
CPM	Communist Party of India (Marxist)
INC	Indian National Congress
IND	Independent
JD	Janata Dal
JP	Janata Party
LS	Lok Sabha Election
NF	National Front
RJD	Rashtriya Janata Dal
SAP	Samata Party
SC	Scheduled Caste
SJP	Samajwadi Janata Party
ST	Scheduled Tribe
VS	Vidhan Sabha Election

1 Electoral Geography: Nature, Scope and Approaches

Electoral geography is a relatively recent sprout of political geography which has come to be identified as an important subfield of political geography only since 1970s.

Electoral studies in geography are essentially concerned with the spatial and environmental aspects of processes of political decision-making. Traditionally, it was held that the role of election studies in political geography was merely to investigate the spatial variations in the distribution of votes cast in favour of or against a particular party/candidate or issue. But, besides the depiction of areal distribution of votes, an electoral geographer is equally concerned with other spatial aspects of political behaviour manifested in and through the outcome of elections.

Electoral geography gained strength after the widespread application of quantitative techniques in human geography in the late 1960s and 1970s, as the electoral data with their great mass of a really defined statistics offered unlimited opportunity for application of quantitative methodology, hypothesis building and testing and theory construction to political studies. At this time, geographers studying elections in a quantitative spatial mode assumed the title of political geographers simply by virtue of the fact that elections are a political phenomenon, and in geography the study of political phenomenon is the domain of political geography. In the late 1970s as the welfare approach set in the discipline, electoral geography became an integral part of political geography. With the change in disciplinary orientation towards the condition of man and justifiable distribution of public goods and services, elections assumed importance as (i) essential first step in gaining access to political power under liberal democracies and (ii) as the most critical element in the process of bringing about equity and social justice. The geographical studies of elections, with their primary focus on the study and analysis of the spatial aspects of political processes involved in achieving power at various levels – local, central and state – became key elements in understanding the role of governments as spatial allocators. 'The nature of government – the spatial bases of support to the ruling party – is the chief determinant in the "where" part of the central question "who gets what and where"? to which modern geographers in increasing numbers are addressing themselves' (Dikshit, 1995, p. 36).

Thus 'Electoral geography' is one of the main sources of fresh insights into the general field of human spatial behaviour (Golledge et al., 1972). Yet until recently it was a neglected aspect of our discipline. Now it is being realized that geography is profoundly affected by governments (Busteed, 1975, p. 54) since in the liberal democracies of the contemporary world, governments are the most effective geographical agents responsible for location of various phenomenon; and the governments, in most of the states, are chosen through elections. Geographers have now realized that 'their emphasis on spatial locations, distribution and interrelationships is particularly well suited to spatial organization of representative areas, the process of political information diffusion and electoral choice and spatial structure of behavioural patterns which result' (Prince and Smith, 1971). The voting responses vary from little to great support in favour of a candidate/issue or party from constituency to constituency or to a bigger political region. It is these variations which are of interest to an electoral geographer who traces out the geographical influences in voting patterns and voting behaviour. 'The geographer brings a characteristic emphasis on spatial location, distribution and spatial interrelationships to the study of electoral behaviour, aspect not normally considered by other disciplines' (Busteed, 1975, p. 3).

Nature of Electoral Studies in Geography

Traditionally, the thrust of electoral studies in geography was on the identification and analysis of areal distribution of votes cast in favour of a particular party, issue or candidate. With the gradual maturity of the field, the concern has widened to theory building with a process oriented perspective in the analysis of the spatial patterns of political behaviour manifested in and through the outcome of elections. Existing approaches in this field are grouped into two broad categories.

Conventional Approaches

Under this head, three main foci of geographical interest in electoral studies may be identified (after Taylor and Johnston, 1979 and Johnston et al., 1990):

Areal Approach

This traditional approach also termed as the 'geography of voting' was primarily concerned with the relationships between the total complex of physical and social environment of a region on one hand and the voting pattern on the other. In this approach, geographers focused on the temporal and spatial variations of voting aggregates and their association with social, economic and environmental variables. Thus these studies analyse the aggregate election data by means of areal association with a view to specify the significant environmental and socio-economic variables.

This traditional areal approach consisted of two main streams. One group of studies lay emphasis on spatial patterns of voting as depicted on maps and the second attempted to seek explanation to the voting patterns by comparing the voting map with maps of other phenomenon, physical as well as socio-economic. The first group of studies is known as 'areal-structural' and the second 'areal-ecological'.

(i) Areal-Structural Approach

This approach examined the spatial pattern and structure of voting choice as revealed by aggregate data of election results which include information regarding the size of electorate in each unit area, the number and percentage of electorate who actually cast their vote, votes polled by each party or candidate, size of majority of victorious candidate as well as proportion of invalid votes. Cartographic techniques, most commonly the choropleth method, are applied to portray the spatial distribution of various election phenomena. These areal cartographic techniques are extremely useful in delineating regions based on political ideological orientations and thereby in identifying areas of stress and strain in the given political system.

(ii) Areal-Ecological Approach

This stream concentrates on explanation of the spatial patterns of election results in terms of their total environmental context, i.e. their ecology. The researcher assumes that 'people will vote according to what they perceive to be their best interests. They then explored the characteristics of votes which might give clue to the nature of their self interest. The areal variations in social and economic class, religion, nationality and race were among the prime factors considered. Using such methods, political geographers seemed to explain the foundations of voting patterns, ... [and] to predict how patterns would change as franchise altered or migration occurred' (Prescott, 1972, p. 84).

Traditionally, the relationships between the spatial patterns of election results and those of selected socio-economic variables were examined through cartographic techniques of map overlay or visual comparison and visual areal correlation. Modern studies, since the 1960s, make use of statistical techniques in examining correlations between voting patterns and socio-economic variables. This method of analysis has been greatly benefited by the use of statistical techniques of inference, particularly by the use of various correlation techniques, which have proved highly valuable in testing hypothesis suggested by map comparisons. The most frequently used techniques are factor analysis and multiple regression analysis.

Spatial Behavioural Approach

Since late 1960s, following the mainstream of contemporary geographical research, the study of voting behaviour also witnessed a shift in emphasis from areal to spatial analysis and from stress on locational attributes to a greater concern for patterns of relative location and spatial interaction. As opposed to the traditional a-spatial approach wherein the voting behaviour was explained strictly as a function of within areal unit economic and social characteristics and the spatial relationships of areal units with one another and the impact of such spatial relationships upon voting behaviour was ignored; more emphasis is laid on the measurement and analysis of such key spatial variables as distance, directional orientation, connectivity and contextual or neighbourhood effect, in the recent spatial behavioural studies. Therefore, in these studies, individual voting behaviour is viewed as the result of not only individual's particular characteristics (or the ecological variables with regard to areal units), but also of his inclusion within a distinct geographical milieu. More emphasis is on investigation of how the factors like distance-biased interpersonal relationships, residential relocation, barriers to spatial interaction are effective in shaping voting response surfaces. Therefore the main focus is on influences of spatial contagion and diffusion of politically relevant information on electoral behavioural pattern.

In Indian context, the ecological studies are found more effective because in India, 'decisions about voting are more often made by groups rather than individuals' (Sharma, 1982, p. 10). 'In the Indian political context individual is seldom the "decision maker" although it is he who slips the paper down into the ballot box. There is a lot to be said in favour of adopting household, village, caste, tribe or some such aggregate of individuals as the decision-making unit' (Das Gupta and Morris-Jones,

1975, p. 352). It is for this reason that this research design has been prepared using areal-structural and areal-ecological approach.

Geography of Representation

Besides the *de facto* organization of voters, *de jure* organization of electoral districts termed as constituencies form the organizational framework of elections and sends the representatives to the parliament or a state assembly. The location of constituency boundaries markedly influences the political complexion of the districts and as a result the complexion of political representation. In this backdrop geographers are keenly interested in evaluating the objectivity or bias in location of electoral boundaries which are major determinants of overall election results.

Non-Conventional Approaches

Geography of Representative Behaviour

The purpose of an election is to allocate power. Similar to influences on voting and representation, geographical underpinnings influence the allocation of power. This approach focuses on the roles and performances of the elected representatives in relation to their respective electorate. 'Such a concern with the outputs of the electoral process is unusual among geographers but is very crucial if the value of the geographical study of whole political system has to be demonstrated' (Cox, 1976 cited in Taylor and Johnston, 1979). The concern is with the level of control over the political decision-making which is allocated to elected representatives. Newton (1976) has typified six such role orientations of representatives:

1. *Delegates or Trustees*: Delegates act in a predetermined way in accordance with the policies debated before the constituents prior to the election. Contrarily, Trustees are members who once elected are free to take decisions on issues at the moment irrespective of the issues discussed during the election campaign.
2. *Party Members or Individuals*: Most of the elections members are successful because of their association with a political party whose backing assures their return to the House. Once elected a party member remains loyal to the party whereas an individual uses personal judgement and may also vote against the party in favour of interests of the electorate.
3. *Local or Territorial Representatives*: Do the elected members own responsibility towards only the localized pockets of their support

or do they have a wider responsibility to the entire electorate whom the House represents?

4. *Policy Makers or Errand Boys*: Policy makers are the representatives who play their main role in the policy making process for the electorate as a whole. Errand boys act as intermediaries between electors and government, as problem solvers for individuals. There may not exist overt localism in the errand boy functions.
5. *Legislative Specialist or Generalist*: Legislative generalists are members who command a detailed knowledge of the entire range of administrative functions under the jurisdiction of the modern state. Legislative specialists are members who specialize, through training or experience, in a particular area of administration which may or may not be of relevance to their constituency.
6. *Independent or Subject to Pressure Groups*: Members may draw support from certain pressure groups which in turn ensure that their sectional interests are protected in the legislatures.

These six different representation role orientations underline twin functions of elected members – representation of electors and formation of governments. An electoral geographer is interested in the relationship between types of representational roles and the geography of representation. The type of representational role of elected candidates is influenced by how the representatives feel they should behave, what they believe their voters expect of them and the importance of courting electors' favours in order to retain power. The representatives' behaviour can be explained in terms of the operational type of electoral system, type of constituency which they represent (safe or marginal) and their youth and experience.

Geography of Power

A decisive implication of geography of representative behaviour is the geography of power. In order to ensure the role of the government strong enough to legislate widely, it is imperative that the party in power should be broadly based in terms of the electorate or parts of country that it represents. The class bias of various parties and spatial segregation of these classes makes equal representation of various parts very difficult. Especially, plurality systems with single member constituencies often give governmental power to a party which has not obtained most votes and is supported only by minority of the total electorate, although it may have obtained more votes than any other party. This representational bias inevitably leads to spatial bias during formulation of policies and distribution of patronage by the government.

Ideology of Place

Reynolds (1990) has noted that till 1970 the standard approach followed in explaining geographies of voting have followed the Social Cleavage model. Thrift (1983) has termed this approach as 'compositional' approach wherein a person's partisan attitudes are viewed as a function of her position in a division of labour, with the result that 'knowledge of society's cleavage structure is considered sufficient to provide excellent predictions of voting behaviour'. Reynolds advocates a more 'contextual' (place-specific) research design and approach.

Agnew (1990) maintains that electoral geography needs to shift its focus from psychology of individual voters and their census attributes to the history of places and parties, since 'national social categories are neither empirically appropriate nor theoretically coherent as causes of individual voting behaviour. All places have their own history, "external" links and peculiar traditions. Consequently *places* are the social contexts in which political expression is determined'. Hence the local/regional influences in moulding peoples' attitudes in particular place need to be studied.

Geography of Political Parties

Dikshit (1995) observes that owing to its overemphasis on division of labour and class conflict and on national level cleavages as the chief determinant of political party programmes, electoral geography often loses touch with the ground realities of electoral politics. Political parties are not frozen entities. Once created, they continuously evolve while transforming their policies and programmes to match the aspirations of their supporters as the society readjusts its ideologies with changing times. Hence focus should be placed on contextual analysis of historical evolution and geography of political parties to identify cores and peripheries of their electoral support. This would require in-depth analysis of party performance in typical constituencies in relation to the geography of organization and electoral mobilization exhibited by political parties.

Concept of Political System

It is often realized that electoral geography has remained an uncoordinated and isolated discipline wherein 'elections are treated as an end in themselves, the actual purpose of election – the producing of legislatures and governments – has been largely forgotten' (Taylor, 1989). The solution lies in finding a synthetic framework to integrate studies on the three major themes – geography of voting, geographical influences in voting and geography of representation – in a coherent overstructure. Easton (1965) has developed the concept of Political System wherein he has divided the entire political process into four elements – input, throughput, output and feedback. In this system, framework geography of voting and geographical influences in voting were seen as input to the electoral system, geography of representation has been seen as a throughput and geographical patterns resulting from resulting governments as output. Feedback loops between input and output round the system and represent the mechanisms by which the elected representatives ensure that their area is well treated by the government so that the constituents repay them by rendering their support in the next election (Figure 1.1).

Figure 1.1

Political System

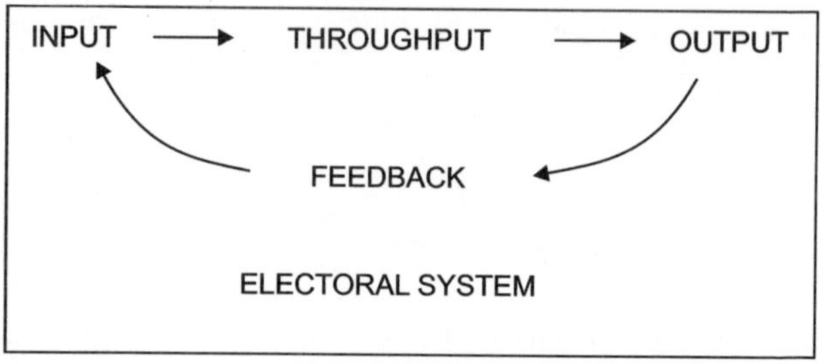

This overarching concept of political system provides electoral studies in geography a wider purpose and focus.

Regulation Oriented Studies

Clark (cited in Johnston et al., 1990) has pointed out another crucial aspect – *geography of the integrity of electoral processes* which has been practically ignored till now. The value of an electoral outcome is intimately related to the election procedures. Hence focus is on the conduct of elections. It includes the regulation of campaigns, regulation of the conduct of elections and regulation of electioneering activities.

A fair electoral process is thought to be an essential ingredient for a just society and as indicative of vitality of democracy. Voter fraud, coercion of voters, booth capturing (some of the many nefarious possibilities) are taken to be serious violations of the ideals and ideology of democracy, even if election outcomes were to be consistent with voter's expectations. If these violations become so widespread that they threaten the very integrity of the electoral process, counting outcomes may be simply a cynical exercise in power and domination. Clark further emphasizes that a broader and more mature electoral geography should integrate these considerations with an appreciation of the regulation of elections. Integrating these aspects will make electoral geography not only broader but also of more consequence for public policy.

Studies in Electoral Geography: Global Perspective

The school of geographical study of elections owes its inception to the pioneer work by Andre Siegfried in 1913, a French geographer, called as the 'Father of Electoral Geography'. His lead was followed in other parts of Europe and the United States and notable contributions were made by Krehbiel (1916), Sauer (1918), Paullin (1932), Wright (1932), Dean (1949), Crisler (1952) and Smith and Hart (1955). In all these studies, geographers concentrated on the temporal and spatial variations of voting aggregates and their association with environmental, social and economic variables. Krehbeil studied British elections and analysed the spatial variations in voting in Great Britain from 1885 to 1910. Rice (1928) in his book *Quantitative Methods in Politics* pioneered a scientific approach to voting analysis wherein a hypothesis is stated and then tested through statistical analysis. Paullin (1932) prepared an 'Atlas of the Historical Geography of the United States' which included a number of maps of voting results portraying the voting trends. Harold Gosnell and Norman Gill (1935) analysed voting in Chicago using correlation and factor analysis techniques. Siegfried (1949) made another significant contribution to the areal-ecological stream through his work, *Geography of Voting in Ardeche Region, France*. He insisted that there was a close correspondence between the nature of the soil, agrarian landscape, type of dwelling, distribution of land ownership, degree of stratification of the society, traditions and political orientation. He identified these aspects of social and economic milieu most likely to underlie the voting decisions and traced those aspects to the physical environment. All the above studied were based on ecological cartographic techniques in which the ecological and voting patterns were correlated through map comparison and visual correlation. Commendable effort in this line was also made by Lewis (1965) who studied the voting behaviour of Flint (Michigan) analysing the relationship between income and Republican voting, Negro population and democratic voting using choropleths and isopleths.

Since 1960s, interpretation of ecological correlations by cartographic methods has been replaced by use of statistical techniques of inference. Lloyd Haring (1959) analysed voting in Tennesse using the multiple regression statistical technique. Roberts and Rummage (1965) used multiple regression with residuals in examining the relationship between labour vote in Britain in 1951 and eleven socio-economic variables selected from 1951 census. Other major works were of Birdsall (1969), Cox (1968a), Brunn et al. (1969), McPhail (1970) who used factor models.

Since late 1960s, emphasis shifted from areal to spatial analysis and 'Spatial Behavioural' studies of voting behaviour received focal attention. Credit of premier work goes to Cox who wrote a series of articles (1968a, 1969a, 1969b, 1971) exploring the spatial influences on voting behaviour. Cox accomplished the most extensive work on the role of neighbourhood and spatial diffusion of political influences on voting. D.R. Reynolds (1974), also made substantive contribution to the school of spatial modelling of electoral behaviour. The research procedures for analysing of electoral behaviour have been standardized in *Geography and Voting Behaviour* by M.A. Busteed (1975) and *Geography of Elections* by P.J. Taylor and R.J. Johnston (1979).

The edited volume *Developments in Electoral Geography* by R.J. Johnston, F.M. Shelley and P.J. Taylor (1990) is a compilation of a series of articles on intellectual development of electoral geography since 1960s; case studies of elections in the countries where the analysis follow the modernization-nationalization tradition of the Lipset and Rokkan social cleavage model; and which suggest new directions for future researches in electoral geography. The validity of inferences drawn from aggregate data analysis has always been a debatable issue in this discipline. Gary King (1997) in *A Solution to the Ecological Inference Problem: Reconstructing Individual Behaviour from Aggregate Data* has extensively discussed the nature of the ecological inference problem and has criticized the past approaches followed by the researchers pointing out their shortcomings. He has constructed a model that remedifies those ills and thereby allows individual behaviour to be inferred from aggregate data.

Indian Socio-Political System and Implications on Election Studies

Elections form the essence of the parliamentary democratic political system in India. Under a liberal democratic setup a single member pluralistic election system returns representatives of people at various levels – Lok Sabha at the Centre, State Legislative Assemblies at the state level, the local bodies like the three-tiered Panchayati Raj system in the rural areas and Municipal bodies in urban areas at the grassroot level. Within the prescribed number of seats in the respective houses seats have been reserved for weaker sections of the population – Scheduled Castes (SCs), Scheduled Tribes (STs) and women candidates. One level of election is inextricably related to other level of election. As a whole this constitutes a network of election politics in contemporary India and is the basic framework of India's democratic regime (Kondo, 2007).

There are several peculiar elements which are characteristic of Indian socio-political milieu. They provide justification for a distinctive orientation in Indian election studies. Some of them have been briefly stated as under:

Evolutionary Change in Nature of Party System (Single Party Dominance to Cleavage Based Multi-party Coalition System)

Indian party system has witnessed drastic changes in its nature and configuration within the short post-independence span of 63 years. Broadly, three phases may be identified:

1. 1947–67: This phase was marked by a stable 'Congress-centred' one party dominant system.
2. 1967–late 1980s: This phase has been a period of transformation characterized by destabilization of the Congress system wherein, for the first time, possibility of dethroning the ruling party was realized. Amidst resurgence and increased political awareness among the downtrodden classes – the SCs, STs and Other Backward Castes (OBCs) – coupled with high social conflicts and political turmoil this period witnessed high political instability and a decline in the ruling party's ability to govern.
3. 1990 onwards: This phase is characterized by the disappearance of Congress System and emergence of a social cleavage based multi-party system, growth and empowerment of regional ethnic parties, frequent changes in ruling parties and coalition politics.

Predominance of Caste Considerations in Political Decision-Making

Several studies have held that in India caste and religion are the most important determinants of party support (Chibber, 1999). Economic class determines voter decisions to a lesser degree whereas social attributes like education are relatively unimportant in determining voter party preferences at both national and state level. Hence the social bases of parties are distinguished by caste, religion and class. These social cleavages have been instrumental in the rise and empowerment of regional ethnic based parties.

Patronage Based Character of Indian Democracy

Last two decades in the country's electoral politics have been marked by phenomenal emergence of ethnic parties at both levels of elections, the growth of which is rooted in the patronage based character of Indian democracy. Chandra (2004) has observed that 'voters expect co-ethnic elites of the party to favour them in the distribution of benefits; elites expect co-ethnic voters to favour them in the distribution of votes under the condition of limited information and ethnic favouritism. This is a self-enforcing and re-inforcing equilibrium'.

Corrupt Practices in Elections

Numerous cases of corrupt practices in the election process as booth capturing, violence or intimidation against weaker sections of the people, provocation and exploitation of communal sentiments, distribution of money among the electorate have often been reported during the elections. The power of Central Election Commission is by and large strong enough to contain major incidents related to these corrupt practices. Nevertheless few such incidents occur which question the sanctity of the election process and the reliability of the aggregate election statistics.

Heterogeneity in Social and Economic Structure

India is a highly heterogeneous and fragmented society. Besides social cleavages based on caste and religion states have distinctive character in terms of language, socio-cultural traditions, economic activities and other such variables. Consequently 'state' as a unit of integrated polity based on common social and cultural traditions has become a significant variable prescribing voting behaviour as a whole including electoral participation as well as party preferences. This necessitates statewise contextual studies for understanding patterns of voter mobilization and electoral preferences. Ecological studies based on aggregate data may fail to reveal the impact of aforesaid variables fully hence there is a need to supplement and verify the conclusions with information collected through case studies and individual based surveys.

Predominant Influence of Candidates as Compared to Ideology and Issues

Voting choice in India is highly influenced by voters' identification with leadership or an individual candidate. The high proportion of independents returning to the respective houses particularly in state level elections and increasing incidents of defection in major parties indicate the influence of personality bias in voting decisions. Party loyalty or caste loyalty outweighs socio-economic attributes such as occupation, age, income, literacy status, etc. Issues – national or international – usually are of lesser importance as compared to issues relating to daily life of the people like rising prices and unemployment except some extraordinary cases as in case of Babri Masjid or assassination of Indira Gandhi. Moreover in India voting decisions are more often made by groups. Household, village, caste, tribe or some such aggregate is often the decision-making unit rather than an individual (Das Gupta and Morris-Jones, 1975).

Shifting Voter Loyalties

An interesting feature of the electoral behaviour in India is the 'split-vote', i.e. differential preferences at different levels of election. Voters may divide his votes into vote for one party to the State Legislative assembly and to another party in the Lok Sabha. Dikshit and Sharma (1993) and Jalan (2006b) in their case studies of Haryana and Rajasthan respectively have found that voter preferences are guided by varying considerations at the two levels of elections which lead to support for different parties in the two sets of electoral contests. Decisions for national level elections have been found to be relatively more secular in nature whereas local level caste and other socio-economic-ethnic conflicts, local issues, personal likes or dislikes and identification with the candidate play greater role in decision-making in state level elections.

Rising Aspirations of Voters

In the last two decades Indian politics has witnessed fluctuating support surfaces of political parties which underline fluctuating voter choices between successive elections. At both levels state as well as national a strong anti-incumbency factor has resulted in complete sway against the ruling party (for example, 1989 Lok Sabha and 1998 Assembly elections in Rajasthan). On one hand this is indicative of the increasing political awareness of the electorate in that the voters evaluate the performance of the ruling government and employ the elections as an opportunity to penalize the ruling party if they fail to fulfill their promises made in the preceding election manifestos. Keeping in view the caste driven and candidate oriented trends of political choice may be considered as maturing democratic decision-making. On the other hand this may also be taken as increased bargaining power of the electorate which may impede a rational legislative functioning of the ruling government and rather resort to appeasement policies. This necessitates an intensive exploration and analysis of the factors underlying these trends in voter behaviour and resultant impacts on democratic governance and development patterns.

Studies in Electoral Geography in India

The trends and directions of studies in electoral geography in India have largely followed evolution of actual electoral politics, especially those of Lok Sabha and the State Legislative Assembly elections. The theoretical developments in election studies in the developed countries especially the United States has had considerable impact in determining the major research questions. Study of voting behaviour, party support surfaces, issues, candidates, social cleavages, voter behaviour with regard to socio-economic status/minority/backward sections of the society have been the major thrust areas of research in India.

In India, study in the field of electoral geography began in 1960s. For a long period, the research in Indian elections was done primarily by political scientists and sociologists. Among the non-geographers, substantial work in Indian election studies has been done by Iqbal Narain in early 1970s. Premier studies in the field of Indian electoral geography were made by K.Z. Amani who dealt with a number of aspects of Indian elections in his four articles published in 1970, 1972, 1973 and 1974. He examined the regional pattern of voting results in Haryana (1970); spatial pattern of voting results in UP during Parliamentary elections in 1967 and 1971 (1972) and in 1973, published another article 'Electoral Geography and Indian Elections' in which he focused on the mechanism of Indian elections and suggested directions for future research. In 1971, B.L. Sukhwal in his book, *India: A Political Geography* discussed the changing political patterns in India since Independence till 1967 Lok Sabha and Assembly elections and also explained the physical and economic base of Indian Republic along with boundary problems and external relations. Other notable contributions at this time were made by Chandidas (1971, p. 72), Varma and Narain (1973) and Brass (1975, 1978). Chandidas in his article 'Poll Participation Slump' examined the trends of voter turnout between 1967 and 1971 elections and the relationship between intensity of interparty competition and socio-economic variables with voter turnout. Varma and Narain (1978) discussed the voting behaviour in Rajasthan in specific context of demographic and socio-economic characteristics. An excellent collection of articles was brought out in the four edited volumes: *Studies in Electoral Politics in Indian States (SEPIS)* by Myron

Weiner and J.O. Field between 1974 and 1977 which dealt with several aspects of Indian political behaviour. *Vol. 1: The Communist Parties of West Bengal* (1974) by John O. Field and Marcus F. Franda (1974) analysed the presence, performance, vote trends and dependability of support of the communist parties in Bengal from 1967 to 1972. *Vol. II: Three Disadvantaged Sectors* (1975a) had contributions by Jagdish N. Bhagwati, Padma Desai, John O. Field, William L. Ritchter and Myron Weiner. *Vol. III: The Impact of Modernization* (1977) had contributions by John O. Field, Francine Frankel, Mary F. Katzensteins and Myron Weiner and *Vol. IV: Party Systems and Cleavages* (1975b) consisted of contributions by M.R. Barnett, Craig Baxter, Paul R. Brass, R. Hammond, R.L. Hardgrave Jr. and Glynn Wood.

Paul R. Brass (1978) in 'Indian Election Studies' underlined the viability of ecological approach in Indian election studies over opinion surveys and discussed the ways in which the problems of ecological analysis can be handled in relation to Indian election studies. Harry W. Blair (1979) attempted to provide an explanation of several statistical approaches for quantitative aggregate analysis of South Asian Elections and also shed light on a number of socio-economic aspects of voting behaviour, viz. examining the role of caste in political mobilization of people with special reference to Bihar, electoral role of Muslim Community in Bihar, impact of rural development programmes on level of rural electoral participation. The book also expounded a number of ways to overcome the problem of matching census and electoral data. Other significant contributions of this period include those of Das Gupta and Morris-Jones (1978), C.P. Singh (1978, 1980, 1981a, 1981b), R.P. Singh (1981), Srivastava (1982).

R.D. Dikshit (1980) examined the content and scope of electoral geography as a part of political geography and advocated that electoral geography formed an applied part of political geography. R.D. Dikshit and J.C. Sharma have individually and together contributed a number of articles (1980, 1981, 1982, 1983) which have greatly enriched the studies of electoral geography in India. Dikshit and Sharma (1981) presented a detailed discourse on choice of a suitable unit of analysis so as to relate the socio-economic data of census units to the electoral data of the constituencies and to meet the requirement of consistency of boundaries for a time series analysis. Two more articles published in 1982 and 1983 were related to ecological analyses of electoral performance of the Congress party in assembly elections from 1952 to 1977 in Punjab and voter turnout in Punjab between 1967 and 1980.

J.C. Sharma (1982) published an article with a detailed discussion on methodology and approaches suited to election studies in Indian context.

Dikshit and Giri (1983, p. 84) examined the changing nature of spatial patterns of the parliamentary voting results in India from 1951 to 1982. They also studied the changing concepts and objectives of electoral geography in the light of new methodological innovations in the field. Hussain and Mir (1984) identified the voting determinants for 1983 Assembly elections in Jammu and Kashmir. Other works include those of Sinha (1985), Dikshit (1988), Dikshit and Sharma (1993), Dikshit (1993), Tripathy (1994), Kaswan and Verma (2002) and Sharma and Chand (2004). Dikshit (1988) carried out areal ecological analysis of spatial pattern of electoral participation during 1982 assembly elections in Haryana. Dikshit and Sharma (1993) examined the differential electoral behaviour at different levels of electoral contest during four pairs of successive assembly and parliamentary elections in Haryana. Tripathy and Padhy (1994) have examined the voting behaviour of tribals in India with special reference to Odisha. *Geography of Elections*, an edited volume by R.D. Dikshit (1995) comprises of excellent compilation of articles related to the nature, scope and development of the discipline; recent intellectual developments in the field; key methodological issues and lines of future research in the discipline with selected case studies from India. Srikant Dixit (2004) has classified the geographical influences on voting decisions of the electorate as socio-economic, political and ecological and asserts that in Indian context social determinants are more important than others.

Election studies dealing with geographical analysis of electoral phenomenon in Rajasthan have so far been few. R.D. Gupta (1985) has analysed various aspects of electoral phenomenon, viz. voter participation, party performances, female participation between 1967 and 1980 assembly elections in Rajasthan using ecological approach. Kuldeep Sharma (1990) has analysed the performance of Congress-I in Rajasthan Assembly election during the period between 1977 and 1985. Sudhir Bansal (1992) has carried out a comparative analysis of spatial patterns of voting behaviour during Assembly and Lok Sabha elections held between 1980 and 1985. Jalan and Gurjar (2002) have endeavoured to identify spatial patterns of electoral participation in north east Rajasthan. Jalan (2006a) has examined the electoral performance of political parties in a federal system. Jalan (2006b) has also underlined this shift in voting preferences of electors Lok Sabha vis-à-vis Assembly elections within a short period of time. She has arrived at the conclusion that the electoral preferences are conditioned by different sets of considerations at different level of elections.

There have been very few attempts to explore the remaining objectives or perspectives – the 'geographical influences in voting' or 'geography of representation'. These are more or less grossly neglected areas in Indian electoral studies. A pioneering attempt at investigation of 'Friends and Neighbours' influence has been made by Dikshit and Singh (1993) for a parliamentary constituency in Haryana. Likewise with a convenient presumption of a robust and fair redistricting process under the aegis of an independent Delimitation Commission in India (Dikshit, 1995; Singh, 2000) very little attention has so far been paid to assess the fairness of constituency boundaries and their impact on election outcomes. J.C. Sharma (2003) has revealed gross violation of procedures (Gerrymandering) laid for delimitation of constituencies in the Delimitation Act 2002 for some assembly and parliamentary constituencies in Himachal Pradesh. Although he does not hold this bias to be necessarily intentional, but the case study is a pacesetter as it breaks the myth of unquestionable procedure of electoral districting in the country and underlines the need for comprehensive nationwide evaluation of constituency boundaries at both levels.

Significant work has also been done in the field of analysis of voting behaviour of particular sections of the society – the backward classes, tribals, minorities or specific communities (Khan, 1969, 1971; Weiner and Field, 1974, 1975a, 1975b, 1977; Blair, 1979; Tripathy and Padhy, 1994; Dikshit, 1995). But such studies are few, isolated and scattered dealing with a particular point in time and to a particular state or constituency at a time, or nation as a whole. A chronological analysis with a wider spatial perspective covering several regions with different social fabric and interlinked studies at different levels of elections can only help in precise theorization of voting behaviour of these sections of population.

It has been observed that enriched with a defined scope and standardized methodology, potential for data based spatial analysis of organized space from a positivist perspective and easy availability of up to date electoral database, the subject attracted substantial research in Indian universities as a theme for doctoral theses over the years. Ironically, the increase in quantity was accompanied by a decline in quality (Dikshit, 1995). The applied research of social utility in this field has not been accomplished to a significant extent. Meaningful and enriching theoretical discussions have been few and therefore the sub-discipline has not kept pace with the contemporary conceptual developments.

2 Understanding North East Rajasthan

Undoubtedly, the electoral system is conditioned broadly by the size and shape of the electoral constituencies, the physiographic favourability and hostility, the climatic particularly the weather conditions during the election process, the polling booth accessibility, socio-economic structure and density of the electors among other large number of factors. This chapter is intended for developing and understanding of broad geographical setup in the region.

Location and Administrative Configuration

North east Rajasthan extends from 25E41' N to 28E31'N latitude and 74E44' E to 78E17' E longitude and comprises of 10 districts, namely Jhunjhunu, Sikar, Jaipur, Alwar, Bharatpur, Dholpur, Karauli, Sawai Madhopur, Tonk and Dausa and a part of Ajmer district (Figure 2.1). The total area of the study region being 61,783.24 sq. km, located in the north-eastern part of the State of Rajasthan, covers 18.05 per cent of the total area of the State. This comprises nine Lok Sabha constituencies out of 25 Lok Sabha constituencies in the State, namely Sikar, Jhunjhunu, Jaipur, Tonk, Alwar, Bharatpur, Bayana, Sawai Madhopur and Dausa (Table 2.1A). Each parliamentary constituency comprises of eight assembly segments thus 72 assembly constituencies of north east Rajasthan are included in the present study. Out of these 72 assembly constituencies, 71 form part of Jhunjhunu, Sikar, Jaipur, Alwar, Bharatpur, Dholpur, Karauli, Sawai Madhopur, Tonk and Dausa districts. Only Kekri assembly constituency, a segment of Tonk parliamentary constituency is an exception which administratively forms part of Ajmer district. The present study deals with the election years 1991, 1993 and1998 during which Lok Sabha and Assembly constituencies in the State have not undergone any change and follows the seventh delimitation of 1976.[1]

Figure 2.1

Lok Sabha and Assembly Constituencies in North East Rajasthan (1976–2008)

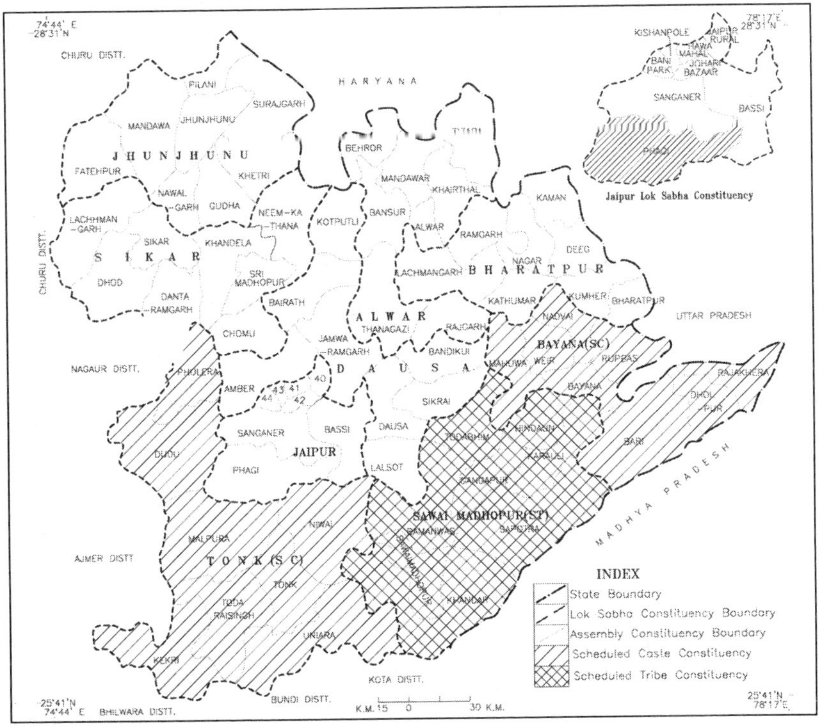

Table 2.1 *Lok Sabha Constituencies and Districtwise Distribution of their Assembly Segments in 1989, 1991 and 1998 (North East Rajasthan)*

A: 1989

No.	*Lok Sabha Constituency*	*Districts and Assembly Segments*					
		District	*No. of Assembly Segments*	*District*	*No. of Assembly Segments*	*District*	*No. of Assembly Segments*
4	Jhunjhunu	Jhunjhunu	7	Sikar	1	—	—
5	Sikar	Sikar	7	Jaipur	1	—	—
6	Jaipur	Jaipur	8	—	—	—	—
7	Dausa	Jaipur	8	—	—	—	—
8	Alwar	Alwar	8	—	—	—	—

Cont'd...

...Cont'd

9	Bharatpur	Bharatpur	5	Alwar	3	—	—
10	Bayana (SC)	Bharatpur	4	Dholpur	3	Sawai Madhopur	1
11	Sawai Madhopur (ST)	Sawai Madhopur	8	—	—	—	—
12	Tonk (SC)	Tonk	5	Jaipur	2	Ajmer	1

B: 1991

No.	Lok Sabha Constituency	Districts and Assembly Segments					
		District	*No. of Assembly Segments*	*District*	*No. of Assembly Segments*	*District*	*No. of Assembly Segments*
4	Jhunjhunu	Jhunjhunu	7	Sikar	1	—	—
5	Sikar	Sikar	7	Jaipur	1	—	—
6	Jaipur	Jaipur	8	—	—	—	—
7	Dausa	Jaipur	4	Dausa	4	—	—
8	Alwar	Alwar	8	—	—	—	—
9	Bharatpur	Bharatpur	5	Alwar	3	—	—
10	Bayana(SC)	Bharatpur	4	Dholpur	3	Sawai Madhopur	1
11	Sawai Madhopur (ST)	Sawai Madhopur	8	—	—	—	—
12	Tonk (SC)	Tonk	5	Jaipur	2	Ajmer	1

There was no change in 1993.

C: 1998

No.	Lok Sabha Constituency	Districts and Assembly Segments					
		District	*No. of Assembly Segments*	*District*	*No. of Assembly Segments*	*District*	*No. of Assembly Segments*
4	Jhunjhunu	Jhunjhunu	7	Sikar	1	—	—
5	Sikar	Sikar	7	Jaipur	1	—	—
6	Jaipur	Jaipur	8	—	—	—	—

Cont'd...

...Cont'd

7	Dausa	Jaipur	4	Dausa	4	—	—
8	Alwar	Alwar	8	—	—	—	—
9	Bharatpur	Bharatpur	5	Alwar	3	—	—
10	Bayana(SC)	Bharatpur	4	Dholpur	3	Sawai Madhopur	1
11	Sawai Madhopur (ST)	Sawai Madhopur	4	Karauli	4	—	—
12	Tonk (SC)	Tonk	5	Jaipur	2	Ajmer	1

Subsequently five new districts have been created in the State in the years 1991 and 1998. In 1990, there were 27 districts in the State which increased to 32 in 1997. Three districts, Baran, Rajsamand and Dausa were created in 1991. Hanumangarh came into existence in 1994. Out of the districts included in the study area, Dausa district which was formerly a part of Jaipur district was newly formed in April 1991 comprising of four assembly segments namely Lalsot (ST), Sikrai (ST), Dausa (SC) and Bandikui (Table 2.1B). Subsequently, in 1997 Karauli district was created (which was formerly a part of Sawai Madhopur district) with four assembly segments namely Karauli, Sapotra (ST), Hindaun (SC) and Todabhim (ST) (Table 2.1C). Thus during the election years from 1991–98, although there was no change in the number and nature of parliamentary and assembly constituencies, the administrative configuration of assembly constituencies was altered due to creation of two new districts.

As a normal principle being adopted in the delimitation of electoral constituencies, an assembly constituency lies within one district. But in the present study two constituencies namely Bayana and Mahuwa are exception to it. Bayana assembly constituency spreads over two districts. Out of total 189 polling stations 115 lay in Bharatpur district and 74 lay in Dholpur district. Similarly out of total 185 polling stations of Mahuwa assembly constituency during the Lok Sabha elections 1998, 147 belonged to Dausa district and 38 belonged to newly formed Karauli district.

Reserved Constituencies

Out of nine Lok Sabha constituencies, three are reserved constituencies. Bayana and Tonk are reserved for SCs and Sawai Madhopur is reserved for STs. Out of the 72 assembly constituencies, 13 are reserved for SC candidates and six are reserved for ST candidates. The location and nature of the various parliamentary constituencies and constituent assembly segments in 1997 have been shown in Table 2.2 and Figure 2.1. Figure 2.2 illustrates the districtwise distribution and nature of the assembly constituencies. Table 2.3 indicates the two assembly spreading over two districts.

Table 2.2 *Districts, Lok Sabha Constituencies and Assembly Segments in North East Rajasthan in 1997 (as per Delimitation of 1976)*

No.	*Name of Lok Sabha Constituency*	*District and Assembly Segments Involved*			
		District	*Assembly Segments*		*No. of Assembly Segments*
			No.	*Name*	
4	Jhunjhunu	Jhunjhunu	23	Pilani	
			24	Surajgarh (SC)	
			25	Khetri	
			26	Gudha	
			27	Nawalgarh	
			28	Jhunjhunu	
			29	Mandawa	7
		Sikar	30	Fatehpur	1
5	Sikar	Sikar	31	Lachhmangarh (SC)	
			32	Sikar	
			33	Dhod	
			34	Danta Ramgarh	
			35	Sri Madhopur	
			36	Khandela	
			37	Neem-ka-Thana	7
		Jaipur	38	Chomu	1
6	Jaipur	Jaipur	40	Jaipur Rural	
			41	Hawa Mahal	
			42	Johari Bazaar	
			43	Kishanpole	
			44	Banipark	
			47	Sanganer	
			48	Phagi	
			53	Bassi	8
7	Dausa	Jaipur	39	Amber	
			54	Jamwa Ramgarh	
			55	Bairath	
			56	Kotputli	4
		Dausa	49	Lalsot (ST)	

Cont'd...

...Cont'd

			50	Sikrai (ST)	
			51	Bandikui	
			52	Dausa (SC)	4
8	Alwar	Alwar	57	Bansur	
			58	Behror	
			59	Mandawar	
			60	Tizara	
			61	Khairthal (SC)	
			63	Alwar	
			64	Thanagazi	
			65	Rajgarh (ST)	8
9	Bharatpur	Alwar	62	Ramgarh	
			66	Lachhmangarh	
			67	Kathumar (SC)	3
		Bharatpur	68	Kaman	
			69	Nagar	
			70	Deeg	
			71	Kumher	
			72	Bharatpur	5
10	Bayana (SC)	Bharatpur	73	Rupbas (SC)	
			74	Nadbai	
			75	Weir (SC)	
			76	Bayana (SC)	4
		Dholpur	77	Rajakhera	
			78	Dholpur	
			79	Bari	3
		Dausa	87	Mahuwa	1
11.	Sawai Madhopur	Sawai Madhopur	82	Khandar (SC)	
			83	Sawai Madhopur	
			84	Bamanwas (ST)	
			85	Gangapur	4
		Karauli	80	Karauli	
			81	Sapotra (ST)	
			86	Hindaun (SC)	
			88	Todabhim (ST)	4
12	Tonk (SC)	Tonk	89	Niwai (SC)	
			90	Tonk	
			91	Uniara	

Cont'd...

...Cont'd

		92	Toda Rai Singh	
		93	Malpura	5
	Jaipur	45	Phulera	
		46	Dudu	2
	Ajmer	102	Kekri (SC)	1

Table 2.3 *Assembly Segments Divided in Two or More Districts*

Lok Sabha Constituency	*Assembly Segment*	*District*	*Polling Stations*	*Total Polling Stations*
Bayana(SC)	76 Bayana (SC)	Bharatpur	115	189
	87 Mahuwa	Dholpur	74	185

Figure 2.2

Districtwise Distribution of Assembly Constituencies in North East Rajasthan (1976–2008)

Physiography

Rajasthan, the land of lofty hills and shifting sand dunes; scorching heat and freezing cold; fertile plain and rugged ravines, is a region of highly varied topography. Geologically the area represents varied facies of rocks ranging from Precambrian to present day alluvium. The crustal part of the region is formed by the Precambrian rocks of Proterozoic era – mostly of middle and upper Proterozoic era whereas unconsolidated sands and alluvium are quaternary in origin. The area is also characterized by the post Delhi intrusives and extrusives. The State has a mature topography, evolved by the denudational processes over a geologically long period of time. Undoubtedly, the present landscape is the product of fluvio-aeolian cycles of erosion which have been in operation since Precambrian era interrupted by Vindhyan tectonics in the south east parts (Sawai Madhopur and Dholpur districts).

The Aravalli range divides the State into two broad divisions:

1. The desert in the west and north west, comprising about three-fifth of the State which is marked by sandy, sterile and inhospitable terrain except the Indira Gandhi Canal command area. Sandy hills and dunes are remarkably distinctive topographic features.
2. The east and the south east division covering about two-fifth of the State, presents a mixed and vivid topography consisting of extensive hill ranges, beckoning valleys, dense forests, fertile table lands and plains. Most of the part of the region is more or less level and open.

Broadly speaking Rajasthan is divided into four major physiographic divisions as under:

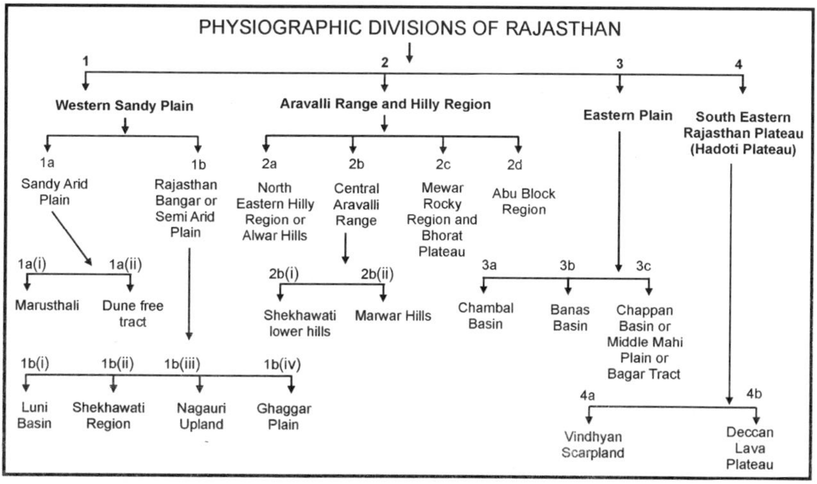

The study region provides a highly interesting case in terms of physiographic landscape owing to its immensely diversified topography in its various parts; incorporating eastern parts of Western sandy plains, Aravalli Region, Eastern Plains as well as South Eastern Rajasthan Plateau (Figure 2.3A).

Shekhawati Region

Western parts of Sikar and Jhunjhunu districts forming the Shekhawati region of Rajasthan Bangar, is a plain area of inland drainage. A range of Aravalli Hills runs through this region from South to North, cutting it into almost two halves and forming a natural boundary between the sandy desert tract of Shekhawati to the north and the fertile plains of Jaipur to the south and south east. The topography of the Shekhawati tract is characterized by an undulating sandy terrain traversed by longitudinal sand dunes. There is only one seasonal river named Kantli which is lost in the sandy terrain soon after its entry in the Churu district.

Aravalli Ranges and Hilly Regions

Eastern parts of Jhunjhunu (Khetri tehsil), Eastern Sikar district (Sikar, Sri Madhopur and Neem-ka-Thana tehsils), Alwar district, Jaipur district, Ajmer and south western part of Tonk district are a part of Aravalli Range and Hilly Region. Within this region remarkable variations are found in the dimensions and relief of the mountain. This region has been divided into sub-regions on the basis of similarity of general physiographic characteristics:

The Alwar Hills

Eastern parts of Jhunjhunu and Sikar district, Alwar and Jaipur district (hilly part) form the north eastern hilly tracts which are called as the Alwar Hills. This region incorporates the isolated hills of Alwar and Jaipur. The offshoots of the ridges (stretching from Delhi towards south west) and hills to the west are found in Sikar, Sri Madhopur, Neem-ka-Thana and Khetri tehsils. Near Khetri and Jaipur, Aravalli attains a character of a continuous range culminating in the peaks of Babai (780m), Kho (920m) in Jaipur, Raghunathgarh (1,055m) and Harshnath (820m) in Sikar. The valleys between the hills are wide and in some cases stretch for many kilometres. Flattered hilltops form small plateaus. The average elevation oscillates between 300–670m. The longitudinal valleys between the ridges are occupied by alluvium. There are several wind gaps in the southern part of this region where bedrock hills are replaced by hills of encroaching sand from the west. These depressions form areas of interior drainage. North of Lake Sambhar, main axis of the range extends north eastwards and reaches Khetri, east of this the northern Aravallis spread out into the Torawati Hills and hills of north east Jaipur; and Alwar on the whole. Around Alwar, the Aravallis form an intricately dissected hill mass rising to nearly 600m above sea level, with a relative relief of about 300m amidst the surrounding plains. Here, around Alwar, the ridges have a N-S trend with longitudinal valleys.

Sambhar Basin

Ajmer, South Western part of Ajmer and South Western parts of Tonk districts form part of the Central Aravalli range which extends from Sambhar lake to Bhorat plateau. This region is an upland marked with scattered ridges. The northern part is a zone of saddle connecting Jaipur Alwar hills with that of Ajmer and Mewar. The levels of valleys and hills are approximately 550m and 700m respectively. These consist of high parallel ridges with barren steep slopes on the quartzites and confused expanse of broken and subdued hills composed of slates and schists. The landscape is marked by sand hills and low depressions with inland drainage and is known as the Sambhar basin. The average level of this region is 550m.

Eastern Plain

Tonk district except south western parts, southern and central part of Jaipur district, Dausa district, Bharatpur district, Karauli and Sawai Madhopur district constitute the eastern plains. Tonk district, southern and central parts of Jaipur districts, Dausa districts, Bharatpur district, most of the Karauli districts except southern strip and Sawai Madhopur district excepts southern parts form the *Chambal Basin*. The landscape of the Chambal basin presents a rather homogeneous topography for hundreds of kilometres characterized by flood plains, river bluffs, interfluves and ravines. The Banas plain in Tonk and Sawai Madhopur districts is a peneplain with erosional surfaces underlying alluvial deposits. More specifically the southern part of this region is called as the Malpura–Karauli plain.

South eastern Tonk district, southern parts of Sawai Madhopur districts form the *Banas plain* which is peneplain with erosional surfaces underlying alluvial deposits. It is a flat upland with 250–350m elevation and occasional sweeps of ridges. Aravallis are prominent near Jaipur. In Kishangarh and Malpura, alluvial deposits are thick where they bury most of the gneissic rocks below with an average elevation of 280–400m. The plain slopes gently towards east and south east.

Figure 2.3

(A) Physiographic Divisions (B) Climatic Regions of NE Rajasthan

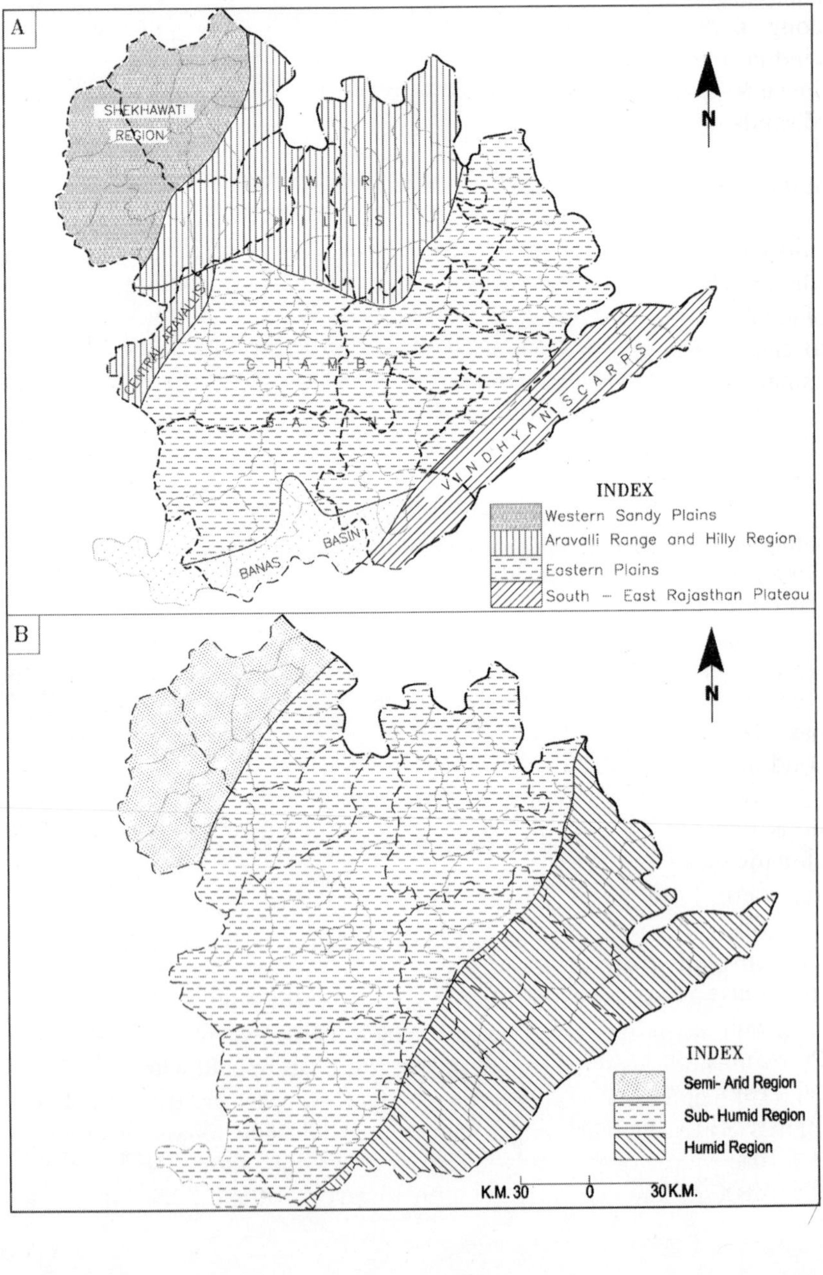

Vindhyan Scarplands

Southern parts of both Sawai Madhopur and Dholpur districts form northern part of Vindhayan scarplands in south east Rajasthan plateau. The region is drained by Chambal river and has a very rugged terrain along the frontier line of the Chambal in Karauli. The lower Vindhayans are well exposed in Karauli tableland and extend from Sawai Madhopur to Bundi and Kota districts. Vidhayan Scarps formed of sandstone mark the topography in the region. Further northwards the topography opens out into flat plains. The height of the scarplands in this region is between 350 and 550m (Figure 2.3).

Climate

Climatic parameters play significant role in the movement and activities of inhabitants in the area concerned. Various schemes have been devised to classify the climates. As per Koppen's scheme of classification of climate, the study area lies in BShw and Cwg types of climatic regions.

Jhunjhunu and Sikar districts form part of BShw climatic region which is characterized by tropical semi arid hot climate with dry winters. Summers also do not receive sufficient amount of rainfall.

Remaining part of the study area lies in Cwg climatic region. Cwg symbolizes warm temperate rainy climates with mild winters. Rains are limited to a few months of summer season. Winters are dry. Temperature maxima occur before the summer rainy season.

According to Thornthwaite's scheme of climatic classification the study area is dominated by DBw type of climate. Only a small portion comprising of northern part of Jhunjhunu and western Sikar districts has DA'W type of climate characterized by semi desertic climatic conditions, hot summers, dry winters and meagre rainfall.

In general, on the basis of the distribution of rainfall and the variations of temperature, the study region has been divided into three climatic regions (Figure 2.3B):

1. *Semi-arid region:* This comprises western parts of Jhunjhunu and Sikar districts. Average annual rainfall ranges between 20 and 40 cms which is quite erratic. Average temperature during summer season ranges from 32°C to 36°C whereas during winter season it ranges from 10°C to 17°C. Winters are short and dry.
2. *Sub-humid Region:* It includes districts of Alwar, Jaipur, Dausa, eastern parts of Jhunjhunu, Sikar and Ajmer districts. This region receives rainfall between 40 and 60 cms which is mainly concentrated in the months of rainy season. The average temperature during summer season ranges from 28°C to 34°C.

3. *Humid Region:* It comprises districts of Bharatpur, Dholpur and Sawai Madhopur. Rainfall varies from 60 to 80 cm. A little rainfall associated with western disturbances occurs in winters also.

On the whole the entire study region has a warm semi arid type of climate with mean annual temperature over 18°C and an annual rainfall between 45 and 88 cms. January is the coldest month of the year when the average temperature dips to 9–10°C. At times due to cold wave temperature reaches the freezing point with occasional frost. May and June are the hottest months, the temperature always range above 30°C. Maximum temperatures are recorded in the month of June which may reach up to 47–50°C in eastern districts. On 1 June 1994, 50°C was recorded in Dholpur. The annual range of temperature lies between 18°C and 20°C. Thus in terms of temperature it may be concluded that the region experiences extremes of temperature with changing seasons: extremely hot summers and chilling cold winters.

Rainfall decreases from east to west. In the east the average annual rainfall is about 70 cm whereas in the West it is 40–50 cms. There are noticeable seasonal as well as regional variations in rainfall. Over 80 per cent of the annual rainfall is concentrated within the four monsoon months – June to September. Winter rains locally known as *Mahavat*, are associated with the western disturbances which may continue sometimes up to May. Alwar, Jaipur, Dausa, Sikar receive fairly moderate proportion of 10–20 per cent to the annual rains from such depressions. The coefficient of variation of annual rainfall is about 30 per cent.

Population Distribution

The distribution of population in the State of Rajasthan is highly governed by the relief, amount of annual rainfall, availability of cultivable fertile land, availability of irrigation facilities level of economic development in terms of urbanization, industrialization and development of means of transport and communication.

The distribution of population in Rajasthan can very well be explained in terms of the carrying capacity of the land which is generally and mostly depended upon relief features, climatic conditions and agricultural potentialities of different areas. In general the population density decreases towards west and north west of the Aravallis and increases towards east and north east. Thus the study area lying to the east of the Aravallis (except Jhunjhunu and Sikar district) is the zone of high concentration of population. As per the 1991 Census in all the districts except Tonk, Karauli and Sawai Madhopur, the density of population is more than 200 persons/km^2. Table 2.4 reveals that the population as increased at different rates in different districts and therefore tremendous variations have taken place in regard to densities of population in the region. District wise densities of population as per Census 1991, 2001 and 2011 are given in Table 2.4.

Table 2.4 *Districtwise Densities of Populations in North East Rajasthan*

District	*Density (persons per sq. km)*		
	1991	*2001*	*2011*
Jaipur	360	471	598
Bharatpur	326	414	503
Dausa	287	384	476
Alwar	274	357	438
Jhunjhunu	265	323	361
Dholpur	247	324	398
Sikar	239	296	346
Sawai Madhopur	171	248	297
Karauli	168	218	264
Tonk	137	168	198

More or less level topography of the eastern plains, adequate rainfall, fertile alluvial soil, sufficient water potential due to presence of rivers like Banas and Chambal and their tributaries, well developed means of transport and communication, high degree of agricultural activities and fast pace of industrial development have collectively contributed to concentration of population in this part of the State.

Despite being a part of the semi arid Bangar tract, the average density is 75–150 persons/km^2. Sikar and Jhunjhunu record high density of population owing to greater facility of irrigation by wells and tubewells. Jaipur district is the most populous district of the State (4,719 lakhs) and contains 10.75 per cent of the total population of the State. Bharatpur (because of its location in the Yamuna basin), Alwar, Dausa, Dholpur, etc. also have very high densities because of fertile and level land, good rains, comfortable climate, seasonal water supply through rivers and irrigation facilities, good deposits of minerals, adequate industrialization and well developed means of transport. Dholpur plain records high population density due to its high productivity. The Karauli table land with a dissected topography, stream with boulder and scrub jungles and much uncultivated land is sparsely populated and in Sawai Madhopur district, population is concentrated in pockets of limited cultivated area. The southern part of the Malpura tract is also sparsely populated. In its northern part, the concentration of population is high owing to its proximity to Jaipur city.

In 1991, the ratio of Scheduled Castes and Scheduled Tribes to total population was 17.04 per cent and 12.21 per cent respectively.

The Meena are mostly concentrated in Sawai Madhopur, Dausa and Jaipur districts. They were formerly rulers of this 'Dhundhad region' and in present times they are either agriculturists or employed in good jobs. The Scheduled Caste population is more or less evenly distributed in all districts. High concentration is found in Sawai Madhopur (21.37%), Bharatpur (21.30%) and Tonk districts (20.63%).

Rationale of the Research Problems

India is a federal democracy with autonomous States functioning within an overall constitutional setup guaranteed by the Central government. Thus, two somewhat parallel and coordinate levels of decision-making bodies exist in India – one in each of the constituent State and the other at the Centre. There are therefore two different sets of electoral contests – one for the Vidhan Sabhas (the State Assemblies) to recruit political elites to supervise and govern the affairs of the respective States and the other for the Lok Sabha (the Parliament) to recruit political elites to supervise all India administration, to arbitrate in inter-state disputes and to take charge of the country's external security and international relations (Wheare, 1963; Dikshit, 1975).

Under this overall federal administrative setup, the day-to-day life of the country's inhabitants is influenced by two sets of political authorities – regional and federal – functioning simultaneously in an enmeshed fashion (Dikshit, 1975). The electorate are guided by different sets of considerations, objectives, interests and expectations while casting votes for electing members of the State Assembly vis-à-vis the election of representatives to the Parliament. While in respect of the State Assembly elections, the voter may prefer to cast his vote in favour of that political party which in his view is likely to be more effective in protecting the State's perceived regional interests, but while exercising one's franchise for the Lok Sabha elections one may prefer an all India party having a proven track record, which can ensure economic stability, internal peace and external security with a favourable foreign policy orientation conducive to national growth and prosperity.

The differences in voting preferences at the two levels of electoral contest also arise from the fact that in the case of State-level elections local issues and caste conflicts tend to dominate electoral preferences in specific constituencies. Such diverse little issues and local level conflicts tend to get lost in the larger context of Lok Sabha elections, since a single parliamentary constituency incorporates eight assembly segments. During Assembly elections, the contestant often belongs to the same region. Owing to higher degree of identification of the candidate among the electorate, personal likes and dislikes and local level conflicts arising from local caste and community differences assume greater importance.

In respect of Lok Sabha contests, even if the candidate is recruited from within the constituency, he would still belong to one of the eight odd assembly segments comprising the constituency thus relatively less known to the voting masses of remaining segments. Thus the influence of personal likes and dislikes, local caste and ethnic conflicts is reduced significantly in Lok Sabha contests.

An individual voter feels very much personally involved in elections to the State Assembly vis-à-vis the Lok Sabha elections because the quality of his immediate government, his day to day life is largely determined by the policies and decisions of the State government. The national government, in comparison, is a distantly removed entity and therefore 'the common voter feels much less personally involved in the electoral process for the recruitment of representatives to the national parliament so that voting decisions tend to be more secular in nature' (Dikshit and Sharma, 1993).

These differences in voting preferences between the two levels of electoral contest form the core of this research work. The main focus of the study is to present a comparative analysis of electoral behaviour, primarily in terms of electoral participation and electoral choice in the Assembly elections vis-à-vis the Lok Sabha elections. To serve this purpose, only such elections were meaningful which were held at relatively short interval of time, since only in such cases could the electoral ecology at State and National level be compared effectively. The present study deals with the following two pairs of elections:

1. Lok Sabha 1991 and Assembly Elections 1993
2. Lok Sabha 1998 and Assembly Elections 1998

To facilitate comparison between the two sets of elections and in view of availability of relevant electoral data, the analysis has been carried out at the level of assembly constituencies. The assembly constituencies form independent units of representation during assembly elections and form part of larger Lok Sabha constituencies during Lok Sabha elections, termed as 'assembly segments' during the latter. To avoid confusion, these electoral units have been referred to as 'assembly units' at places where comparative analysis has been undertaken.

Rajasthan is the largest State of the country, divided into 25 Lok Sabha and 200 assembly constituencies. Instead of the whole State, the study has been restricted to north eastern part of the State, covering 72 assembly constituencies and 9 Lok Sabha constituencies because dealing with all the assembly constituencies at a time would have rendered an in-depth study and quality work almost impossible.

The organization of space for purposes of electoral representation has been of prime concern for the geographers because it conforms to their traditional interest in building a region. 'The process of political redistricting would appear to offer an ideal opportunity for the application of geographical principles of regionalization' (Morill, 1973, p. 463). The criteria which are used in constructing these electoral areas and their boundaries, viz. equal population, recognition of settlement patterns, accessibility and special regional interests are of significant concern in geographical studies. 'The examination of shape, size and areas, the alignment of boundaries, the spatial distribution of voter and related social characteristics are such tasks for which geographer alone is best qualified to carry out' (Dikshit, 1993, p. 13). At the very outset of this research work, a detailed discourse has been made regarding the basis of delimitation of electoral areas of the region, examination and measurement of spatial variations existing among the electoral districts of both levels, State and National, with respect to their geographical area and electorate size and identification of factors responsible for them.

The political decision-making of each individual voter comprises of decision-making at two levels while exercising one's franchise. The first decision is related to the electoral participation, i.e. whether to vote or not, in the first place and second, regarding the party/candidate to support, i.e. whom to vote for? In a democratic political system, the study of political participation assumes importance because it can potentially lend insight into the extent of citizen support for a political system (Dikshit, 1988). Of the many preconditions to the successful functioning and sustenance of a democratic regime, the extent of participation is one. In politics where elections are a means to select rulers, the number of citizens exercising their franchise and the extent of the legitimacy enjoyed by the ruling elites are complimental political realities (Dahl, 1966, pp. 246–48). Palmer (1976) has pointed out that voting is the most common and most widely discussed form of political participation related to the electoral process. Thus identification of the spatial patterns and trends of voter turnout in a region can be used as an effective tool to assess the level of political awareness of a region. In view of the above facts, a comprehensive and elaborate analysis has been taken up in this study of the spatial distribution and temporal variation in the degree of effective electoral participation in the study area and to assess the extent to which socio-economic milieu of the electoral units has affected the spatial patterns of voter participation in electoral process during various election years at State and National levels of electoral contests.

While analysing the patterns of election results and degree of electoral support for various political parties, the importance of policy programmes and promises offered by the political parties in fray and the issues of national and regional importance in the air at that time, cannot be undermined. The swings in favour of or against a party are often a manifestation of emotional impact of such issues and election planks. 'For the country (India), political parties do actually end up winning or losing a sizeable chunk of votes based on what they have to say or do not say' (Roy, 1999, p. 200).

The manifestos of all political parties are designed and manipulated in accordance with the major issues of the time, putting forward the party's views and proposed strategies to meet them. Issues assume far greater importance in the Assembly elections. 'In the case of State level elections local issues and socio-economic conflicts arising from local and regional complexities of ethnic group relations tend to dominate electoral preferences in specific constituencies (Dikshit, 1993). The image and degree of voter identification of the candidate, intraparty dissent and defection, personal likings and dislikings of the electorate are also crucial in determining the voter's response. Attempt has been made in the study to identify the major issues standing before the electorate during the respective elections and to outline the poll planks of the major parties which may have played crucial role in determining the voting choice of the people.

The long and exhaustive exercise of the political parties which commences from declaration of elections, passes through the tough ordeal of wooing the masses in their favour by all means, fair or unfair, legal or illegal culminates in polling and ultimately its success or failure finds expression in the patterns of elections results. These election results are of utmost importance for an electoral geographer as they create variations in the space giving rise to patterns which he wants to analyse in conjunction with particular socio-economic and politico-cultural characteristics. This aspect of study focuses on the analysis of the voter's decision regarding 'whom to vote for?' The spatial variations found in the population structure, occupational structure and issue strata both at the national and regional level are associated with voting for an individual/party or issue and spatial variations in these phenomenon give rise to areal variations in support for various parties. While performing ecological analysis the geographic nature of these varying voting response surfaces is examined.

Owing to seemingly dualistic political structure under a federal system, electoral preferences of the voters are guided by different sets of considerations in elections to the Assembly vis-à-vis the Parliament (Dikshit and Sharma, 1993). The patterns of electoral support for a party are quite well defined in case of Lok Sabha elections whereas there is absence of any clearly defined pattern in the Assembly contest. This may be accounted for by the fact that in case of the recruitment of representatives for the State legislature, caste affiliation and other local/regional interests and conflicts play a more pronounced role in influencing voter's choices which often leads to significant differences in the patterns of voting even between such constituencies whose political and economic characteristics are similar. Such differences are mitigated in the much wider national perspective during the Lok Sabha contests and regions with similar socio-economic base tend to exhibit similar voting behaviour. Thus it implies that secular factors exercise greater influence on voter preferences in the parliamentary contests vis-à-vis the assembly ones.

'The areal definition of support in socio-economic terms is not uniform for all the parties; it is greater for parties whose ideologies, programmes and appeals to particular sections of the community are more sharply drawn' (Das Gupta and Morris-Jones, 1975, p. 216). Thus the socio-economic base of BJP is likely to be more well defined than for Congress, for which relatively inconsistent and hazy results are expected, owing to the aggregative nature of the party which, as a general rule, draws support from all sections of the society even though the actual complexion of this support may vary from one election to the next (Dikshit and Sharma, 1993, 1982; Brass, 1975). Finally, an attempt has been made in the study to examine and compare the degree of success of the two main political parties, i.e. INC and BJP in Rajasthan, the spatial patterns of party support, patterns of party performance, vote trends and stability of support and to determine the ecological bases of support for both the parties in both sets of elections.

Objectives

In the background of the above discourse, the objectives of this study were as follows:

1. To examine the patterns of spatial organization of electoral areas in the study region and to assess the level of disparity existing among the electoral units regarding their geographical area and electorate size.
2. Spatial and ecological analysis of the voting behaviour of the electorate during Lok Sabha elections (1991–98) and Assembly elections (1993–98).
3. To establish a relationship between the voting behaviour of the electorate and geographical socio-political milieu at the time of elections.
4. To compare the spatial patterns of electoral behaviour and the influence of selected ecological variables at the two levels of electoral contests, i.e. Assembly and Lok Sabha elections.
5. To identify the differences in voting behaviour in the urban and rural, general and reserved constituencies.

6. To examine the election results in the light of contemporary issues and social, economic and cultural policies of various parties.
7. To determine the degree to which the spatial patterns of voter participation and party performances are consistent over time.

Hypotheses

The research proceeded with primarily to test the following hypotheses with respect to north east Rajasthan:

1. Level of active participation of the electorate in election process is positively related to the level of development and advancement in the cultural traits of the electorate.
2. Caste, religion, gender and class (economic and social) play important roles in the decision-making process of the electorate.
3. Socio-economic configuration of an area definitely fashions people's attitude towards electoral involvement. Highly developed areas record higher level of turnout.
4. Level of electoral participation is positively related to closeness of contest among the rival parties/degree of inter party competition.
5. The level of electoral participation is higher in Assembly elections than in Lok Sabha elections.
6. The reserved constituencies generally record low voter turnout.
7. The spatial pattern of electoral support for a party is more clearly defined in Lok Sabha elections whereas there is absence of any well defined pattern during Assembly elections.
8. Socio-economic factors exert a more decisive influence on voting preferences in elections for the Lok Sabha than in respect of Assembly contests.
9. The areal pattern of support in socio-economic terms will be more conspicuous for a party whose ideologies, programmes and appeals for particular sections of community are more sharply defined.
10. Owing to aggregative nature of the Congress Party (which draws support from all sections of society) no specific context displays any significant role or consistent relationship in influencing preferences in favour of it.

Methodology

Voting is the outcome of numerous events and interactions among complex sets of phenomena, but the identification and measurement of all the factors involved is practically very difficult. In this study the selection of variables has been made in accordance with the hypotheses which are based on the findings of the previous researches in this field.

The analysis has been based on 'areal-structural' and 'areal-ecological' approaches. These approaches have already been dealt with in Chapter 1. Assembly segments have been taken as the unit of analysis.

The methodology of the present research work consists of three steps:

1. *Collection of Data:* The electoral data have been collected from the published election reports of the State Election Department. The data related to the selected socio-economic variables have been acquired from the respective District Census Handbooks (1991 Census). The information regarding the contemporary local and national issues, party strategies have been derived from the contemporary newspapers mainly the *Rajasthan Patrika* and the *Indian Express*. Party manifestos have been obtained from the respective party offices.
2. *Data Generation:* Since the data related to the socio-economic attributes of the population were available for Census divisions rather than electoral divisions, Census data have been aggregated from village/ward level to the assembly segment/constituency level to make them comparable.
3. *Analysis of Data:* The analysis of data has been carried out mainly in two steps:
   (i) identification of spatial patterns of distribution of electoral phenomenon; and
   (ii) explanation of patterns so identified in relation to their total environmental context, i.e. ecological analysis.

The analysis has been accomplished using a multitude of statistical and cartographic techniques.

The spatial patterns of electoral phenomena during each election have been defined using tools of descriptive statistics, in terms of averages, standard deviation, coefficient of variation and frequency distribution. The spatial variation in the intensity of a phenomenon has been studied in terms of Z-scores (standard deviates) since their use facilitates comparative assessment of data in different units owing to the fact that the mean of Z-scores is always zero and standard deviation one.

Z-scores have been computed according to the following formulae:

$$\text{Z-score} = (X_i - \overline{X}) / SD$$

where X_i = variable X at ith observation

$\overline{X}$ = mean of X variable

SD = standard deviation of X variable.

Choropleth maps have been prepared to illustrate the spatial distribution of various phenomena.

Contextual explanation to the spatial patterns thus identified has been sought by examining the relationships between electoral patterns and the selected voting determinants using Pearson's product moment correlation, partial correlation, multiple regression, stepwise regression, multiple coefficient of determination and factor analysis (principal component method).

Nature and degree of bivariate association between two variables has been determined using Pearson's Product Moment Correlation technique. For performing multivariate analysis, R^2 values (Multiple coefficient of determination) have been derived by multiple regression of all variables on the respective electoral variable, which indicates the total explanation of variance in voting patterns accounted for by all the variables related to the socio-economic-political contexts as a whole. Multiple Regression equation expressed below has been applied:

$$Y_{ijt} = a_{it} + \sum_{k=1}^{n} b_{kit} X_{kj}$$

where Y_{ijt} = electoral variable i in assembly unit j in election year t.

X_{kj} = factor score of context X_k or independent variable in assembly unit j.

b_{kit} = regression coefficient of X_k for electoral variable i in election t.

a_{it} = intercept for electoral variable i in election t.

n = number of independent variables or socio-economic contexts.

t = LS 1991, VS 1993, LS 1998, VS 1998

Multiple coefficient of determination (R^2) has been derived from the multiple regression equation through the following formula:

$$R^2 = \left(\frac{\sigma_y'}{\sigma_y} \right)^2$$

where σ_y' = standard deviation of the predicted values of electoral variable (dependent variable)

σ_y = standard deviation of actual observed values of dependent variable.

Stepwise Regression technique has been employed to assort those variables which exercised decisive influence on voting patterns. Partial correlation coefficients have been determined in the analysis of voter turnout, to assess the relative importance of each independent socio-economic variable in a multivariate situation which takes into account the coexisting correlation of remaining variables too.

Factor analysis (principal component method) has been performed to compress the hypothesized socio-economic variables into socio-economic contexts of significantly interrelated variables. Grouping identical variables into fewer 'contexts' has many advantages in the explanation of voting patterns. When contexts are used as independent variables, the emphasis is on the environmental contexts. It, therefore, provides an appropriate ecological perspective since we know that 'people with similar personal attributes (such as education, age or occupation) behave differently in varying environments or situations (Elkins, 1975, p. 2).

With a view to facilitate interpretation of the contexts, factors having eigen values higher than unity were rotated to normal varimax position. Factor scores, the values of each factor for individual areal units, were used as independent variables in the regression equation while analysing the performance of political parties.

Note

1. Allocation of seats in the House of the People and division of the State into territorial constituencies is done as per the provisions of Article 82 of the Constitution of India. Originally it had to be done every 10 years after the census. The provision has been amended in 1976 by the Delimitation of Parliamentary and Assembly Constituencies Order, 1976 whereby the allocation of seats and division of States into constituencies was deferred till the first census of 21st century i.e. until after the year 2001. The last delimitation of constituencies was done in 1976 by the Delimitation Commission and ever since the boundaries have remained unchanged.

3 Constituencies and Electorate

A constituency is a geographical area within a State which is represented in the Parliament or State Assembly by an elected member. The constituencies are delimitated from time to time by the Delimitation Commission on the basis of some principles laid down at the time of carrying out such exercise. At the time of conducting this research in 2007 there were 4,061 Vidhan Sabha (Assembly) constituencies and these were grouped together to form 543 Lok Sabha (Parliamentary) constituencies. Even during the period of delimitation exercise carried out as per Delimitation Order, 2008 the number of Assembly and Lok Sabha constituencies have been retained. Each Lok Sabha constituency consists of eight Assembly constituencies which are called as Assembly segments. Electorate refers to the group of adult persons enrolled as electors in a constituency. Thus an electorate is only a proportion of the total population residing in constituency who have obtained eligibility and further have been enrolled as electors in the electoral rolls prepared by the Election Commission of India.

Delimitation of Constituencies

Delimitation of constituencies refers to the task of drawing geographical boundaries for constituencies throughout the country. The guidelines for allotment of seats to each State/Union Territory in the House of the People and division of each State/Union Territory into territorial constituencies have been laid down in Article 81 of the Constitution of India. Article 170 of the Constitution lays down the directives for the determination of number of seats in the Legislative Assembly of a State and the division of the State into Assembly constituencies. Article 327 of the Constitution empowers the Parliament to make provisions with respect to all matters relating to election to either House of Parliament or the State Legislatures including laws relating to the preparation of electoral rolls and the delimitation of constituencies. In exercise of the power conferred upon, the Parliament of

India has enacted the Representation of People's Act 1950 and 1951. Article 328 provides power to the Legislature of the State to make provisions regarding the elections to such Legislature.

In pursuance of Article 81, the allocation of seats to various states in the Lok Sabha is made on the basis of population of the respective State, in such a manner that the ratio between this number and the population of the State is almost the same for all states. Each State is then divided into territorial constituencies in such manner that the ratio between the population of each constituency and the seats allotted to it, so far as practicable, is almost the same throughout the State.

Similarly, as per Article 170 of the Constitution, the Legislative Assembly of each State may consist of 60 to 500 members chosen by direct election from the territorial constituencies in the State. For this purpose the State is divided into territorial constituencies in such manner that the ratio between the population of each constituency and the number of seats allotted to it, is almost the same throughout the State. For a State, the total number of seats assigned to the Legislative Assembly is an integral multiple of the number of seats in the House of the People allocated to that State. Article 82 of the Constitution has stipulated a necessary readjustment of allocation of seats in the House of the People to the States and division of States into territorial constituencies after each Census. However, the provision has been amended in 1976 by the Delimitation of Parliamentary and Assembly Constituencies Order, 1976 whereby the readjustment of number of seats and territorial division of States for the Lok Sabha as well as Legislative Assembly was deferred till the first census of 21st century, i.e. until 2001. According to the Eighty-Fourth Amendment Act, 2001, no readjustment is necessary in the allocation of seats in the Lok Sabha to the states and division of State into territorial constituencies, as readjusted on the basis of 1971 Census. Thus the expression 'population' taken as the criteria for demarcation of territorial constituencies, refers to the population of the respective geographical area as per 1971 Census.

In India the demarcation of boundaries of constituencies is done by the Delimitation Commission. The Parliament by law enacts a Delimitation Act after each Census. Under this Act, the Central government constitutes a Delimitation Commission which carries out the task of demarcation of boundaries of the Parliamentary and Assembly constituencies as per the provisions of the Delimitation Act. The delimitation of constituencies adopted in the present study was done as per the provisions of the Delimitation Act, 1971 and the constituencies were carved out on the basis of 1971 Census, having regard to the provisions of Articles 81, 170, 330 and 332. While demarcating the boundaries of the constituencies, it has been ensured that all constituencies, as far as practicable, are geographically compact areas paying due regard to physical features, existing boundaries of administrative units, facilities of communication and public convenience. Every Assembly constituency was so delimited as to fall wholly within one Parliamentary constituency.

Reservation of Constituencies

Article 330 and 332 of the Constitution lay down the provisions for the reservation of seats for Scheduled Caste (SC) and Scheduled Tribe (ST) in the House of People and Legislative Assemblies of the states respectively. As per Article 330, the allocation of seats for SCs/STs in the Lok Sabha is made in such a manner that the number of seats reserved in a State for SCs or STs bears the same proportion to the total number of seats allotted to that State in the Lok Sabha as the population of SCs or STs in the State bears to the total population of the State. It is ensured that the reserved seats are distributed in different parts of the State and are located in those areas where the proportion of their population to the total is comparatively large. Similarly according to Article 332, the number of seats reserved for the SCs and STs in the Legislative Assembly of any State bears the same proportion to the total number of seats in the Assembly as the population of the SCs or STs in the State bears to the total population of the State.

Lok Sabha and Assembly Constituencies in Rajasthan: Historical Background

Assembly Constituencies

The first general election for Rajasthan Legislative Assembly was held in 1952. The total number of constituencies in Rajasthan (excluding Ajmer) was 140 out of which 120 were single member and 20 were double member constituencies. In all the total number of seats was 160 out of which 21 seats were reserved – 16 for SCs and 5 for STs. In 1957 elections, there were 136 constituencies, out of which 96 constituencies were single member and 40 were double member constituencies. Thus total number of seats were 176 out of which 48 seats were reserved, 28 seats for SCs and 20 seats for STs.

A major change in the history of territorial delimitation of constituencies occurred in 1962 when Parliament abolished the system of double member constituencies by Double Member Constituencies Abolition Act, 1960. Double member constituencies were split and their extent delimited. Thus in 1962 general elections, the number of constituencies increased to 176 out of which 48 were reserved seats – 28 seats for SCs and 20 seats for STs.

In the fourth general election of 1967, the total number of Assembly constituencies was increased to 184. In the fifth general elections, there was no change in the number, size and nature of constituencies. In the 1977 Assembly elections, the number of Assembly constituencies was increased to 200. Fifty six seats were reserved out of which 32 seats were reserved for SCs and 24 seats were reserved for STs. Since 1977, the total number of constituencies has remained unchanged. In the seventh general election of 1980, Reodar of Sirohi district, a general Assembly constituency was converted into an SC reserved constituency. Since 1980 till 2008, the number, size and nature of Assembly constituencies of Rajasthan remained unchanged with 200 constituencies in total and 57 reserved constituencies out of which 33 are reserved for SCs and 24 are reserved for STs. It was in 2008 that the exercise for the delimitation of constituencies was undertaken and as a result thereof the size and nature of constituencies were redefined, though total number of constituencies remained 200. A summary of the temporal changes in the total number and number of reserved Assembly constituencies in Rajasthan till 1998 has been given in Table 3.1. The 200 Assembly constituencies, their names and location existing in 1998 has been illustrated in Figure 3.1 and Table 3.2.

Table 3.1 *Assembly Constituencies in Rajasthan (1952–98)*

Year of Election	*No. of Constituencies*			*Total*
	Reserved for SC	*Reserved for ST*	*General*	
1952	16	5	139	160
1957	28	20	128	176
1962	28	20	128	176
1967	31	21	132	184
1972	31	21	132	184
1977	32	24	144	200
1980	33	24	143	200
1985	33	24	143	200
1990	33	24	143	200
1993	33	24	143	200
1998	33	24	143	200

Source: Compilation from the record of the Chief Election Officer, Government of Rajasthan, Jaipur.

Figure 3.1

Lok Sabha and Assembly Constituencies of Rajasthan
(As Per Delimitation of 1976)

Lok Sabha Constituencies

The State of Rajasthan was divided into 22 Lok Sabha constituencies during the 1952 Lok Sabha Elections. Out of these two were reserved for SCs and one for STs. In 1957 and 1962 Lok Sabha elections, although the total number of seats remained 22, but the number of reserved constituencies increased to five out of which three were reserved for SCs and two for STs. During 1967 and 1971 elections, the total number of Parliamentary constituencies increased to 23, out of which four were reserved for SCs and three for STs. In 1977, the total number of seats allotted to the State of Rajasthan in the House of

Table 3.2 *Lok Sabha Constituencies and their Assembly Segments in Rajasthan (as per Delimitation Order 1976)*

1.	*Ganganagar (SC)*	*6.*	*Jaipur*	*11*	*Sawai Madhopur(ST)*	*16*	*Banswara(ST)*	*21*	*Pali*
1	Bhadra	40	Jaipur (Rural)	80	Karauli	128	Kushalgarh (ST)	159	Jaitaran
2	Nohar	41	Hawamahal	81	Sapotra (ST)	129	Danpur (ST)	160	Raipur
3	Tibi (SC)	42	Johari Bazar	82	Khandar (SC)	130	Ghatol (ST)	161	Sojat
4	Hanumangarh	43	Kishanpole	83	Sawaimadhopur	131	Banswara	162	Kharchi
5	Sangaria	44	Banipark	84	Bamanwas (ST)	132	Bagidora (ST)	163	Desuri (SC)
6	Ganganagar	47	Sanganer	85	Gangapur	133	Sagwara (ST)	164	Pali
7	Kesrisinghpur (SC)	48	Phagi (SC)	86	Hindaun (SC)	134	Chorasi (ST)	165	Sumerpur
8	Karanpur	53	Bassi	88	Todabhim (ST)	135	Dungarpur (ST)	166	Bali
2	Bikaner	7	Dausa	12	Ajmer	17	Salumber (ST)	22	Jalore (SC)
9	Raisinghnagar (SC)	39	Amer	94	Kishangarh	127	Pratapgarh (ST)	167	Sirohi
10	Pilibanga	49	Lalsot (ST)	95	Ajmer East (SC)	136	Aspur (ST)	168	Pindwara-Abu (ST)
11	Suratgarh	50	Sikrai (ST)	96	Ajmer West	137	Lasadia (ST)	169	Reodar (SC)
12	Lunkaransar	51	Bandikui	97	Pushkar	144	Salumber (ST)	170	Sanchore
13	Bikaner	52	Dausa (SC)	98	Nasirabad	145	Sarada (ST)	171	Raniwara
14	Kolayat	54	Jamwaramgarh	99	Beawar	146	Kherwada (ST)	172	Bhinmal

Cont'd...

...Cont'd

15	Nokha (SC)	55	Bairath	100	Masuda	147	Phalasai (ST)	173	Jalore (SC)
192	Jayal (SC)	56	Kotputli	101	Bhinai	148	Gogunda (ST)	174	Ahore
3	Churu	8	Alwar	13	Tonk (SC)	18	Udaipur	23	Barmer
16	Dungargarh	57	Bansur	45	Phulera	138	Vallabh Nagar	175	Siwana (SC)
17	Sujangarh (SC)	58	Behror	46	Dudu (SC)	139	Mavli	176	Pachpadra
18	Ratangarh	59	Mandawar	89	Niwai (SC)	140	Rajsamand (SC)	177	Barmer
19	Sardarshahar	60	Tizara	90	Tonk	141	Nathdwara	178	Gudamalani
20	Churu	61	Khairthal (SC)	91	Uniara	142	Udaipur	179	Chohtan
21	Taranagar	63	Alwar	92	Todaraisingh	143	Udaipur Rural (ST)	180	Sheo
22	Sadulpur	64	Thanagazi	93	Malpura	149	Kumbhalgarh	181	Jaisalmer
193	Ladnu	65	Rajgarh (ST)	102	Kekri (SC)	150	Bhim	182	Shergarh
4	Jhunjhunu	9	Bharatpur	14	Kota	19	Chittorgarh	24	Jodhpur
23	Pilani	62	Ramgarh	103	Hindoli	108	Ladpura	183	Jodhpur
24	Surajgarh (SC)	66	Lachhmangarh	104	Nainwa	115	Ramganj Mandi	184	Sardarpura
25	Khetri	67	Kathumar (SC)	105	Patan (SC)	121	Begun	185	Sursagar (SC)
26	Gudha	68	Kaman	106	Bundi	122	Gangrar (SC)	186	Luni

Cont'd...

...*Cont'd*

27	Nawalgarh	69	Nagar	107	Kota	123	Kapasin	187	Bilara
28	Jhunjhunu	70	Deeg	109	Digod	124	Chittorgarh	188	Bhopalgarh
29	Mandawa	71	Kumher	110	Pipalda (SC)	125	Nimbahera	189	Osian
30	Fatehpur	72	Bharatpur	111	Baran	126	Badi Sadri	190	Phalodi
5	Sikar	10	Bayana (SC)	15	Jhalawar	20	Bhilwara	25	Nagaur
31	Lachhmangarh (SC)	73	Rupbas (SC)	112	Kishanganj (ST)	151	Mandal	191	Nagaur
32	Sikar	74	Nadbai	113	Atru (SC)	152	Sahada	194	Deedwana
33	Dhod	75	Weir (SC)	114	Chhabra	153	Bhilwara	195	Nawan
34	Dantaramgarh	76	Bayana	116	Khanpur	154	Mandalgarh	196	Makrana
35	Srimadhopur	77	Rajakhera	117	Manohar Thana	155	Jahazpur	197	Parbatsar (SC)
36	Khandela	78	Dholpur	118	Jhalrapatan	156	Shahpura (SC)	198	Degana
37	Neem-ka-Thana	79	Bari	119	Pirawa	157	Banera	199	Merta
38	Chomu	87	Mahuwa	120	Dag (SC)	158	Asind	200	Mundwa

Source: Statistical report of General Elections, 1998 to the 11th Vidhan Sabha, Election Department, Rajasthan, Jaipur.

the People increased to 25. Four seats were reserved for SCs and three seats were reserved for STs. Since 1977, the total number of Lok Sabha constituencies in Rajasthan and their nature and configuration has remained unchanged. Table 3.3 provides a summary of the changes which have occurred in the organization of Lok Sabha constituencies in Rajasthan during 1952–98.

Table 3.3 *Lok Sabha Constituencies in Rajasthan (1952–98)*

Year of Election	*No. of Constituencies*			*Total*
	Reserved for SC	*Reserved for ST*	*General*	
1952	2	1	19	22
1957	3	2	17	22
1962	3	2	17	22
1967	4	3	16	23
1971	4	3	16	23
1977	4	3	18	25
1980	4	3	18	25
1984	4	3	18	25
1989	4	3	18	25
1991	4	3	18	25
1996	4	3	18	25
1998	4	3	18	25

Source: Chief Election Officer, Government of Rajasthan, Jaipur.

Lok Sabha and Assembly Constituencies in Rajasthan: 1991–98

As per the delimitation of Lok Sabha and Assembly constituencies done in 1976, the State of Rajasthan was divided into 25 Lok Sabha and 200 Assembly constituencies from which representatives were elected through direct elections to the 25 seats in the House of People and 200 seats in the State Legislative Assembly respectively. Thus a constituency may informally be termed as a seat also. In Rajasthan each Parliamentary constituency comprised of eight Assembly constituencies.

Out of the 25 Parliamentary constituencies, four constituencies (16%) namely Ganganagar, Bayana, Tonk and Jalore were reserved for SCs and three constituencies (12%) namely Banswara, Sawai

Madhopur and Salumber were reserved for STs till the redelimitation of constituencies in 2008 whereby nature of constituencies was redefined. The SC reserved Parliamentary constituencies cover 12.98 per cent of the total area of the State whereas ST reserved constituencies cover 8.22 per cent of the total area of Rajasthan. Figure 3.2 illustrates the location and nature of Lok Sabha constituencies of Rajasthan.

Figure 3.2

Lok Sabha Constituencies of Rajasthan (After Delimitation of 1976)

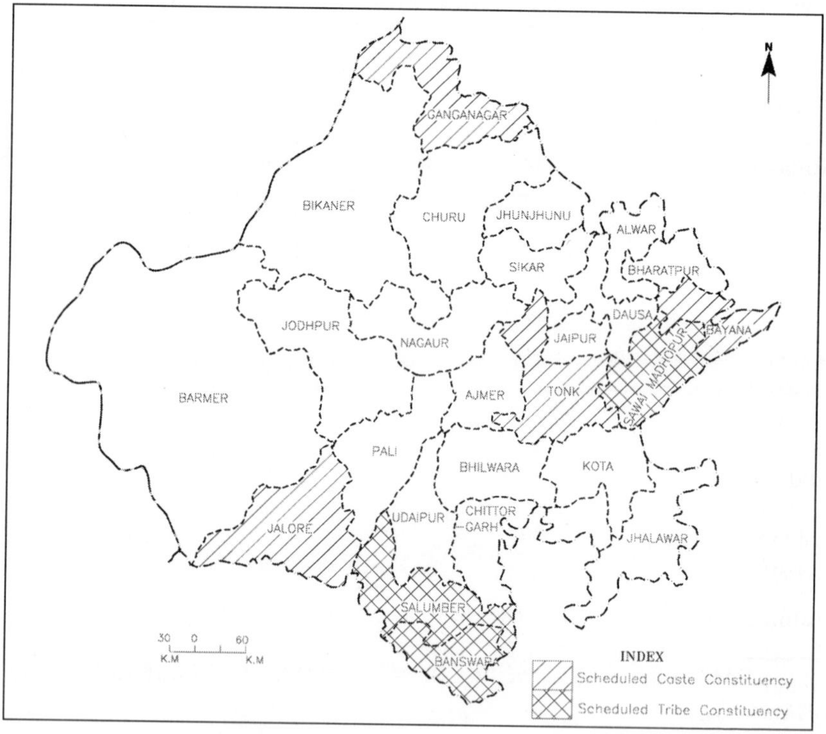

In case of Assembly constituencies 57 out of 200 were reserved constituencies. Thirty three constituencies were reserved for SCs and 24 are reserved for the STs. The names of all Lok Sabha constituencies of the State and their constituent Assembly segments as existed till 2008 are listed in Table 3.2. Thus 16.5 per cent and 12 per cent of the total number of Assembly seats in Rajasthan were reserved for SCs and STs respectively. As per 1971 census, the SC population of the State was 40.75 lakhs and the ST population was 31.25 lakhs which constituted 15.8 per cent and 12.12 per cent of the total population of the

State respectively. The general seats covered 2,64,600 km^2 (77.31%) of the total area, constituencies reserved for SC candidates covered 47,259.31 km^2 (13.81%) and ST constituencies spread over 30,379.32 km^2 (8.88%) of the total area of the State. The SCs constituencies were mainly scattered in the central and northern part of the State whereas the STs constituencies were mainly concentrated in the southern and eastern part of Rajasthan. In the South, the ST Assembly constituencies spread over southern part of Udaipur, Dungarpur and Banswara districts whereas in the east, they were confined to Dausa, Sawai Madhopur and eastern part of Kota districts.

Lok Sabha and Assembly Constituencies in North East Rajasthan

This study comprised nine Lok Sabha constituencies of north east Rajasthan, each comprising of eight Assembly segments and thus 72 Assembly constituencies in total. These constituencies spread over 11 districts of north east Rajasthan. A detailed note on north east Rajasthan has already been given in Chapter 2 (Figures 3.1 and 3.2).

In north east Rajasthan, the SC reserved Parliamentary constituencies and the ST reserved constituency, i.e. Sawai Madhopur covered 27.41 and 14.98 per cent respectively of the total area. The remaining 57.61 per cent of the area was covered by general category of constituencies. In case of Assembly constituencies under consideration, 13 were SC reserved constituencies spreading over 22.62 per cent of the total area and six were ST reserved constituencies covering 10.08 per cent of the total area. Almost 67.30 per cent of the total area was covered by general category of Assembly constituencies. The extent of different nature of constituencies in the study area has been summarized in Table 3.4.

Table 3.4 *Nature of Constituencies in North East Rajasthan (1976–2008)*

Nature of Seat	*Assembly*			*Lok Sabha*		
	Number of Seats	*Area in Km^2*	*Area (% of TA)*	*No. of Seats*	*Area in Km^2*	*Area (% of TA)*
General	53	41,583	67.30	6	35,593.62	57.61
SC	13	13,974.1	22.62	2	16,934.03	27.41
ST	6	6226.16	10.08	1	9255.59	14.98
Total	72	61783.2	100.00	9	61783.24	100.00

Note: TA stands for total geographical area of the study area.

Source: Records of Chief Election Officer, Government of Rajasthan and partly generation by the author.

It is interesting to note that significant proportion of the area – 26.39 per cent constituencies covering 32.70 per cent of the total area in case of Assembly constituencies and 33.33 per cent constituencies covering 42.39 per cent of the total area in case of Lok Sabha constituencies was occupied by reserved constituencies. It clearly reflects high concentration of SC/ST population in the area which certainly played a crucial role in the final electoral outcomes in the region.

Relationship Between Population and Electorate

As explained in the previous section, the geographical size of constituencies is determined by size of its population. While drawing the territorial boundaries of the Assembly and Lok Sabha constituencies, the ratio between the population of the constituency and the number of seats allotted to it is kept almost the same for all constituencies. Thus it may be said that the entire geographical area of the State is divided into territorial divisions of more or less equal population size.

Thus the guiding principle of elections is that each elected representative whether for Lok Sabha or Vidhan Sabha should represent almost the same number of people. But this general principle does not work at ground level because of the following two reasons:

1. The population of constituencies grow at widely different rates.
2. Only the citizens of India who are equal or above to 18 years of age are eligible to cast their vote at the time of elections. Thus whereas the geographical area of the constituency is determined by the size of entire population of the respective area, in reality the fate of the candidate is decided by only a part of that population, i.e. number of voters in that area. In accordance with the Article 326 of the Constitution, the elections to the House of the People and to the Legislative Assemblies of the States are conducted on the basis of adult suffrage. All people who are citizens of India and are not less than 18 years of age (Sixty-First Amendment Act, 1989) and have not otherwise been disqualified to cast their vote, are entitled to be registered as a voter in an election. This segment of population which is eligible to vote for the election in a constituency is termed as the 'electorate' of that constituency. As per the population and electorate figures of the election year 1991 the total population of the study area was 1,60,20,847 and the total electorate was 95,68,806 which constituted 59.73 per cent of the total population. The proportion of total electorate to total population at the Assembly segment level was highest in Mahuwa (75.79%) and lowest in Jaipur Rural (41.60%). The variability of the ratio of electorate size to population size was 0.06 when

measured in terms of standard deviation and the coefficient of variation was 9.45 per cent.

As per 1991 Census, the average population of the study area, per Assembly unit was 2,20,029, ranging between the minimum of 1,60,673 in Mahuwa and maximum of 4,79,722 in Johari Bazaar. The standard deviation of population size of Assembly segments was 45,876 and the coefficient of variation was 20.62 per cent.

Thus there existed considerable variation among the constituencies regarding size of population and electorate. The constituencies, both Assembly and Parliamentary were demarcated on the basis of 1971 Census population figures. Thereafter the boundaries have been redrawn in 2008. Due to differential rate of growth of population in different parts of the State since 1971, great variations occurred in the size of population of various constituencies and therefore it necessitated the redelimitation in 2008.

The total population of Rajasthan as per 1971 Census was 2,57,65,806. Thus on an average, the size of population of one Assembly constituency at the time of delimitation in 1976 was 1,28,829. In 1991, the population of Rajasthan increased to 4,40,05,990 and the average population per Assembly constituency increased to 2,20,029. For the delimitation of Lok Sabha constituencies, the size of population per constituency was approximately 10 lakhs at the time of delimitation of 1976. If the same is calculated on the basis of 1991 Census figures, it comes out to be approximately 17 lakhs.

Thus in view of constantly increasing population at differential rate of growth in various parts of the State, a uniformity of the ratio of number of seats to population of a constituency can be maintained only if fresh boundaries are drawn by way of redelimitation of constituencies after each Census as was originally conceived in Article 82 of the Constitution. Since the exercise for delimitation took place only in 2008, great variations had taken place among the Assembly as well as Lok Sabha constituencies in terms of this size of population and electorate.

In addition, due to differential age structure of the population, the ratio of size of electorate to total population of the constituency had also highly varied among constituencies.

Size of Assembly and Lok Sabha Constituencies in North East Rajasthan

As it has been pointed out earlier, the size of a Lok Sabha or Assembly constituency in terms of area is dependent on the size of population. Since 'more or less uniformity in population size of all constituencies' is the guiding principle of the delimitation process, it implies that the geographical area of a constituency will be more if the region is sparsely populated and it will be less if it spreads over a region having high density of population. Thus it may be said that there is an inverse relationship between the geographical area and the density of population of a constituency.

In Rajasthan, Barmer with an areal extent of 70,391.28 km^2 is the largest Parliamentary constituency and Jaipur (3,655.25 km^2) is the smallest one. Among the 200 Assembly constituencies Jaisalmer, with an area of 34,920 sq. km, is the largest and Jodhpur (3.49 km^2) is the smallest. The reason is obvious, Barmer and Jaisalmer, lying in the western sandy plains, are located in the Great Indian Desert. Hostile climatic conditions, meagre rainfall, scarce resources, under-developed economy and harsh living conditions have made this region the least populated region of the State, having population density less than 50 person/km^2.

Similarly, small size of Jaipur Lok Sabha constituency and Jodhpur Assembly constituency could be attributed to the high density of population in these areas. The then Jaipur Parliamentary constituency was located in the fertile plain area east of the Aravallis, having moderate climatic conditions, moderate rainfall, sufficient irrigation facilities and fertile soil. In addition to that being the capital of the State, Jaipur city along with the areas adjoining the capital city had developed economy and infrastructure leading to high density of population. Jodhpur Assembly constituency being a part of Jodhpur city acted as a trade, educational, commercial, tourist, transportation and administrative centre with extremely high concentration of population.

North east Rajasthan forms part of the eastern plains, the relatively densely populated region of the State whereas the areal extent of Assembly constituencies in Rajasthan ranged from 3.49 sq. km (Jodhpur) to 34,920 sq. km (Jaisalmer), it ranged between 6.23 sq. km (Hawa Mahal) and 2,126.42 sq. km (Sapotra) in north east Rajasthan. Excluding five Assembly constituencies, namely Malpura, Uniara, Dudu, Khandar and Sapotra, all the remaining Assembly constituencies in north east Rajasthan were smaller than the average size of Assembly constituencies in Rajasthan (1,626.9 sq. km).

In the following discussion, an attempt has been made to examine the variation in the geographical area of Lok Sabha and Assembly constituencies in north east Rajasthan. For this purpose, the mean area of constituencies was calculated and the variation was measured in terms of coefficient of variation and per cent deviation from mean.

Lok Sabha Constituencies

The variation in the size of Parliamentary constituencies has been examined in the following two ways:

1. Variation among various Parliamentary constituencies – Inter constituency variation.
2. Variation among the Assembly segments of a Parliamentary constituency – Intra constituency variation.

The nine Lok Sabha constituencies in north east Rajasthan constituted 18.05 per cent of the total area of Rajasthan. The size of these constituencies in terms of area ranged between 3,655.25 sq. km (Jaipur) and 11,223.18 km (Tonk). Jaipur, the smallest constituency covered 1.07 per cent of the total area of Rajasthan. It was not only the smallest constituency in north east Rajasthan but it was smallest in the entire State too. Tonk, the largest constituency of north east Rajasthan constituted 3.28 per cent of the total area of Rajasthan. Thus the areal extent of Tonk Parliamentary constituency was approximately thrice the Jaipur Parliamentary constituency. It is interesting to note that if the distribution of population was considered, Jaipur had the highest whereas Tonk had the least density of population. Thus the inverse relationship between areal extent of constituencies and their population density was evident. If the constituencies were arranged in ascending order of area Jaipur was followed by Bharatpur, Alwar, Bayana, Dausa, Jhunjhunu, Sikar, Sawai Madhopur and Tonk in the end (Table 3.5). The sequence remained the same if the constituent districts were arranged in descending order of their population densities.

Great variation was observed when the Parliamentary constituencies were compared on the basis of the size of their Assembly segments. The coefficient of variation of the areal extent of eight Assembly segments of each constituency was calculated. This revealed that the highest variation in the size of Assembly segments amounting to 122.05 per cent, occurred in Jaipur Lok Sabha constituency. Hawa Mahal, spreading over 0.17 per cent of the total area of Jaipur Lok Sabha constituency was the smallest Assembly segment whereas Phagi which spread over 41.68 per cent of the total area was the largest Assembly segment of this constituency. The difference in geographical area of these two segments was 1,517.14 km^2, Phagi being approximately 245 times bigger in size than Hawa Mahal. Not only Hawa Mahal, four out of the eight Assembly segments of Jaipur Parliamentary constituency namely Banipark, Johari Bazaar, Kishanpole and Hawa Mahal had an area less than 31 sq. km. The extremely small size of these four Assembly segments could be explained by their large population size, being situated in highly urbanized areas of the capital city of Jaipur.

Table 3.5 *Variability among Lok Sabha Constituencies with Respect to Geographical Size (1991)*

(Area in sq. km)

Lok Sabha Constituency			*Assembly Segment*		*C.V.*
Name	*Area in sq. km*	*% of Total Area of Raj.*	*Largest*	*Smallest*	
Jaipur	3,655.25	1.07%	Phagi(SC) (41.68)	Hawa Mahal (0.17)	122.05
Bharatpur	5,203.91	1.52%	Lachhmangarh (21.46)	Bharatpur (7.13)	33.43
Alwar	5,493.00	1.61%	Thanagazi (22.12)	Alwar (5.50)	38.22
Bayana (SC)	5,710.85	1.67%	Bari (26.51)	Dholpur (9.63)	45.42
Dausa	6,726.31	1.97%	Jamwaramgarh (16.47)	Bandikui (8.68)	21.69
Jhunjhunu	7,028.85	2.05%	Mandawa (16.47)	Gudha (9.30)	19.83
Sikar	7,486.30	2.19%	Lachhmangarh (SC)(16.59)	Sikar (8.06)	26.42
Sawai Madhopur (ST)	9,255.59	2.70%	Sapotra (ST) (22.97)	Todabhim (ST) (5.02)	53.70
Tonk (SC)	11,223.18	3.28%	Dudu (SC) (16.86)	Phulera (8.07)	27.35

Note: Figures in parentheses indicate area as percentage of total area of the respective constituency. C.V. (Coefficient of Variation) is based on the Mean and SD of the area of the eight Assembly segments of the respective constituency.

Source: Records of Chief Election Officer, Government of Rajasthan and partly generation by the author.

Sawai Madhopur Lok Sabha constituency stood next to Jaipur Lok Sabha constituency with coefficient of variation of 53.70 per cent. The smallest Assembly segment in this constituency was Todabhim, a ST reserved constituency which spread over 464.86 km^2, forming 5.02 per cent of the total area of the constituency. Todabhim was located in relatively densely populated plain and level part of Sawai Madhopur district. Sapotra (2,126.42 km^2) was the largest segment of Sawai Madhopur Parliamentary constituency, forming 22.97 per cent of the total area of the constituency. Sapotra was the largest Assembly segment of not only Sawai Madhopur Parliamentary constituency, but also in the entire north east Rajasthan. It was the largest of all the Assembly segments in all the nine Lok Sabha constituencies of north east Rajasthan. Sapotra was located in the hilly and rugged portion of Sawai Madhopur district which was very sparsely populated owing to its dissected topography. Sawai Madhopur was followed by Bayana, Alwar, Bharatpur, Tonk, Sikar, Dausa and lastly Jhunjhunu, in descending order of intra constituency variability of Assembly segment size. The coefficient of variation of Jhunjhunu Lok Sabha constituency was 19.83 per cent. The smallest Assembly segment of Jhunjhunu is Gudha (653.81 km^2) and the largest was Mandawa (1,158 km^2). Thus the Manda was approximately twice the size of Gudha.

Concludingly, it may be said that high degree of variability existed among the Lok Sabha constituencies in both the respects. The Parliamentary constituencies varied in terms of their geographical extent as well as the area of Constituent Assembly segments within themselves. Jaipur exhibited an extraordinarily high degree of variability (122.05%) whereas in the remaining constituencies the variation ranged between 19.83 per cent and 53.70 per cent. Table 3.5 gives a detailed account of the area, largest and smallest Assembly segment and variability in the size of Assembly segments of various Lok Sabha constituencies.

Assembly Constituencies

To investigate the variation in the size of Assembly constituencies of north east Rajasthan in terms of area, deviation of the area of individual constituencies from mean area was calculated. These deviation values were then converted into percentage deviation values. The 72 Assembly constituencies were then classified on the basis of the per cent deviation of their area from the mean area. The per cent deviation values ranged from 147.81 per cent for Sapotra to –99.27 per cent for Hawa Mahal. The entire distribution was then classified into seven classes with a class interval of 40 per cent (Table 3.6).

Table 3.6 *Frequency Distribution of Assembly Constituencies on the Basis of Geographical Area (1977–2008)*

Area in sq. km

d	*Frequency*		*% of total area*	*Assembly Constituency*			
	f	*%f*		*Largest*	*Area*	*Smallest*	*Area*
–80 to –120	4	5.56	0.12	Johari Bazaar	30.85	Hawa Mahal	6.23
–40 to –80	4	5.56	2.50	Todabhim(ST)	464.86	Alwar	302.00
0 to –40	36	50.00	39.40	Lalsot(ST)	856.45	Deeg	548.19
0 to 40	15	20.83	25.11	Dantaramgarh	1,169.61	Nawalgarh	880.60
40 to 80	8	11.11	17.40	Phagi(SC)	1,523.37	Thanagazi	1,215.00
80 to 120	2	2.78	5.73	Uniara	1,776.44	Malpura	1,766.30
120 to 160	3	4.17	9.73	Sapotra(ST)	2,126.42	Dudu(SC)	1,892.00

Note: d= per cent deviation from mean area
f = number of Assembly constituencies in a class of % deviation from mean, i.e. d/mean*100
% f =(f/total no. of constituencies (72))*100
% of total area = area under a class/total area of study region (61,783.24 sq. km)

Hawa Mahal, with an areal extent of 6.23 sq. km was the smallest constituency in the region and Sapotra (2,126.42 km^2) was the largest. The mean area of the 72 constituencies was 858.10 km^2. The frequency distribution of the constituencies revealed the following facts:

1. There was a clear clustering of constituencies around the mean value. Seventy per cent of the constituencies are of size which deviated –40 per cent to +40 per cent from the mean size. Ten per cent constituencies are extraordinarily small or large in size, lying on the extreme ends of the distribution. Another 5.56 per cent have an area with –120 to –80 per cent deviation from mean and 4.17 per cent of them deviate 120 to 160 per cent from mean area.
2. Four constituencies belonged to the class ranging from –120 to –80 per cent deviation from mean area being the smallest of all constituencies. These constituencies together covered 75.38 km^2 area which was 0.12 per cent of north east Rajasthan. Johari Bazaar (30.85 km^2) was the largest and Hawa Mahal was the smallest of the four constituencies of this class. It was noted that all these four constituencies were located in Jaipur city. This explained their exceptionally small size to a great extent.
3. The size of four constituencies deviates –40 per cent to –80 per cent from the average. These four constituencies together covered 1,547.10 km^2 or 2.50 per cent of north east Rajasthan. Todabhim having an area of 464.86 km^2 was the largest constituency in this class and Alwar (302 sq. km) was the smallest. Alwar, Bharatpur, Todabhim and Jaipur Rural, all the four constituencies comprising this class were densely populated urban and semi urban areas. Alwar and Bharatpur were urban constituencies located in cities of Alwar and Bharatpur respectively which were highly populated pockets of north east Rajasthan. Similarly, Jaipur Rural spread over the Jamwa Ramgarh tehsil of Jaipur district and had high population density owing to its adjacency to Jaipur city. Todabhim was located in the plain and fertile part of Sawai Madhopur district.
4. Fifty per cent of the constituencies (36) are of size which deviated less than 40 per cent from the mean on the negative side. These constituencies covered 24,343.55 sq. km area which constituted 39.40 per cent of the total area. The size of constituencies in this category ranged from 548.19 sq. km (Deeg) to 856.45 km^2 (Lalsot). Out of 36, eight constituencies belonged to Alwar district, eight were part of Bharatpur district, five constituencies

were located in Dausa and Jaipur district each, four in Jhunjhunu, two in Sikar and Dholpur each and one in Sawai Madhopur and Karauli each. Bharatpur, Alwar, Dausa and Jaipur were the highest populated districts of Rajasthan. Owing to level topography, fertile soil, adequate rainfall and irrigation facilities, well developed transport network and their proximity to the developed parts of North India, both agriculture and industry were fairly developed in the region. Thus the region had a moderate to high density of population of above 250 person/km^2. It was noteworthy that two constituencies of this category, Gangapur and Hindaun, belonging to Sawai Madhopur and Karauli district respectively figured as exceptions since all other constituencies (except Todabhim) belonging to these districts had area more than the mean area. These districts had a low population density in general but both Gangapur and Hindaun are thickly populated pockets owing to their the locational benefits.

5. The size of 15 constituencies deviated between the mean value and 40 per cent deviation from the mean. This was the second largest category in terms of frequency and comprised of constituencies covering 25.11 per cent of the total study area spreading over 15,510.78 sq. km. The category comprises of five constituencies of Sikar district, three located in Jhunjhunu district, three belonging to Jaipur district and one constituency from the districts of Tonk, Sawai Madhopur, Karauli and Alwar each.
6. Eight constituencies fell in the class of 40 to 80 per cent deviation from mean area. These together cover 10,750.25 sq. km area which constituted 17.40 per cent of the total study area, Phagi (1,523.37 sq. km) was the largest constituency of this category and Thanagazi (1,215 sq. km) was the smallest. The constituencies comprising this category were located in Tonk (2), Jaipur, Dholpur, Sawai Madhopur, Sikar, Ajmer and Alwar district (1 each).
7. Two constituencies, namely Uniara and Malpura, both belonging to Tonk district were of size ranging between 80 to 120 per cent from the mean area. These constituencies, 2.78 per cent of the total number of constituencies of the study area, spread over 5.73 per cent of the total study area extending over 3,542.74 km^2 of geographical area.
8. Three constituencies (4.17%) formed the category of largest constituencies in the region, those of size deviating more than 120 per cent from the mean area. These three constituencies spread

over 9.73 per cent of the total study area, covering a geographical area of 6,013.44 km^2. These three constituencies are Dudu (Jaipur district), Khandar (Sawai Madhopur district) and Sapotra (Karauli district). Khandar and Sapotra were located in the hilly and undulating areas of the Vindhayan Scarps, thus having a very low density of population.

The distribution of Assembly constituencies among the above seven categories according to their size revealed some very interesting facts as under:

1. The 15 Assembly constituencies of Jaipur district figured in all the classes except one (80 to 120% deviation category). Whereas all the constituencies constituting the class of smallest constituencies were located in Jaipur district, Dudu was one of the largest constituencies in the region. Ten out of the 15 constituencies of Jaipur district were of size less than the mean size in terms of area. This might be attributed to the uneven distribution of population in the district which was highly concentrated in and around the capital city and decreased away from it in all directions, particularly in the west and south west.
2. All the constituencies of Bharatpur district were smaller than the mean size. Bharatpur, being located in the Yamuna Basin, had a level topography with well developed agriculture, fast developing industries and a well developed transport network. Thus it was a region of high population density, the average density of the district being 327 persons per sq. km (1991), the rural density being 270 persons per sq. km and urban density being 2,457 persons/km^2.
3. Similarly, eight out of the 11 constituencies of Alwar district were of size less than 40 per cent above the mean. The reason is the relatively high density of population in the district.
4. The constituencies belonging to Sawai Madhopur, Karauli and Tonk were distributed on the higher side of the mean, with a few exceptions where the constituency spreads over an urban area.

The size of 38.89 per cent (28) Assembly constituencies were larger than the mean whereas 64.11 per cent (44) constituencies were smaller than the mean size in terms of area. Figure 3.3 illustrates the spatial distribution of Assembly constituencies comprising various categories of geographical area.

Since the size of the four constituencies of Jaipur namely Hawa Mahal, Johari Bazaar, Kishanpole and Banipark was extraordinarily small, when the distribution of the remaining constituencies according to their size is studied in terms of deviation of their area from mean

Figure 3.3

Area of Assembly Constituencies in NE Rajasthan (1976–2008)

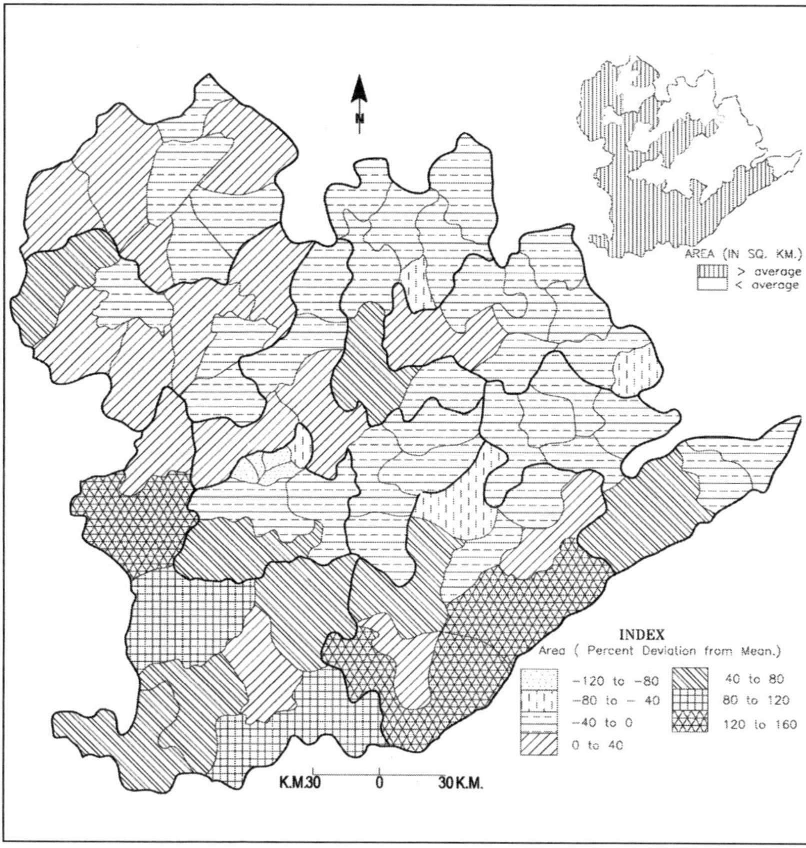

area, the mean value was influenced by the extreme values. Excluding the above, the size of Assembly constituencies ranged between 302 sq. km (Alwar) to 2,126.42 km^2 (Sapotra). When the size of constituencies was studied as per cent deviation from the mean value of area for the remaining 68 constituencies, significant changes occurred in the previous distribution pattern.

The mean value of area, excluding the four constituencies of Jaipur, was 907.47 sq. km. The range of per cent deviation from mean area was between – 66.72 per cent to 134.32 per cent for Alwar and Sapotra respectively. The apparent differences in size were reduced to a significant extent when the extreme values were excluded from the distribution. Approximately 80 per cent (54) of the Assembly constituencies clustered around the mean value within the range of 40 per cent deviation from mean on both sides.

Spatial Distribution of Electorate

Electorate is defined as that segment of the total population of a constituency which is equal to or above 18 years of age on the date fixed by law. The age structure of population residing in an area is a function of the socio-cultural characteristics as well as the level of economic development of the region. The ratio of electorate to the total population tends to be higher in areas which provide good employment opportunities. Thus trade, commercial, administrative, mining or transport centres; areas bearing favourable conditions for intensive agriculture; and areas located near well developed urban centres have higher concentration of working population as well as population seeking employment, leading to concentration of main workers, marginal workers as well as non-workers in the area.

It is the size of electorate in a constituency which ultimately forms the base of the electoral response scenario in the region. It is the electorate who decides the fate of the political parties in form of election outcomes through their right to exercise vote in an election. Therefore size of electorate of constituency plays a crucial role in determining the level of voting turnout in a constituency and subsequently the share of votes polled by the individual parties. In order to understand the spatial patterns of voting turnout and election results, it is important to understand the spatial distribution of electorate in the region. The following section examines the spatial distribution of electorate in the study region in two ways:

1. Assembly unitwise size of electorate in terms of absolute number of electorate.
2. Spatial variation in electorate size in terms of per cent deviation from mean.

Attempt has also been made to examine the temporal changes in electorate size of various Assembly units and to identify areas where such changes had been substantial. For the purpose of studying the temporal variations, the elections have been grouped into two pairs of successive elections:

1. Lok Sabha Elections 1991 and Assembly Elections 1993
2. Lok Sabha Elections 1998 and Assembly Elections 1998

Absolute Size of Electorate

For each election year, the Assembly units of the study area have been classified into seven categories at an interval of 20,000 (Table 3.7).

Table 3.7 *Frequency Distribution of Assembly Units on the Basis of Absolute Number of Electorate*

Electorate Class	*LS 1991*		*VS 1993*		*LS 1998*		*VS 1998*	
	f	*%f*	*f*	*%f*	*f*	*%f*	*f*	*%f*
Below 1,00,000	3	4.17	—	—	—	—	—	—
1,00,000–1,20,000	15	20.83	12	16.67	9	12.5	9	12.5
1,20,000–1,40,000	30	41.67	23	31.94	22	30.56	19	26.39
1,40,000–1,60,000	21	29.17	29	40.28	29	40.28	31	43.06
1,60,000–1,80,000	—	—	5	6.94	7	9.72	8	11.11
1,80,000–2,00,000	—	—	—	—	2	2.78	2	2.78
Above 2,00,000	3	4.17	3	4.17	3	4.17	3	4.17

f: number of Assembly units in a class
%f: relative frequency (f/72)*100)

Lok Sabha Elections 1991

During Lok Sabha elections 1991, the average per Assembly segment size of electorate was 1,32,783 persons which ranged between 90,891 in Kaman and 2,44,404 in Banipark. In three Assembly units the size of electorate was below 1,00,000. In 15 Assembly units it was between 1,00,000 and 1,20,000; in 30 Assembly units it ranged between 1,20,000 to 1,40,000 and in 21 Assembly units it was between 1,40,000 to 1,60,000 persons. In three Assembly units, all of which were urban Assembly units of Jaipur city namely Kishanpole, Johari Bazaar and Banipark, the electorate size was extraordinarily large as compared to the remaining Assembly units. The electorate size was above 2,00,000 in these Assembly units.

A close examination of Figure 3.4A reveals that the electorate size of Assembly units of Alwar, Bharatpur, Dausa, Dholpur and Tonk districts was smaller than 1,40,000 in general. Alwar and Bharatpur segments were exceptions where the electorate size was more than 1,40,000. Kaman, Deeg and Rupbas had the lowest electorate in the entire region. Five Assembly units of Jhunjhunu district, six Assembly units of Sikar and Jaipur districts each, Todabhim and Hindaun had relatively larger electorate population which ranged between 1,40,000 to 1,60,000.

The exceptionally large electorate size in the three Assembly units of Jaipur city is well explained by the highly commercialized and urbanized character of these areas which resulted in excessively high population density in these areas. Almost 91.67 per cent of the Assembly units had electorate size ranging between 1,00,000 to 1,60,000.

Figure 3.4

Assembly Unitwise Absolute Size of Electorate (1991, 1993, 1998)

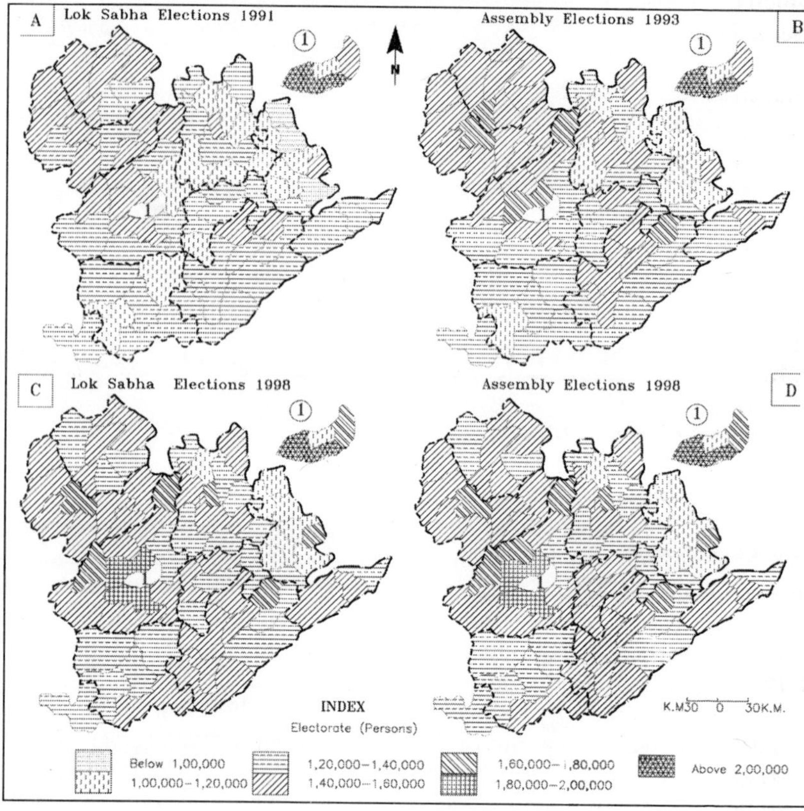

Assembly Elections 1993

In Assembly Elections 1993, the average per seat number of electorate increased to 1,42,275 persons. The electorate size of individual Assembly units varied from 1,00,263 in Hawa Mahal to 2,80,877 in Banipark.

As evident from Table 3.7, there was a general increase in the frequency of classes of larger electorate size consequent upon increase in the size of electorate of various Assembly units. The number of Assembly units having electorate size between 1,00,000 to 1,40,000 declined from 48 to 35 and the Assembly units with electorate size greater than 1,40,000 increased to 37 as compared to 24 in 1991. A detailed frequency distribution has been given in Table 3.7.

The districtwise distribution of Assembly units comprising various classes of electorate size has been illustrated in Figure 3.4B.

All the districts (except Kekri of Ajmer district) invariably exhibited a shift of frequencies towards the higher end of the scale, which underlines a common trend of increase in electorate size in all of them. The increase in size of electorate was consequent upon increase in the population size of the respective areas, especially due to migration and also due to increase in the number of registered voters as more people attain the required age and become eligible for voting.

The category of 1,00,000 to 1,20,000 comprised of Assembly units of Alwar and Bharatpur districts. Toda Rai Singh also figured in this class. Assembly units of Tonk, southern Sawai Madhopur, Dausa, Dholpur and southern part of Jaipur districts had an electorate size ranging between 1,20,000 to 1,40,000. Jhunjhunu, Sikar, northern and central part of Jaipur, northern part of Sawai Madhopur, some parts of Alwar district had relatively larger electorate size, above 1,40,000. Highest electorate size was recorded in the urban Assembly units of Jaipur. Hawa Mahal was an exception where the electorate size was exceptionally low, minimum among all the Assembly units of the study area. Almost 88.9 per cent of the Assembly units recorded an electorate size between 1,00,000 to 1,60,000.

Lok Sabha Elections 1998

In Lok Sabha elections 1998, the average per Assembly unit size of electorate increased to 1,49,214 persons. The electorate size in individual Assembly units varied between 1,07,069 in Hawa Mahal to 3,49,553 in Banipark. The frequency distribution of various classes of electorate size exhibited further shift towards the higher end of the scale (Table 3.10). In nine Assembly units, the size of electorate was between 1,00,000 and 1,20,000; in 22 Assembly units it was between 1,20,000 to 1,40,000; in 29 of them it ranged between 1,40,000 to 1,60,000; and in seven Assembly units it was between 1,60,000 to 1,80,000. Amer and Sanganer recorded a marked increase in electorate which stood between 1,80,000 and 2,00,000. Highest electorate was again recorded in the three urban Assembly units of Jaipur city.

There were some areas of notable exception in Jhunjhunu where a reduction in the number of electorate occurred in Mandawa, Khetri, Gudha and Nawalgarh. The Assembly unitwise distribution of electorate in Lok Sabha elections 1998 has been illustrated in Figure 3.4C. It is evident from the map that larger concentration of electorate occurred in Sikar, Jaipur, western Dholpur and Sawai Madhopur districts. Areas of highest concentration were the urban areas of Jaipur city, Sikar, Phulera, Kotputli, Alwar, Bharatpur and Hindaun. Bharatpur stood as a contrast among all other Assembly units of the district which had the lowest concentration of electorate in the study area.

Assembly Elections 1998

Assembly elections 1998 were held in the month of November, after a short duration of only nine months from the Lok Sabha elections 1998 which took place in the month of February. In Assembly elections 1998, the average per seat electorate size was 1,50,090 persons. The electorate size in individual Assembly units ranged from 1,08,031 in Deeg to 3,68,861 persons in Banipark. The frequency distribution of Assembly units among various categories of electorate size was very similar to the preceding Lok Sabha elections except some minor changes (Table 3.7). The number of Assembly units in the category of 1,20,000 to 1,40,000 decreased to 19 whereas the frequency of the category 1,40,000 to 1,60,000 increased to 31 and that of 1,60,000 to 1,80,000 increased to eight. The proportion of Assembly units having electorate size less than 1,60,000 decreased to 81.95 per cent.

Figure 3.4D illustrates the distribution of electorate in the Assembly units of the study area during 1998 Assembly elections.

The spatial pattern of distribution of electorate was more or less similar to the preceding Lok Sabha election except Lalsot, Sikrai, Chomu and Gudha, which recorded significant increase in their electorate size.

Spatial Variation in Size of Electorate

The spatial variation in the size of electorate in the study area, during various elections under study, has been defined in terms of per cent deviation of the number of electorate in the respective Assembly unit from the mean electorate per Assembly unit of the study area. The analysis consists of four steps as below:

1. Calculation of mean electorate size per Assembly unit.
2. Calculation of percentage deviation of the electorate size of individual Assembly units from the average electorate size, according to the following formula:

$$\% \text{ deviation from mean} = \frac{X - \overline{X}}{X} \times 100$$

Where, X = size of electorate of an Assembly unit

X= mean electorate size in the study area

3. Categorization of Assembly units into eight categories of per cent deviation from mean. For preparing the frequency distribution, the class interval has been taken as 10 per cent and the first and the last classes have been left open ended.
4. Identification of high and low electorate regions by broadly classifying the Assembly units as (a) those with more than average electorate and (b) those with less than average electorate.

Figure 3.5

Spatial Variation in Electorate Size in North East Rajasthan (1991–93)

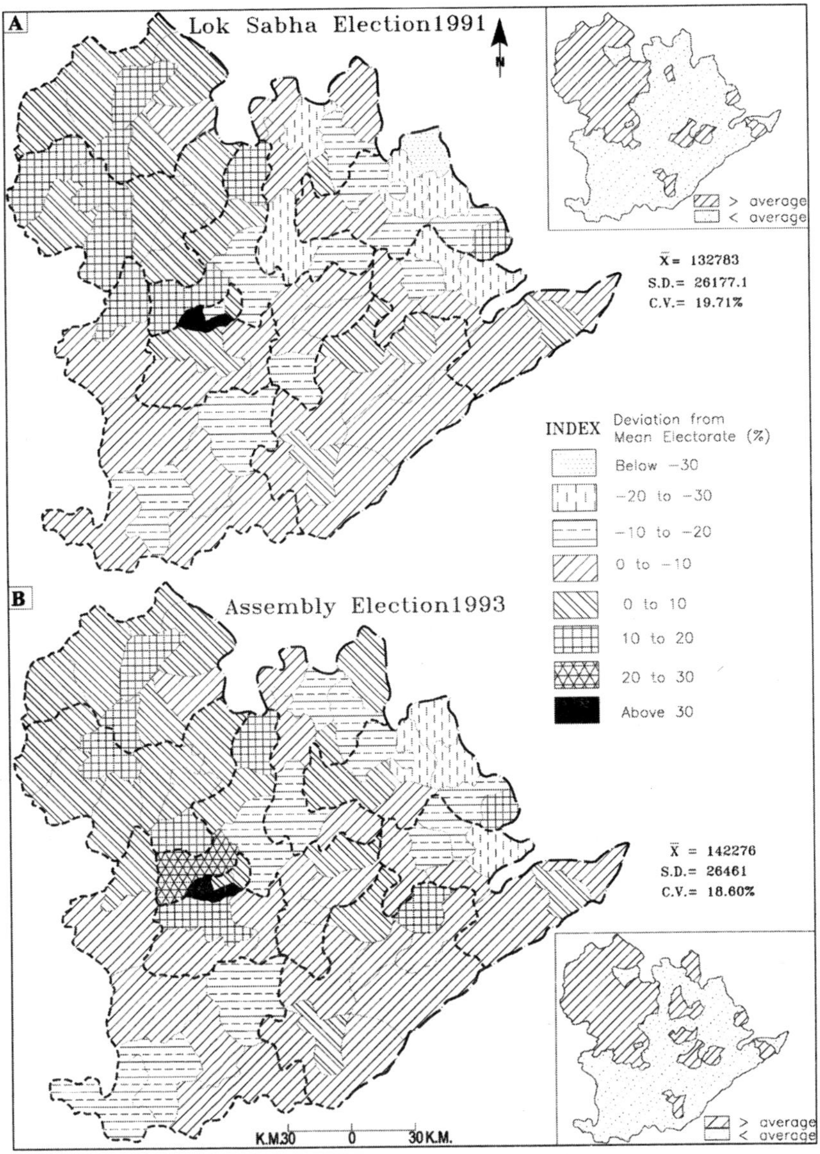

Lok Sabha Elections 1991

During Lok Sabha elections 1991, the mean size of electorate per Assembly unit was 1,32,783 with a standard deviation of 26,177 and a coefficient of variation of 19.17 per cent (Table 3.8).

Table 3.8 *Parameters of Distribution of Electorate*

Election	*Mean Electorate*	σ	*C.V.*
LS 1991	1,32,783	26,177	19.71
VS 1993	1,42,276	26,461	18.60
LS 1998	1,49,214	35,445	23.75
VS 1998	1,50,090	38,095	25.38

Note: σ = standard deviation, C.V. = coefficient of variation.

In 58.33 per cent (42) Assembly units, the electorate size was less than average. Whole of Tonk, Dausa, Sawai Madhopur, Alwar, Bharatpur and southern part of Jaipur district were included in this category. Among these Alwar, Bharatpur, Dholpur, Todabhim, Hindaun and Sawai Madhopur Assembly units were exceptions where the electorate size was higher than average. The 41.67 per cent (30) Assembly units which had more than average size of electorate included all Assembly units of Jhunjhunu district (except Khetri), whole of Sikar district and northern and central part of Jaipur district (Figure 3.5A).

Table 3.9 displays a comparative view of frequency distribution of Assembly units into various categories of electorate size in terms of percentage deviation from mean during all election years under study. As evident from the table, in 1991 very few Assembly units differed substantially from the average size, lying on extreme ends of the scale. Only 13.89 per cent of the Assembly units deviated more than 20 per cent from mean on either side whereas 86.11 per cent (62) Assembly units had electorate size between 20 per cent on both sides from the mean.

On the extreme ends of the distribution, Kaman, having the lowest electorate in the entire study area was the only Assembly unit in the category of more than 30 per cent deviation on the negative side. six Assembly units of Alwar and Bharatpur districts had electorate which deviated between 20 to 30 per cent from mean on the negative side. Electorate size of 11 Assembly units deviated between 10 to 20 per cent on negative side of the mean. The areal distribution of the Assembly units comprising these categories has been illustrated in Figure 3.5A.

On the higher side, nine Assembly units had electorate size 10 to 20 per cent greater than the mean. Three Assembly units had extremely high concentration of electorate, deviating more than 30 per cent from mean, actually amounting to 69.13 per cent in Kishanpole, 74.22 per cent in Johari Bazaar and 84.06 per cent in Banipark. If these Assembly units are excluded, the coefficient of variation of spatial distribution of electorate in the region drops to 12.22 per cent.

Table 3.9 *Frequency Distribution of Assembly Units on the Basis of Electorate Size (% Deviation from Mean)*

Class	*Lok Sabha 1991*		*Vidhan Sabha 1993*		*Lok Sabha 1998*		*Vidhan Sabha 1998*	
	f	*%f*	*f*	*%f*	*f*	*%f*	*f*	*%f*
Less than –30	1	1.39	0	0	0	0	0	0
–20 to –30	6	8.33	6	8.33	9	12.50	9	12.50
–10 to –20	11	15.28	10	13.89	9	12.50	12	16.67
0 to –10	24	33.33	24	33.33	26	36.11	24	33.33
0 to 10	18	25.00	20	27.78	17	23.61	16	22.22
10 to 20	9	12.50	8	11.11	6	8.33	6	8.33
20 to 30	0	0.00	1	1.39	2	2.78	2	2.78
More than 30	3	4.17	3	4.17	3	4.17	3	4.17

Note: f = frequency, %f = relative frequency in per cent.

There was considerable variation among the Lok Sabha constituencies of the study area with regard to their respective size of electorate and inter segment distribution of electorate. The average size of electorate, Assembly segments having maximum and minimum electorate and coefficient of variation of inter segment disparities in electorate size of constituent Assembly segments of each Lok Sabha constituency has been shown in Table 3.10.

In 1991, Bharatpur had the minimum electorate size of 9,01,890 persons and Jaipur had maximum with an electorate size of 13,46,629 persons. The inter segment disparity in voter population was also highest in Jaipur with a coefficient of variation of 32.84 per cent. Hawa Mahal had the minimum and Banipark had the maximum number of electorate in Jaipur Lok Sabha constituency.

Highest uniformity in inter segment distribution of electorate obtained in Sikar Lok Sabha constituency, for which the value of coefficient of variation was 4.83 per cent. The electorate size in constituent Assembly segments varied between a minimum of 1,36,331 in Khandela to a maximum of 1,58,617 in Sikar.

Table 3.10 *Intra Constituency Variability in Size of Electorate (LS 1991)*

LS Constituency	*Electorate*	*Mean*	σ	*C.V.*	*Minimum*	*Maximum*
Sikar	11,60,797	1,45,100	7,014.42	4.83	Khandela (11.74)	Sikar (13.66)
Jhunjhunu	11,42,564	1,42,821	7,662.02	5.36	Khetri (11.38)	Jhunjhunu (13.37)
Sawai Madhopur (ST)	10,52,967	1,31,621	8,822.68	6.70	Sapotra(ST) (11.42)	Hindaun (SC)(13.79)
Tonk (SC)	9,99,712	1,24,964	10,751.21	8.60	Toda Rai Singh (11.27)	Phulera (14.68)
Bayana (SC)	9,44,735	1,18,092	12,456.51	10.55	Rupbas(SC) (10.56)	Bari (13.54)
Alwar	9,62,311	1,20,289	13,153.44	10.93	Mandawar (10.67)	Alwar (14.66)
Dausa	10,48,801	1,31,100	14,510.67	11.07	Jamwa Ramgarh (10.98)	Amer (14.72)
Bharatpur	9,01,890	1,12,736	19,051.86	16.90	Kaman (10.08)	Bharatpur (16.58)
Jaipur	13,46,629	1,68,329	55,278.89	32.84	Hawa Mahal (8.19)	Banipark (18.15)

Note: Mean refers to average electorate of constituent Assembly segments.
Figures in parenthesis stand for electorate size of Assembly segment as per cent of total electorate of the LS Constituency.

Bharatpur Lok Sabha constituency, although having smallest electorate size, ranked next to Jaipur in terms of intra constituency variation in electorate. The coefficient of variation of inter Assembly segment distribution of voter population for Bharatpur was 16.90 per cent, which was nearly half as compared to Jaipur Lok Sabha constituency.

The spatial patterns of distribution of electorate and its variability at the level of Assembly units as well as Lok Sabha constituencies may be explained through an examination of geographical characteristics of the respective areas. The size of electorate primarily depends upon two factors:

1. The size of total population in an area.
2. The proportion of population of 18 years of age or above in that area.

The correlation between population and electorate in the study area, at the level of Assembly units, was +0.84 in 1991. This implies that the Assembly units having low population are the ones having small electorate size in the region and vice versa. The average ratio of electorate to population per Assembly unit was 59.97 per cent which varied between a minimum of 41.60 per cent in Jaipur Rural to a maximum of 75.79 per cent in Mahuwa.

Therefore, the factors which govern the distribution of population in a region by and large determine the distribution of electorate also. Most important of these factors are as under:

1. Physical factors
   - (i) Topography or relief
   - (ii) Availability of drinking water
   - (iii) Climatic conditions
   - (iv) Fertility of soil
2. Socio-economic factors
   - (i) Irrigation facilities
   - (ii) Connectivity and accessibility of an area, i.e. development of transport network
   - (iii) Level of economic development and employment opportunities in the region

Besides the above listed factors, several historical and cultural factors also play a crucial role in determining the spatial distribution pattern of population in a region. All these factors together not only influence the absolute size of population in a region but also condition the compactness of settlement type, age structure and occupational structure of population which ultimately determines the ratio of electorate to total population in the region.

When the Assembly unitwise variation in electorate size in 1991 is analysed in the light of the geographical characteristics of the respective areas, it is observed that by and large, the Assembly units having less than average electorate are located in areas of uneven or dissected topography, lacking in adequate transportation network, i.e. low connectivity through State or National highways and railway network or are predominantly rural areas. Contrastingly, the Assembly units having electorate size larger than the average are those which comprise of urban and sub urban areas; spread over district, tehsil or sub divisional headquarters; are located on transport foci or industrial centres in the region. All these conditions are inter-related and together provide impetus to the concentration of working population as well as population seeking employment in an area which results in higher concentration of population and larger electorate size in such areas.

The spatial variation in the distribution of electorate among the various Assembly units of the study area may thus be explained as under:

1. Assembly Units Having Electorate Size Less than Average

The areas where the electorate size was less than the per unit average, particularly those areas which deviated more than 10 per cent on the negative side included Assembly segments of Alwar and Bharatpur districts; Toda Rai Singh, Niwai, Hawa Mahal and Jamwa Ramgarh. Except Hawa Mahal all these Assembly units were located in predominantly rural areas spreading over those parts of the respective districts where major proportion of rural population of the district resides. For example, Rupbas and Nagar recorded the maximum proportion of rural population in the district in 1991 census. Kaman, having minimum voter population, had an uneven topography with hilly terrain in its western and central part and an uneven intervening land. The percentage of electorate to population was 49.37 per cent in Kaman in 1991. This explains the small population and electorate size in this area to a large extent. Hawa Mahal is an exception in the category which is one of the most populated segments of the study area but has a small voter population. In 1991, 49.54 per cent of the population of Hawa Mahal formed the electorate. Hawa Mahal is an urban Assembly unit, lying in the heart of Jaipur city and a centre of business activity in the capital.

Assembly units in which the electorate size deviates less than 10 per cent on the negative side form part of Alwar, Dausa, Dholpur, Sawai Madhopur and Tonk districts. Bayana, Bassi, Dudu and Phagi also figure in this category. These segments, in general, spread over small towns or other areas with fairly high concentration of population in the respective districts, being either trade, administrative or commercial centres or being located on major roads or railway routes. Proximity of a city, concentration of industrial units in the area were other factors which had resulted in migration of population from nearby rural areas towards these areas. For example, Gangapur, Karauli and Tonk were urban centres; Bandikui and Behror had developed as important towns owing to their location on important railway routes and national highway respectively; Bassi and Dudu enjoyed the locational advantages of proximity to Jaipur city and situation along national highways; Khetri was an important mining centre in north east Jhunjhunu and likewise.

2. Assembly Units Having Electorate Size More Than Average

The Assembly units having electorate size on higher side of the average included all Assembly units of Sikar district, whole of Jhunjhunu except Khetri, 10 of the 15 Assembly units of Jaipur district and Todabhim and Hindaun of Sawai Madhopur district. These were densely populated areas enjoying favourable location with regard to resource potential, both agricultural and mineral, for industrial development; high connectivity through rail and road network; proximity to large urban centres; and had developed into market, trade and commercial centres or transport foci.

Jhunjhunu and Sikar districts with a mixed economy had large number of urban centres distributed uniformly over the entire district. These districts possessed substantial mineral as well as agro resource base, a well developed transport network especially road network and hence large proportion of population was employed in non agricultural activities. Thus the voter population in these areas was large as well as uniformly distributed. The electorate size of Amer, Sanganer and Jaipur rural is largely explained by their proximity to Jaipur city. Kotputli, Sawai Madhopur, Alwar, Bharatpur and Dholpur were large urban centres with large concentration of industries enjoying nodal position on road as well as broad gauge railway routes. Chomu, located near the State capital had a big *mandi*. Gudha was an important mining centre. Hindaun and Phulera had developed because of their location on broad gauge railway line. Neem-ka-Thana, Sri Madhopur and Danta Ramgarh formed part of Khetri Jaipur industrial belt. Fatehpur, Lachhmangarh, Khandela, Nawalgarh and Mandawa were important urban centres well connected through rail and roads. Sikar and Jhunjhunu were district headquarters.

Kishanpole, Johari Bazaar and Banipark, located in highly urbanized capital city of Jaipur were centres of business and commercial activities and therefore recorded exceptionally large electorate size. It is noteworthy that electorate formed 48.22 per cent of the total population in Johari Bazaar whereas this ratio was more than 70 per cent in Kishanpole and Banipark.

Concludingly, it may be generalized that the distribution of electorate was predominantly governed by the nature of economy, level of urbanization and spacing of urban centres in the area. Rural areas being sparsely populated and having low ratio of electorate to total population had relatively small voter population. Contrastingly, densely populated urban areas having higher ratio of electorate to total population record relatively larger voter population. The intra-constituency variability largely depended upon the spacing of urban centres. In districts where urban centres were closely spaced as in Jhunjhunu and Sikar, variability was low. In areas where large disparities existed in the level of socio-economic development in different parts of a district, as in districts lying in eastern part of the study area where urban centres were few and far apart, variability was high.

Assembly Elections 1993

In 1993, the average electorate per Assembly unit was 1,42,276. The standard deviation of distribution of electorate was 26,461 and coefficient of variation was 18.60 per cent. The slight decline in the magnitude of coefficient of variation indicated relatively higher uniformity in the distribution of electorate.

Forty (55.6%) Assembly units had electorate size below average which were mainly those located in the eastern and southern parts of the study region in Alwar, Bharatpur, Dausa, Dholpur, Sawai Madhopur and whole of Tonk district. And 44.4 per cent (32) Assembly units had electorate size above average. These were mainly located in Jhunjhunu and Sikar districts, major part of Jaipur district and some scattered pockets in the eastern part of the study area encompassing district headquarters and trade, transport or industrial centres (Figure 3.5B).

The frequency distribution of Assembly units over various categories of electorate size as per cent deviation from mean was more or less the same as in 1991. A comparison of the frequency distribution in 1991 and 1993 has been made in Figure 3.6.

It is evident from the graph that there were small shifts in the frequencies of various categories from lower to higher categories but no drastic changes were observed. There was a slight decline of one unit in the number of Assembly units having electorate size deviating between –10 to –20 per cent from the mean. The number of Assembly units in the category of 0 to 10 per cent deviation increased by two units whereas the frequency of the category of 10 to 20 per cent deviation declined by one unit (Table 3.9). In one Assembly unit, i.e. Amer, the electorate size was 20 to 30 per cent higher than the mean.

The spatial distribution pattern of electorate as depicted in Figure 3.5B did not exhibit any marked shifts as compared to 1991. In general the lowest voter population was recorded in Bharatpur district along with some parts of Alwar and Tonk districts. The highest electorate population was recorded in Assembly units of Jaipur city.

As evident from Figure 3.6 and Table 3.9, maximum concentration of Assembly units occurred close to the average. In 86.11 per cent (62) Assembly units, the electorate size varied between 20 per cent on both sides of the average whereas in 61.11 per cent Assembly units, electorate size varied within 10 per cent from the average on both sides, which is quite insignificant.

Although the deviation values ranged between –29.53 per cent in Hawa Mahal and 97.12 per cent in Banipark, in 69 (95.8%) Assembly units the deviation figures varied between –29.53 per cent to 20.64 per

Figure 3.6

Spatial Distribution of Electorate
(Lok Sabha 1991 and Assembly Elections 1993)

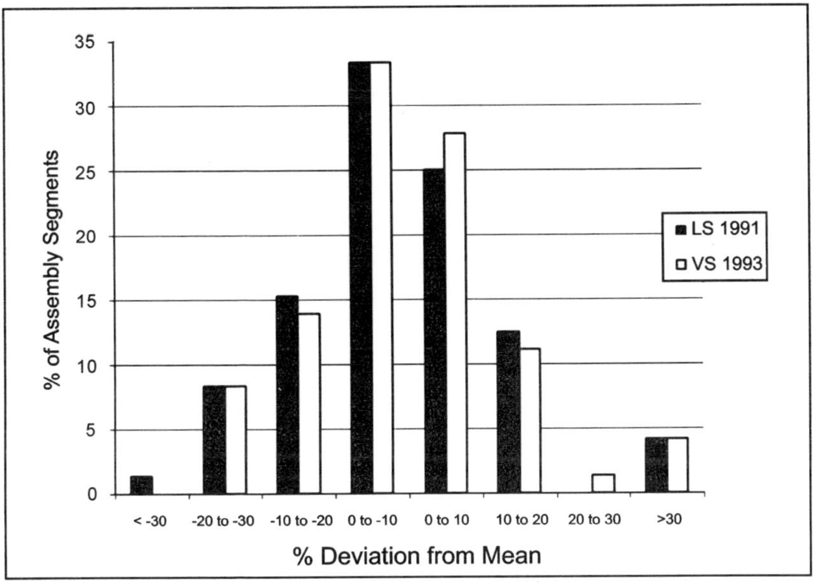

cent. If the three Assembly units of Jaipur – Banipark, Kishanpole and Johari Bazaar are excluded, the coefficient of variation for the remaining study area declines to 11.8 per cent.

Lok Sabha Elections 1998

During Lok Sabha elections 1998, the mean size of electorate per Assembly segment was 1,49,214 persons. The standard deviation of Assembly unitwise distribution of electorate was 35,445 and the coefficient of variation was 23.75 per cent. Thus there was an increase in the variability in the distribution of electorate in the region as compared to the previous elections.

In 61.11 per cent (44) Assembly units, the size of electorate was less than the average. The Assembly units comprising this category were predominantly located in eastern and southern parts of the study area. Small part of southern Jhunjhunu and western Sikar were also included in this category. In 28 (38.89%) of Assembly units the electorate size was higher than average. These areas included northern part of Jhunjhunu district, major part of Sikar and Jaipur districts and some isolated patches in the eastern part of the study area (Figure 3.7A)

As revealed by the frequency distribution of Assembly units among various classes of electorate size as per cent deviation from mean (Table 3.9), 80.5 per cent of the Assembly units had electorate size within the range of 20 per cent deviation above or below average.

In 59.7 per cent Assembly units, the voter population was within the range of 10 per cent deviation from the average on both sides of the mean. In nine Assembly units, the voter population deviated between 20 to 30 per cent from the mean on negative side, majority of which were located in Bharatpur district. Mandawar also figured in this category. Five Assembly units with exceptionally high concentration of electorate amounting to more than 20 per cent positive deviation from the average were located in the highly urbanized areas of Jaipur city. Kishanpole, Johari Bazaar and Banipark had extraordinarily large electorate population with magnitude of deviation between 58.72 per cent in Kishanpole and 134.25 per cent in Banipark. Excluding these three Assembly units, the electorate size of 95.83 per cent Assembly units ranged between –28.24 and +27.17 per cent deviation from the mean with a coefficient of variation of 12.54 per cent. The spatial pattern of Assembly unitwise variation in size of electorate in the study area in 1998 Lok Sabha elections has been illustrated in Figure 3.7A.

A comparative statement of Lok Sabha constituencywise size of electorate and inter segment variation in electorate size during 1998 Lok Sabha elections has been given in Table 3.11.

Table 3.11 *Intra-Constituency Variability in Size of Electorate (LS 1998)*

LS Constituency	*Total Electorate*	*Mean*	*S.D.*	*C.V.*
Jhunjhunu	11,53,561	1,44,195	8,122.22	5.63
Sikar	12,43,952	1,55,494	8,845.96	5.69
Sawai Madhopur (ST)	11,77,149	1,47,144	11,082.69	7.53
Tonk (SC)	11,09,239	1,38,655	13,343.42	9.62
Bayana (SC)	10,53,793	1,31,724	14,069.48	10.68
Dausa	12,23,211	1,52,901	18,381.85	12.02
Alwar	11,25,267	1,40,658	19,292.76	13.72
Bharatpur	10,34,598	1,29,325	19,898.26	15.39
Jaipur	16,22,629	2,02,829	81,251.48	40.06

The average electorate per constituency was 11,98,730 which varied from a minimum of 10,34,598 in Bharatpur Lok Sabha constituency to a maximum of 16,22,629 in Jaipur Lok Sabha constituency. The coefficient of variation of inter constituency distribution of

Figure 3.7

Spatial Variation in Electorate Size (1998–99)

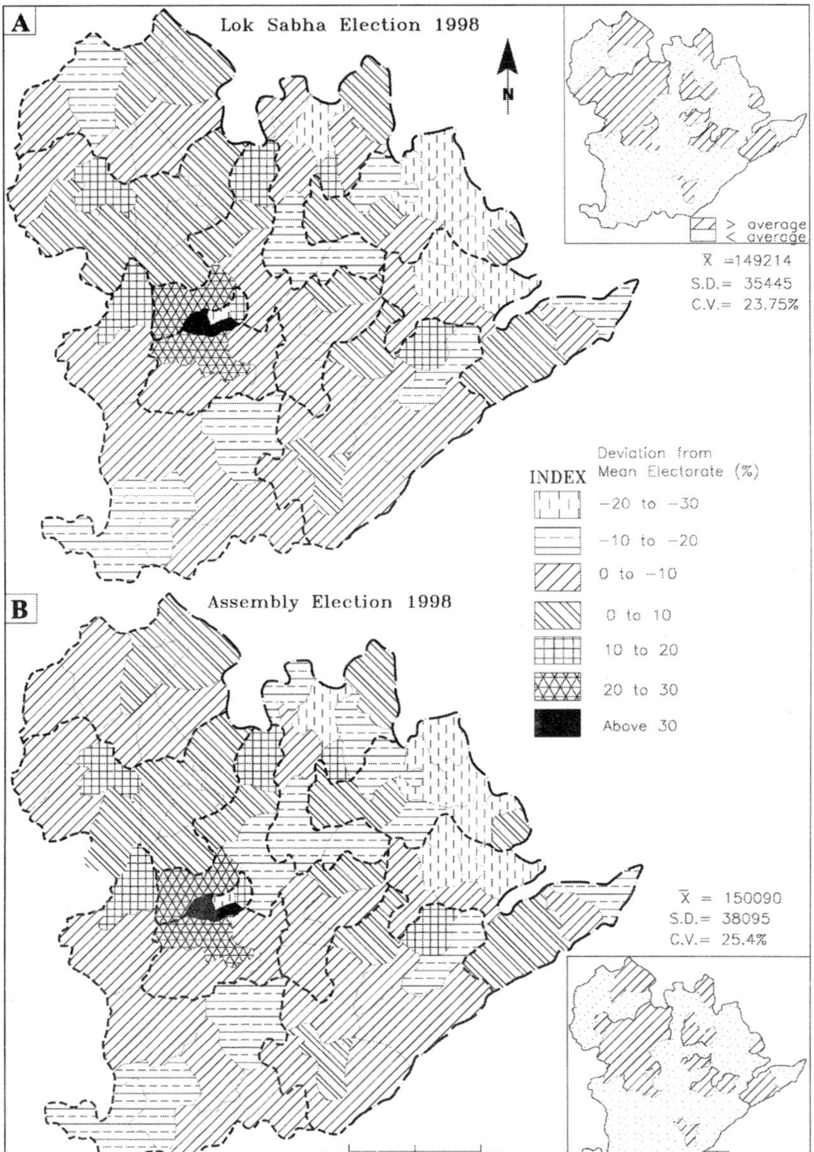

electorate was 15.58 per cent. Excluding Jaipur constituency the coefficient of variation for the remaining constituencies was 6.54 per cent. This underlines the exceptionally high concentration of voter population in Jaipur constituency.

The intra constituency variation in Assembly segmentwise distribution of voter population as indicated by values of coefficient of variation of individual constituencies was minimum in Jhunjhunu and maximum in Jaipur. In Jhunjhunu, the electorate size of individual segments varied between 1,34,102 in Mandawa and 1,54,481 in Surajgarh, with a coefficient of variation of 5.63 per cent.

The coefficient of variation in Jaipur Lok Sabha constituency was 40.06 per cent which indicates high disparity in distribution of electorate in the region. The electorate size of constituent Assembly segments of the constituency varied from a minimum of 1,07,069 in Hawa Mahal to a maximum of 3,49,553 in Banipark.

Bharatpur constituency with coefficient of variation of 15.39 per cent stood next to Jaipur. Deeg, with 10.51 per cent of the total electorate of the constituency had the least voter population whereas Bharatpur, with 15.81 per cent share of total electorate of the constituency, had the highest voter population.

Assembly Elections 1998

Assembly elections 1998 were held at a short interval of nine months after the 1998 Lok Sabha elections. The spatial pattern of variation in electorate size at the Assembly unit level cannot be expected to change significantly in such a short span of time. In Assembly elections 1998, the mean electorate size per constituency was 1,50,090 persons. The standard deviation of distribution of electorate was 38,095 and coefficient of variation was 25.38 per cent. Thus there was slight increase in the strength as well as variability of distribution of electorate in the region as compared to the preceding Lok Sabha elections.

Figure 3.8 provides a comparison of the distribution of Assembly units among various categories of electorate size during the two elections.

It is evident from the Figure 3.8 that there was slight decline in the number of Assembly units having electorate size within the range of 10 per cent on both sides of mean whereas the number of Assembly units with electorate size of 10 to 20 per cent less than the average increased. The frequencies in the remaining categories remained unchanged (Table 3.9).

62.5 per cent (45) Assembly units had more than average electorate whereas 37.5 per cent (27) of them had less than average

Figure 3.8

Spatial Distribution of Electorate
(Lok Sabha 1998 and Assembly Elections 1998)

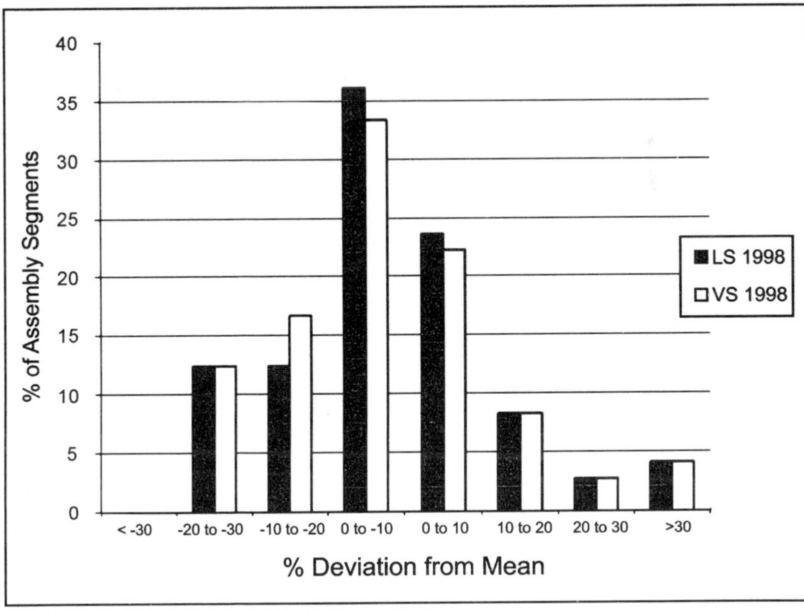

electorate. The spatial distribution pattern of Assembly units having high and low electorate size was exactly similar, except for Dhod which stepped down to below average category due to negative change in its voter population (Figure 3.7B).

As evident from Table 3.9, there was a slight decline in the number of Assembly units centring around the average. Nearly 55.55 per cent of Assembly units had voter population which deviated less than 10 per cent on both sides of mean. But the proportion of Assembly units within the range of 20 per cent deviation around the mean remained unchanged at 80.5 per cent. The electorate size of individual constituencies deviated between –28.02 per cent in Deeg and 145.76 per cent in Banipark. Excluding the three urban Assembly units of Jaipur having the extraordinarily high electorate size, the values for remaining 95.8 per cent units ranged between –28.2 per cent in Deeg and 29.89 per cent in Sanganer with a coefficient of variation of 12.67 per cent.

A comparison of Figure 3.7A and B clearly reveals that the spatial pattern of distribution of electorate in the region was by and large similar to that during Lok Sabha elections. No marked changes had occurred except for some parts of Alwar district, Jamwa Ramgarh and Dhod, which stepped down by one category and positive change in Mandawa.

Comparative Analysis

A careful examination of the distribution and variation of electorate during the four elections under consideration reveals the following facts:

1. There was an increase in the total electorate and mean electorate in the region (Assembly unit level) in each successive election. This is a natural phenomenon as increasing number of people attain the voting age with passage of time.
2. The variability in the distribution of electorate over the study area, measured as standard deviation and coefficient of variation, also registered a constant increase in magnitude, from 19.71 per cent in Lok Sabha 1991 to 25.38 per cent in Vidhan Sabha 1998 (Table 3.8).
3. The value of mean electorate, standard deviation and coefficient of variation of electorate size of individual Assembly units was highly affected by extremely large size of electorate of three Assembly units namely Johari Bazaar, Kishanpole and Banipark. In each election, the electorate size of 95.83 per cent (69) Assembly units varied within the limits of –30 to +30 per cent deviation around the mean and excluding the above three Assembly units, the coefficient of variation valued between 11.5 per cent and 12.6 per cent. If the three Assembly units of Jaipur, occurring in the category of more than 30 per cent deviation in all four elections are included, the values of coefficient of variation increase considerably ranging from 18.6 per cent to 25.38 per cent.
4. More than 50 per cent of the Assembly units had less than the mean size of electorate. The number was minimum in Vidhan Sabha 1993 elections (40) and maximum (45) in Vidhan Sabha 1998 elections.
5. Nearly 60 per cent of the Assembly units, in all elections, had electorate within the range of –10 per cent to +10 per cent deviation from their respective means.
6. Bharatpur Lok Sabha constituency had the lowest electorate size and Jaipur Lok Sabha constituency had the highest number of electorate. Jaipur Lok Sabha constituency also had the highest variability in the size of electorate of its constituent Assembly units. Bharatpur recorded next highest variability after Jaipur. Jhunjhunu and Sikar had the most uniform distribution of electorate among their Assembly segments.

7. Broadly speaking the eastern and southern parts of the study area had relatively low electorate size and the northern, western and central parts had higher electorate size. In Lok Sabha 1991 and Assembly 1993 elections, this demarcation was relatively more pronounced.

Temporal Variations in Spatial Distribution of Electorate

To examine the temporal changes in the electorate size at the Assembly unit level, the election years under consideration were dealt as two pairs of successive elections, LS 1991 – VS 1993 and LS 1998 – VS 1998. The spatial pattern of changes in electorate size were described in terms of per cent difference (increase or decrease) in number of electorate over the previous election year. This was calculated according to the following formulae.

$$\% \text{ change} = \frac{a_x b_x}{a_x} \times 100$$

Where, a_x = size of electorate of Assembly unit 'x' during former election year.

b_x = size of electorate of Assembly unit 'x' during consecutive election year.

The spatial patterns of change were then identified by classifying the Assembly units on the basis of the magnitude of per cent negative or positive change into seven classes, with a class interval of 5 per cent.

Lok Sabha 1991 and Assembly Elections 1993

There was an overall increase in the size of electorate in the study area except for Hawa Mahal, Kishanpole and Johari Bazaar where it recorded a decline.

As evident from the Table 3.12, in 12 Assembly units, the change in electorate size was less than 5 per cent which was quite insignificant. In 44 Assembly units there was a positive change ranging between 5 and 10 per cent. In 13 Assembly units, there was substantial rise in size of electorate, from 10 to 15 per cent. Kaman was the only Assembly unit which registered an increase of more than 20 per cent in its voter population.

The spatial pattern of magnitude of change in electorate size shown in Figure 3.9A reveals that in major part of the study area including south-eastern part and Pilani of Jhunjhunu district; central and eastern part of Sikar; northern part of Tonk; whole of Sawai Madhopur (except

Hindaun); major part of Dausa (except Lalsot); south western, southern and eastern part of Jaipur district; north eastern and south western part of Bharatpur district; western and eastern Dholpur district; and major part of Alwar district recorded a moderate increase in voter population amounting to 5 to 10 per cent. Central part of Jaipur district especially the hinterland of Jaipur city viz. Sanganer, Amer, Chomu and Kotputli; Lalsot, Hindaun, north eastern and central part of Alwar; Kaman, Nagar, Nadbai and Rupbas in Bharatpur districts recorded substantial increase (more than 10%) in electorate.

Table 3.12 *Frequency Distribution of Assembly Units in Various Classes of Per cent Change in Size of Electorate*

Class	*A*		*B*	
	f	*%f*	*f*	*%f*
–5 to –10	2	2.78	0	0
0 to –5	1	1.39	31	43.06
0 to 5	11	15.28	40	55.56
5 to 10	44	61.11	1	1.39
10 to 15	13	18.06	0	0.00
15 to 20	0	0	0	0.00
20 to 25	1	1.39	0	0.00

Note: A = Lok Sabha Elections 1991 and Assembly Elections 1993
B = Lok Sabha Elections 1998 and Assembly Elections 1998
f = number of constituencies/Assembly segments
%f = relative frequency in per cent.

Among the Assembly units which recorded a negative change in electorate size, the change was very small and insignificant in Johari Bazaar. In Hawa Mahal and Kishanpole the decline was –9.10 per cent and –8.15 per cent respectively.

Lok Sabha 1998 and Assembly Elections 1998

As stated earlier, owing to the short interval of time, no major changes in electorate size could be expected between the two elections held in 1998. The magnitude of change during these elections ranged from –2.79 per cent in Surajgarh to 5.52 per cent in Banipark. It is evident from the frequency distribution of Assembly units among various categories of percentage change given in Table 3.12 that in 98.6 per cent of the Assembly units the change in electorate size was less than 5 per cent on both sides, which is quite insignificant. Only in Banipark there was a positive change of more than 5 per cent. But in Banipark

Figure 3.9

Temporal Changes in Electorate Size (Assembly Unitwise), 1991–93, 1998–98

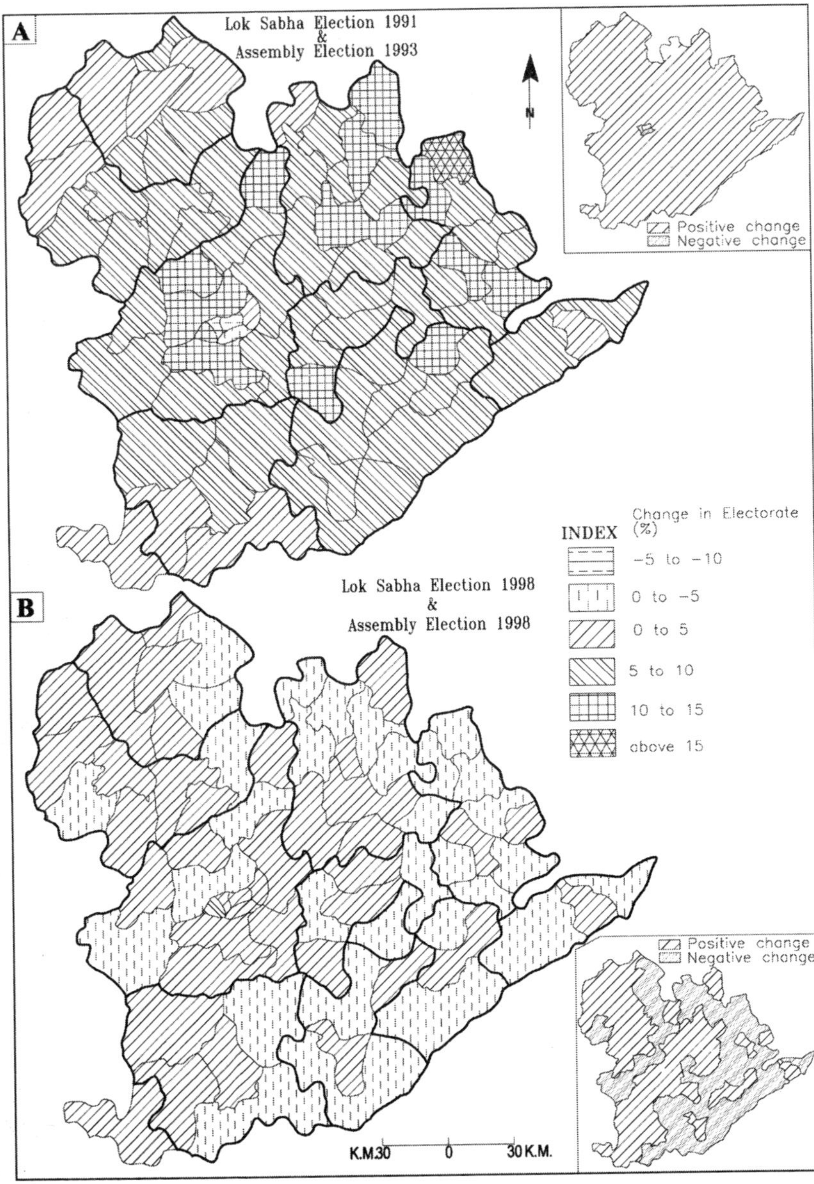

too the increase in electorate size was only 5.52 per cent which is not very substantial.

Thirty one Assembly units recorded a negative change whereas 40 Assembly units recorded a positive change in voter population. Figure 3.9B portrays the spatial pattern of change in electorate size in the study area during the elections held in 1998. No well defined areas of growth or decline are identifiable and the Assembly units recording positive and negative growth were scattered over the entire region. But broadly speaking, it may be said that there was a positive change or growth in electorate size in the north western, central and south western part of the study area whereas in the northern, eastern and south eastern part there was, by and large, decline in the size of electorate.

The following factors were responsible for the changes, positive as well as negative, occurring in the electorate size of an area:

1. Inclusion of new electorate in the electoral rolls during the exercise of revision of electoral rolls by way of attaining the age of 18 years.
2. Deletion of names because of natural death.
3. Immigration to and migration of electorate from a constituency.
4. Lapse on the part of enumerators to include names in the list or on part of electorate to get themselves registered at the time of revision of electoral rolls.
5. Voluntary addition and deletion of names in the electorate of particular constituencies desired by the electorate themselves.

Density of Electorate

Due to high degree of variation among the Assembly units with respect to their geographical area as well as size of electorate, great variations were observed both at the Lok Sabha and the Assembly segment levels regarding density of electorate which was measured as number of electorate per sq. km of area.

An attempt was made to identify the spatial variation in density of electorate during the four election years under study by classifying the Assembly units on the basis absolute density (electorate per sq. km). The Assembly units were classified into eight classes of density of electorate, 50–100, 100–150, 150–200, 200–300, 300–500, 500–1,000, 1,000–10,000 and more than 10,000 electorate per sq. km. The class interval was exclusive and unequal as there was great variation in density values in the region which were more concentrated in the lower end of the range and few Assembly units had high to very high density values. Therefore to highlight the distribution characteristics of electorate density properly, varying class interval were adopted. The last class was left open ended. The spatial pattern of density variation was defined in terms of frequency and relative frequency of each class.

Lok Sabha Elections 1991

As density of electorate is a function of area and number of electorate of the respective constituency, the smallest Assembly units in the region are the ones having highest density of electorate and vice versa. During Lok Sabha elections 1991, the density of electorate in the study region as a whole was 155 persons per sq. km. Among the nine Lok Sabha constituencies under study, highest density of electorate occurred in Jaipur Lok Sabha constituency, the density being 368 persons per sq. km. This high value could be attributed to the small area and large electorate size of the four urban Assembly units of Jaipur – Hawa Mahal, Johari Bazaar, Kishanpole and Banipark. In Jaipur Lok Sabha constituency, Kishanpole had the highest density (26,084 persons per sq. km) and Phagi had the lowest (81 persons per sq. km) density of electorate. Phagi was the largest Assembly segment of Jaipur constituency and Kishanpole was the smallest of the three segments (in terms of area) having the largest electorate size in the region.

Tonk Lok Sabha constituency had the lowest density of electorate (89 persons per sq. km). It is noteworthy that Tonk was the largest of all Lok Sabha constituencies in terms of area. Phulera, the smallest in terms of area, had the maximum density (162 persons per sq. km) and Dudu, the largest segment, had the least density (68 persons per sq. km).

If the intra-constituency variation in density of the Assembly segments of the respective constituencies was considered, the variation was highest among the segments of Jaipur Lok Sabha constituency (C.V. 129.24%) and was lowest in Jhunjhunu Lok Sabha constituency (C.V. 19.34%). Density values in Jhunjhunu constituency ranged between 123 persons per sq. km in Mandawa and 211 persons per sq. km in Jhunjhunu. The mean density of Lok Sabha constituencies and statistics regarding inter segment variation of electorate density of constituent Assembly segments during Lok Sabha 1991 elections has been given in Table 3.13.

At the level of the Assembly segments, electorate density varied from a minimum of 57 persons per sq. km in Sapotra to a maximum of 26,084 persons per sq. km in Kishanpole. It is noteworthy that Sapotra was the largest Assembly segment in the study region. The mean density in the study region, including the density values of the four Assembly segments of Jaipur was 984 persons per sq. km whereas if these were excluded, the mean density of the remaining 68 Assembly segments came down to 167 persons per sq. km, with maximum density of 467 persons per sq. km in Alwar (Table 3.14).

Table 3.13 *Parameters of Lok Sabha Constituencywise Density of Electorate (LS 1991)*

Constituency	*Density*	*Mean*	*ó*	*C.V.*	*Highest*	*Lowest*
Jhunjhunu	163	168	32.50	19.34	Jhunjhunu (211)	Mandawa (123)
Dausa	156	162	35.82	22.11	Bandikui (226)	Jamwa Ramgarh (104)
Bayana	165	181	46.22	25.53	Dholpur (245)	Bari (84)
Sikar	155	166	51.31	30.91	Sikar (263)	Dhod (121)
Tonk	89	96	33.75	35.16	Phulera (162)	Dudu (68)
Bharatpur	173	191	88.05	46.10	Bharatpur (403)	Lacchmangarh (115)
Alwar	175	207	113.40	54.78	Alwar (467)	Thanagazi (87)
Sawai Madhopur	114	150	86.62	57.74	Todabhim (304)	Sapotra (57)
Jaipur	368	7,535	9,737.98	129.24	Kishanpole (26,084)	Phagi (81)

Note: Density = number of electorate per sq. km.
Figures in parentheses indicate absolute density of the respective Assembly units.
Mean stands for average density of constituent Assembly segments of respective Lok Sabha constituency.

Table 3.14 *Frequency Distribution of Assembly Units on the Basis of Density of Electorate (1991–93)*

Density	*LS 1991*			*VS 1993*		
	f	*%f*	*% area*	*f*	*%f*	*% area*
50 to 100	11	15.28	28.76	10	13.89	26.76
100 to 150	14	19.44	24.82	12	16.67	22.01
150 to 200	26	36.11	30.55	26	36.11	32.07
200 to 300	13	18.06	13.24	16	22.22	16.54
300 to 500	4	5.56	2.50	3	4.17	2.02
500 to 1,000	0	0.00	0.00	1	1.39	0.49
1,000 to 10,000	2	2.78	0.10	2	2.78	0.10
More than 10,000	2	2.78	0.02	2	2.78	0.02

Note: Density = number of electorate per sq. km.

In 11 Assembly units the density ranged between 50 and 100 persons per sq. km. These were located mainly in southern part of the study area in Tonk district, south western part of Jaipur district, southern Sawai Madhopur and western part of Dholpur district. Thanagazi was also included in this category. All these Assembly units covered 28.76 per cent of the study area. The density of electorate varied between 100 and 150 persons per sq. km in 14 Assembly units which included major part of Sikar district, Mandawa and small parts of Jaipur, Alwar, Tonk, Dausa and Sawai Madhopur districts. In 26 Assembly units the density of electorate was between 150 and 200 persons per sq. km spreading over 30.55 per cent of the total study area which included predominantly the Assembly units of northern and north eastern part of the study area comprising northern and eastern part of Jhunjhunu district, almost whole of Bharatpur district, major part of Alwar district, central part of Dausa and peripheral parts of Jaipur district. The density ranged between 200 and 300 persons per sq. km in 13 Assembly segments which mainly included the semi urban areas of all districts and covered 13.24 per cent of the entire study area. Alwar, Bharatpur, Todabhim and Jaipur Rural, together covering 2.5 per cent of the study area had high electorate densities ranging between 300 and 500 persons per sq. km. Johari Bazaar, Banipark, Hawa Mahal and Kishanpole had extremely high densities ranging from 7,499 persons per sq. km in Johari Bazaar to 26,084 persons per sq. km in Kishanpole. The spatial variation in electorate density in the study area in 1991 has been portrayed in Figure 3.10A.

Assembly Elections 1993

The geographical boundaries of the constituencies, both Assembly and Lok Sabha, did not undergo any revision since 1976 till 2008. Therefore their geographical area remained unchanged till 2008. Any change whether positive or negative in the electorate density of an Assembly unit is directly related to the respective change in number of electorate. Between 1991 and 1993, the change in density of electorate was substantial only in a few areas like Amer, Alwar, Kotputli, Banipark Todabhim and Kaman. Figure 3.11 illustrates the relative changes in the electorate densities during 1991 and 1993.

During Assembly elections 1993, the density of electorate in the region was 166 persons per sq. km. In individual constituencies it varied between a minimum of 61 persons per sq. km in Sapotra to a maximum of 23,959 persons per sq. km in Kishanpole. The mean density per constituency, excluding the four urban constituencies of Jaipur city which had electorate density of more than 7,000 persons per sq. km, was

Figure 3.10

Spatial Pattern of Electorate Density of North East Rajasthan

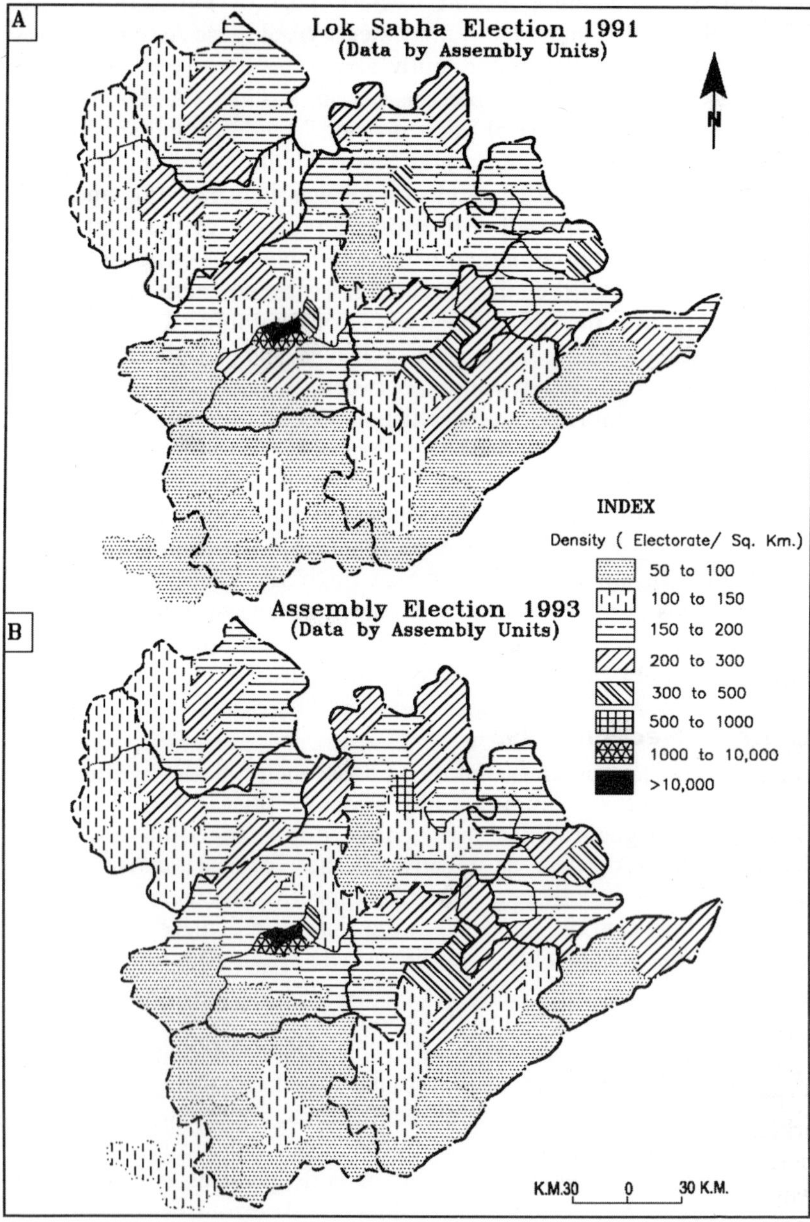

Figure 3.11

Assembly Unitwise Density of Electorate (Lok Sabha Elections 1991 and Assembly Elections 1993)

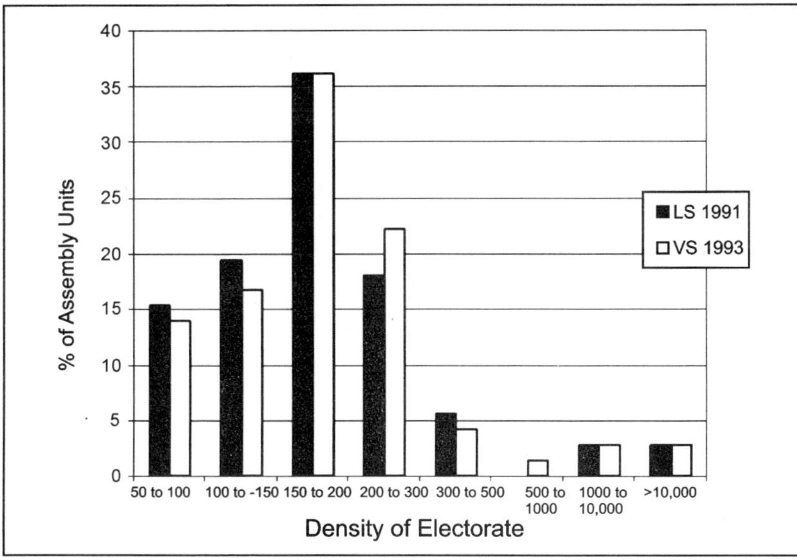

180 persons per sq. km with maximum density in Alwar (501 persons/km^2). As evident from Table 3.14, there were small changes in the densities of various Assembly units during this period. Ten Assembly units had density within the range of 50 to 100 persons per sq. km which spread over 26.76 per cent of the total area of the study region. Twelve Assembly units had densities between 100 to 150 persons per sq. km covering 22.01 per cent of the total area. In 26 Assembly units, spreading over 32.07 per cent of the total area, the density of electorate was between 150 to 200 persons per sq. km. In 16 Assembly units it was from 200 to 300 persons per sq. km and in three of them, it ranged between 300 and 500 persons per sq. km covering 16.54 per cent and 2.02 per cent of the total area respectively. Alwar was the only Assembly unit where the density was between 500 and 1,000 persons per sq. km. Figure 3.10B illustrates the spatial distribution pattern of Assembly units on the basis of density of electorate. As evident from Figure 3.10A and B, the spatial pattern of variation in electorate density did not undergo any marked changes during 1991 and 1993, except for a few pockets like Amer, Lalsot, Neem-ka-Thana, Kotputli, Rajakhera, Khairthal, Kekri, Alwar and Kumher where an increase in density is apparent and Sanganer where a decline is observed.

Lok Sabha Elections 1998

During Lok Sabha elections 1998, the density of electorate in the study area increased to 174 persons per sq. km. Among the Lok Sabha constituencies, the density of electorate varied between a minimum of 99 persons per sq. km in Tonk to a maximum of 444 persons per sq. km in Jaipur. The intra constituency variability of density at the level of Assembly segments was the highest in Jaipur with a coefficient of variation of 122.10 per cent and the lowest in Jhunjhunu with a Coefficient of Variation of 20.14 per cent. The Lok Sabha constituencywise electorate density and degree of intra constituency variability during 1998 Lok Sabha elections have been summarized in Table 3.15.

Table 3.15 *Parameters of Lok Sabha Constituencywise Density of Electorate (LS 1998)*

Constituency	*Density*	*Mean*	*ó*	*C.V.*	*Highest*	*Lowest*
Jhunjhunu	164	170	34.21	20.14	Jhunjhunu (210)	Mandawa (116)
Dausa	182	188	38.98	20.71	Bandikui (258)	Jamwa Ramgarh (121)
Bayana	185	201	47.21	23.48	Dholpur (261)	Bari (100)
Sikar	166	179	59.95	33.41	Sikar (289)	Lacchmangarh (SC)(117)
Tonk	99	107	38.63	36.09	Phulera (184)	Dudu 76)
Bharatpur	199	218	92.63	42.54	Bharatpur (441)	Lachhmangarh (137)
Sawai Madhopur	127	168	95.53	56.99	Todabhim (328)	Sapotra (64)
Alwar	205	245	147.98	60.45	Alwar (590)	Thanagazi (100)
Jaipur	444	8,313	10,150.03	122.10	Kishanpole (27,506)	Phagi (92)

Note: Density = number of electorate per sq. km.
Figures in parentheses indicate absolute density of the respective Assembly units.
Mean = mean density of the constituent Assembly segments of the respective Lok Sabha constituency.

On the level of Assembly segments, the electorate density in the region varied between 57 persons per sq. km in Sapotra to 26,084 persons per sq. km in Kishanpole. Excluding the extraordinarily high densities in the urban segments of Jaipur, the mean density of 94.4 per cent Assembly segments was 187 persons per sq. km.

As evident from the above table, in 89 per cent of Assembly units the density of electorate was below 300 persons per sq. km; in seven segments covering 20.25 per cent of the total study area, it was below

100 persons per sq. km. These included Assembly units of south western and southern part of the study area in Tonk, Sawai Madhopur and southern part of Jaipur districts. In 14 Assembly units spreading over 26.90 per cent of the study area, the electorate density ranged between 100 and 150 persons per sq. km. These included southern and western part of Sikar district, Mandawa, north eastern part of Tonk, parts of Alwar district, Sawai Madhopur, western part of Dholpur district and Jamwa Ramgarh (Figure 3.12A). The density of electorate was between 150 and 200 persons per sq. km in 23 Assembly units which constituted 29.35 per cent of the total study area. These were predominantly concentrated in eastern part of Jhunjhunu and Sikar districts, central part of Jaipur district, Sikrai and Lalsot in Dausa and major part of Bharatpur and Alwar districts. Sawai Madhopur was also included in this category. Twenty segments, covering 20.87 per cent of the total study area had electorate density ranging from 200 to 300 persons per km^2, comprising of semi urban areas of Jaipur, Sikar, Jhunjhunu and Sawai Madhopur districts and scattered areas in Dholpur, Dausa, Bharatpur and Alwar districts.

Table 3.16 *Frequency Distribution of Assembly Units on the Basis of Density of Electorate (1998–98)*

Electorate per sq. km

Density		*LS 1998*			*VS 1998*	
	f	*%f*	*% area*	*f*	*%f*	*% area*
50 to 100	7	9.72	20.25	7	9.72	20.25
100 to 150	14	19.44	26.90	14	19.44	26.90
150 to 200	23	31.94	29.35	24	33.33	30.51
200 to 300	20	27.78	20.87	19	26.39	19.71
300 to 500	3	4.17	2.02	3	4.17	2.02
500 to 1000	1	1.39	0.49	1	1.39	0.49
1,000 to 10,000	1	1.39	0.05	1	1.39	0.05
More than 10,000	3	4.17	0.07	3	4.17	0.07

Note: f = frequency, %f = relative frequency in per cent.
% area = relative area in per cent.

The density was from 300 to 500 persons per sq. km in Todabhim, Bharatpur and Jaipur Rural. Alwar and Johari Bazaar had densities ranging between 500 to 1,000 and 1,000 to 10,000 persons

Figure 3.12

Spatial Pattern of Electorate Density

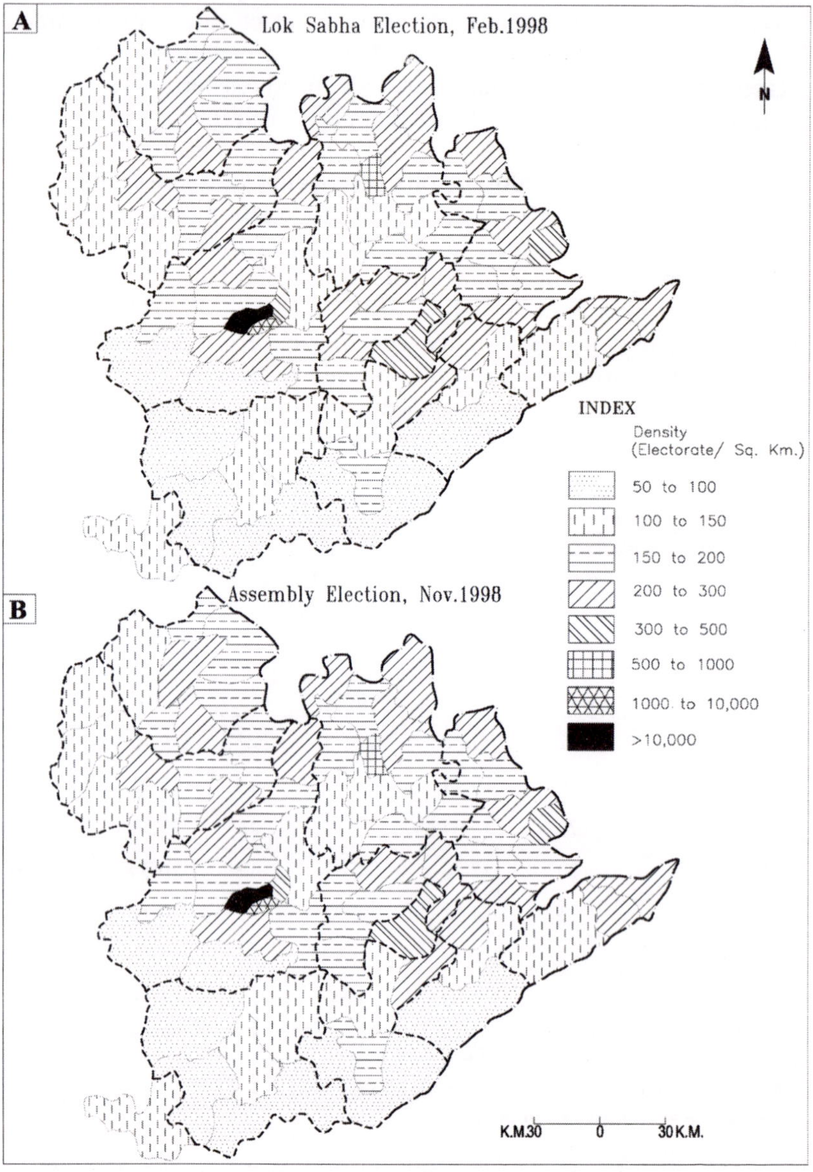

per sq km respectively. The remaining three urban segments of Jaipur had extremely high densities of more than 10,000 persons per sq km. The above discussed spatial pattern of electorate density in the study area at the Assembly segment level has been illustrated in Figure 3.12A.

Assembly Elections 1998

During Assembly elections 1998, the density of electorate in the study region increased to 175 persons per sq. km. In individual constituencies it varied between 64 persons per sq. km in Sapotra to 28,659 in Kishanpole. Excluding the four Assembly constituencies of Jaipur having extremely high densities, the mean density per constituency was 188 persons per sq. km, with maximum density in Alwar (594 persons per sq. km).

In Figure 3.13 a comparison has been made between the broad distribution of Assembly units among various categories of electorate density during Lok Sabha and Assembly elections 1998.

As evident from Figure 3.13 there was very little change in the distribution during the two elections. Although variations occurred both on the negative and the positive side in majority of the Assembly

Figure 3.13

Assembly Unitwise Density of Electorate

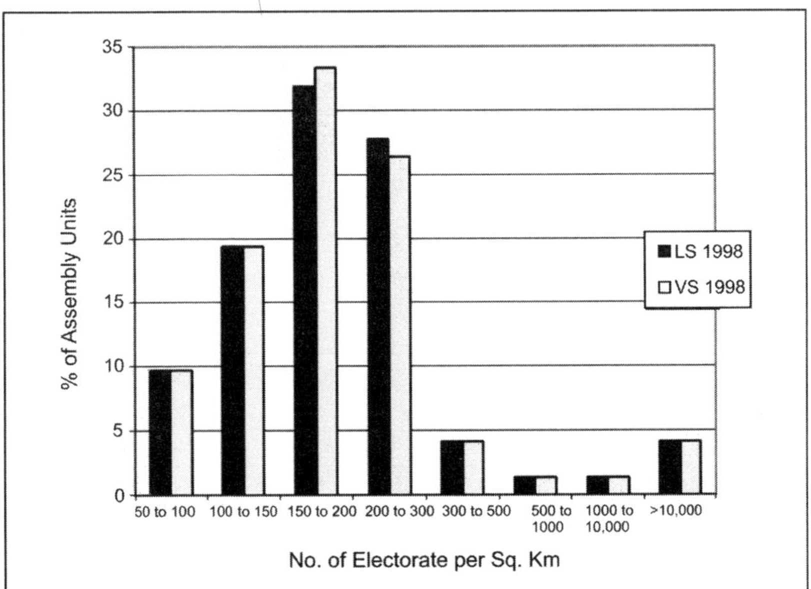

units but they were too small to be significant except substantial rise in density in the urban areas of Jaipur city.

The spatial pattern of electorate density during Assembly elections 1998 has been illustrated in Figure 3.12B. A comparison of Figure 3.12A and B also reveals that no marked shifts occurred in the density of electorate in various Assembly units in Assembly elections 1998 as compared to the preceding Lok Sabha ones.

Concludingly it may be said that extreme disparities existed among both Lok Sabha and Assembly constituencies with regard to density of electorate. During the four elections under study the electoral density ranged between 50 and 300 persons per sq. km in approximately 90 per cent of the Assembly units. Extremely high density (more than 1,000 persons per sq. km) occurred in the four smallest and highly urbanized Assembly units located in Jaipur city. The spatial pattern of electoral density in north east Rajasthan remained by and large unchanged over the period between 1991 and 1998. Consequent upon change in electorate size there was gradual increment or decline in the densities of individual Assembly units over consecutive elections but such changes were quite small and insignificant in majority of them. The temporal changes were marked and substantial only in a few urban and semi urban areas.

4 Trends and Patterns of Voting Turnout

Voting turnout is measured as the percentage of registered voters in each constituency who actually exercise their voting right at the time of election. The study of political participation is important because it can potentially lend insight into the extent of citizen support for a political system (Dikshit, 1988). Palmer (1976) has pointed out that voting is the most common and the most widely discussed form of political participation related to the electoral process. Thus identification of the spatial patterns and trends of voter turnout can be used as an effective tool to assess the level of political awareness in a region. The voting behaviour of the voters can be effectively understood in the light of the socio-economic characteristics of constituencies in which they live. Brass (1978) has noted that among the analysts of Indian elections, ecological analysis, i.e. the correlation of available demographic and socio-economic aggregate data from Census and similar sources with election results to identify patterns and variations in turnout, interparty competition and party support – continues to vie with the opinion survey as a preferred form of election studies.

Methodological Framework

This chapter deals with identification of spatial patterns of voter turnout during various election years and correlating these patterns with socio-economic characteristics of the study area using appropriate statistical techniques. The discussions in the chapter possibly answer the following three questions:

1. What is the spatial pattern of voting turnout?
2. How do the spatial patterns of voting turnout vary with time?
3. Why does the spatial pattern of voting turnout have that form?

Answers to the first two questions were sought using tools of descriptive statistics. The level and spatial variations of turnout were examined in terms of average turnout, standard deviation and coefficient of variation. Choropleth maps were prepared illustrating the spatial distribution of different levels of voting (measured in terms of votes polled as percentage of total electorate) and spatial variation in voting turnout (depicted in form of Z-scores of per cent votes polled). Z-score values were interpreted as per scheme outlined in Table 4.1.

Table 4.1 *Interpretation of Z-Score Values*

Z-score Values	*Intensity of Electoral Participation*
Positive	
Above 2.25	Extremely high
1.50 to 2.25	Very high
0.75 to 1.50	Moderately high
0.00 to 0.75	High
Negative	
0.00 to –0.75	Low
–0.75 to –1.50	Moderately low
–1.50 to –2.25	Very low
Below –2.25	Extremely low

Frequency distribution diagrams were prepared to investigate the extent of spatial variation in Assembly unitwise voter turnout.

Temporal changes in voting turnout were examined by comparison of averages, measures of variability and calculating Assembly unitwise increase or decrease in turnout during successive elections.

Explanations to the spatial patterns of voter turnout were sought by examining relationships between voting turnout and 13 selected voting determinants related to political, demographic and socio-economic attributes of the study area. Pearson's product moment correlation technique was used to assess the nature and degree of bivariate association between voting turnout and the selected variables. R^2 values (Multiple coefficient of determination) have been derived by multiple regression of all variables on voter turnout which indicate the total variance in voter turnout accounted for by all the socio-economic variables as a whole. Multiple regression equation expressed below has been applied:

$$Y_{jt} = a_t + \sum_{k=1}^{10} b_k X_{kj}$$

Where, Y_{jt} = percentage voter turnout of Assembly segment 'j' in election year 't' (1991, 1993, 1998).

a_t = intercept for election 't'

b_k = value of regression coefficient of variable X_k

k = socio-economic variables (1 .... 10)

j = Assembly units

Multiple coefficient of determination (R^2) is derived from the multiple regression equation through the following formula:

$$R^2 = \left(\frac{\sigma_{y'}}{\sigma_y} \right)^2$$

Where, $\sigma_{y'}$ = standard deviation of predicted values of voter turnout (dependent variable)

σ_y = standard deviation of actual observed values of voter turnout

Stepwise regression was carried out to identify the variables which have exercised decisive influence on voter turnout in each election. Partial correlation coefficients were determined to assess the relative importance of each independent socio-economic variable in a multivariate situation where the coexisting correlation of remaining variables is also taken into account.

Voting is the outcome of numerous events and interactions in a complex set of phenomena. Thus any attempt to explain voting behaviour patterns with reference to only one or two independent variables would be of little value. At the same time, identification and measurement of all the factors involved is too difficult task to accomplish. The voting determinants incorporated in the analysis have been selected in the light of empirical values of the findings and conclusions drawn in previous researches and the effectiveness of the same has been tested in explaining the level of turnout in the study area. An extensive review of literature on the ecological study of voting behaviour in India has led me to incorporate the following variables in the analysis to measure the impact of polling booth accessibility, intensity of party competition and level of socio-economic development of the area on spatial patterns of voter turnout; and to examine the voting behaviour of the reserved category of electors as well as to determine the extent of female participation in the elections (Table 4.2).

Table 4.2 *List of Selected Voting Determinants*

Variable	*Acronym*
Ratio of polling booths per village	N_ PS
Proportion of small villages	N_SV
Margin of victory	M_V
Density of electorate	D_E
Proportion of urban population (per cent of total population)	U_P
Literacy rate (per cent of total population)	L_R
Proportion of working population (per cent of total population)	W_P
Proportion of workers employed in other services (per cent of total working population)	W_OS
Proportion of agricultural labourers (per cent of total working population)	A_L
Proportion of agricultural workers (per cent of total working population)	A_W
Proportion of Scheduled Caste electorate (per cent of total electorate)	SC_E
Proportion of Scheduled Tribe electorate (per cent of total electorate)	ST_E
Sex-ratio of electorate (female electorate per thousand male electorate)	S_R_E

Conceptual Base

Two variables – ratio of polling booths to villages and proportion of villages with a population less than 900 persons (referred to as small villages), were chosen as measures of polling booth accessibility. Brass (1978) has stated that only after determining how much of the variance in turnout is explained by the convenience of polling booth accessibility, it makes any sense to look for socio-economic correlates to explain the unexplained variance in turnout. He found high positive correlation between ratio of polling booth to villages and voter turnout. Chandidas (1972) observed significant negative correlations between voter turnout and proportion of small villages.

The guidelines of Delimitation Commission require that a polling station should be provided for a well defined polling area normally covering about 800 to 1,000 electors. Thus small villages of population less than 800 are clubbed together in a manner ensuring that no voter is required to travel more than two kilometres for casting one's vote. These conditions may be technically satisfied, i.e. a village attached to a polling booth may be within the prescribed radius of two kilometres, but the actual path to the polling station may be very arduous. This impedes people from voting. Therefore, 'wherever more than one village is attached to a polling station, the rate of participation definitely drops' (Chandidas, 1972, p. 1,368). In the present study, the population of 900 persons has been taken as the delimiting figure to ascertain the number of villages sharing a polling booth with other villages.

Several studies have established that party competition is a very important factor in mobilizing voter participation. Milbrath (1965) has observed that the more competitive the parties, the greater is the likelihood of high rates of participation. Chandidas (1972) and Dikshit (1988) have also stated that 'closeness of the vote' is positively related to voter turnout. Das Gupta and Morris-Jones (1975) have also pointed out that 'there would be higher turnout in areas with a greater degree of competition among the parties, whereas the voters would be less keen to vote in areas where the level of contest was minimal'. Margin of victory has been chosen as a measure of intensity of interparty competition.

Voter turnout is also significantly influenced by the composite of environmental, demographic and ecological variables which provide a community a structural context. Das Gupta and Morris-Jones (1975) have concluded that turnout is positively related to development. Lipset (1960) has also noted that 'as the process of development advances, the rate of voter turnout increases'. Das Gupta and Morris-Jones (1975) and Chandidas (1971, p. 72) have emphasized on the positive relationship between literacy and turnout. Milbrath (1965) has concluded that 'education has a greater impact on political behaviour than the other components of socio-economic status'. Literacy rate as proportion of literate population to total population, has been used as a measure of level of education.

Chandidas (1972) has also observed that density of population stimulates voter participation through enhancing opportunity for interaction and communication. Field et al. (1977) studied the urban electoral participation in India and concluded that 'urban constituencies are more politicized than the Indian countryside'. Das Gupta and Morris-Jones (1975) and Chandidas (1972) also observed high positive correlation between proportion of urban population and voter turnout. It is assumed that the abundance of opportunities for higher interaction and communication, exposure to higher level of political information and various media of communication and nearness to the centres of power which are located in urban areas, makes an average urban elector highly politicized. Due to this increased political awareness among urban voters, electoral participation tends to be higher in urban areas. For the purpose of analysis, the proportion of urban population to total population of an Assembly unit has been used as measure of degree of urbanization of the area.

Varma and Narain (1973) discussed the voting behaviour in Rajasthan in the specific context of demographic and socio-economic characteristics, level of political information, various media of communication, exposure to and participation in campaigning, etc. They have concluded that in urban areas participation is higher among population engaged in white collar occupations than in manual and semi-skilled workers. In rural constituencies, participation is higher among farmers and lowest among agricultural labourers. In line with these findings, the variables – proportion of agricultural labourers and agricultural workers to total working population and population engaged in other services have been included in the analysis.

Dikshit and Sharma (1995) observed that the rate of voter turnout is usually lower in reserved constituencies than in general ones. Two pioneer studies of voting behaviour of tribal constituencies have been carried out by Weiner and Field (1975) and Mishra et al. (1982). To investigate the voting trends in SC/ST majority areas the variables – proportion of SC and ST electorate to total electorate have been chosen.

Chandidas (1972) and Dikshit and Sharma (1993) are of the view that the level of voter turnout ought to be higher in Assembly elections than the Lok Sabha elections because the degree of voter identification of the contenders and issues is higher in the contest for lower level of political office. Surely 'voter identification with contestants for political office is an important stimulus to go and vote' (Chandidas, 1972).

Sex ratio of electorate has been incorporated in the analysis to examine the level of female participation in electoral process. Since only that segment of population which is above 18 years of age comprises the electorate, voter turnout has been analysed in relation to density of electorate instead of density of population.

Voter Turnout: Trends and Patterns

Spatial Patterns of Voter Turnout

Lok Sabha Elections 1991

The average per Assembly unit voter turnout during the Lok Sabha Elections 1991 being 45.51 per cent was the least among all the four elections under consideration. The turnout was the highest in Kaman segment (70.73%) of Bharatpur constituency and the lowest in Bari segment (29.06%) of Bayana constituency. The coefficient of variation of voter turnout being 17.97 per cent was the highest among all the four elections (Table 4.3).

Table 4.3 *Parameters of Distribution of Voter Turnout*

Election	*Average (% voter turnout)*	*SD*	*CV (%)*	*Max*	*Min*
Lok Sabha 1991	·45.51	8.18	17.97	70.73	29.06
Vidhan Sabha1993	62.47	6.47	10.36	77.96	47.69
Lok Sabha 1998	58.77	7.57	12.87	72.55	43.81
Vidhan Sabha 1998	64.87	6.84	10.55	74.32	46.89

Note: SD = standard deviation, CV = coefficient of variation.

On the whole the level of electoral participation being 45.51 per cent was quite low. About 54.17 per cent of the Assembly units recorded a turnout below average whereas in nearly three fourth (73.61%) of the Assembly units less than half of the registered voiers went to poll. Just 2.78 per cent of the Assembly units recorded a fairly high turnout of over 60 per cent which were Nagar and Kaman Assembly units of Bharatpur constituency (Table 4.4).

Table 4.4 *Percentage Frequency Distribution of Assembly Units Under Various Vote Categories (1991, 1993, 1998)*

Voter Turnout	*LS 1991*	*VS 1993*	*LS 1998*	*VS 1998*
Less than 40	26.39	0	0	0
40–45	27.78	0	2.78	0
45–50	19.44	1.39	16.67	5.56
50–55	11.11	12.5	15.28	2.78
55–60	12.50	16.67	15.28	13.89
60–65	0.00	34.72	25.00	19.44
65–70	1.39	26.39	22.22	33.33
Above 70	1.39	8.33	2.78	25.00
Less than average	54.17	50.00	45.83	40.28
More than average	45.83	50.00	54.17	59.72
More than 50%	26.39	98.61	80.56	94.44
More than 60%	2.78	69.44	50.00	77.78

Note: LS and VS refer to Lok Sabha and Vidhan Sabha respectively.

A detailed appreciation of Assembly unitwise percentage voter turnout reveals that the entire southern, eastern and some northern parts of the study area recorded below average turnout. All Assembly units of Bayana and Tonk Lok Sabha constituencies, all Assembly units of Jaipur Lok Sabha constituency except Hawa Mahal, Dausa Lok Sabha constituency except Sikrai, Jhunjhunu Lok Sabha constituency except Jhunjhunu and Fatehpur Assembly segments and Alwar Lok Sabha constituency except Khairthal recorded below 50 per cent voter turnout. The rate of voter participation was relatively high in Bharatpur

Figure 4.1

Spatial Pattern of Voter Turnout in North East Rajasthan (1991–93)

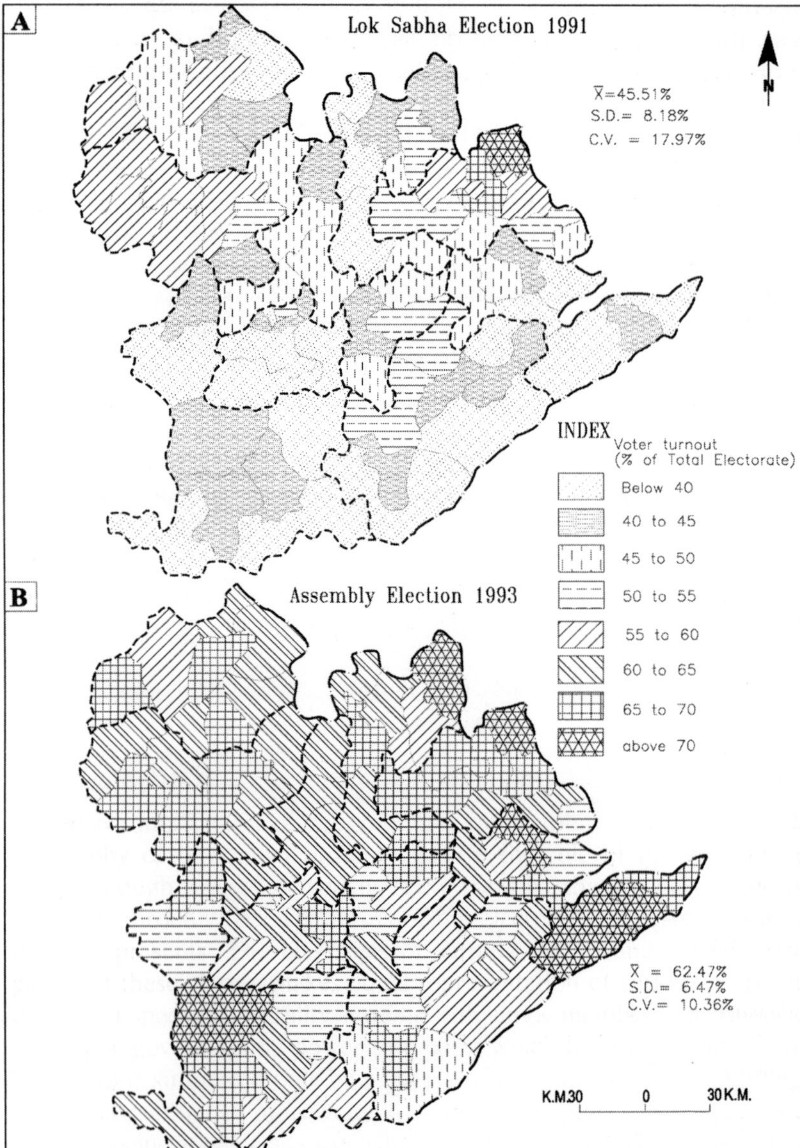

and Sikar Lok Sabha constituencies where most of the Assembly segments recorded turnout between 50 per cent and 60 per cent. Two Assembly segments of Bharatpur Lok Sabha constituency – Nagar and Kaman recorded an exceptionally high voter turnout of above 65 per cent. Figure 4.1A illustrates the spatial distribution of various levels of voter turnout during Lok Sabha election 1991. As the average rate of electoral participation in the Lok Sabha elections of 1991 was quite low, the real picture of spatial variation in turnout can be examined more accurately by identifying the areas of high and low turnout on the basis of Z-scores of percentage voter turnout. As revealed in Figure 4.2A, the southern and eastern parts including whole of Tonk, Bayana (except Mahuwa), Jaipur (except Hawa Mahal), major parts of Sawai Madhopur and Alwar and eastern parts of Jhunjhunu districts recorded low to very low voter turnout. The rate of voter participation was high to very high in Sikar (except Chomu), major part of Dausa and entire Bharatpur Lok Sabha constituency. Two segments of Bharatpur Lok Sabha constituencies – Kaman and Nagar registered an extremely high voter turnout. A striking feature of the spatial pattern of voting turnout during this election was a clear division into areas of high and low turnouts (Figure 4.2A inset) with southern, eastern and northern parts of the study area recording a low rate of voter turnout and north western, north eastern and central parts (with few exceptions) recording a high rate of poll participation. Constituencywise variations in level of voter turnout during Lok Sabha elections 1991 have been summarized in Table 4.5.

Table 4.5 *Lok Sabha Constituencywise Variations in Voter Turnout, 1991*

LS Constituency	*Voting Turnout (%)*	*Mean Turnout (%)*	*SD*	*CV (%)*	*Highest*	*Lowest*
Jhunjhunu	46.82	46.27	8.61	18.6	Fatehpur (57.35)	Surajgarh (32.12)
Sikar	54.16	53.86	5.86	10.88	Sikar (59.99)	Chomu (42.49)
Jaipur	41.58	41.75	3.93	9.42	Hawa Mahal (50.79)	Bassi (38.49)
Dausa	46.68	47.29	3.31	7.00	Sikrai (52.97)	Kotputli (42.90)
Alwar	43.93	43.68	5.52	12.64	Khairthal (51.35)	Bansur (37.65)
Bharatpur	54.71	56.16	8.81	15.68	Kaman (70.73)	Bharatpur (46.30)
Bayana (SC)	39.35	39.52	6.74	17.05	Mahuwa (49.18)	Bari (29.06)
Sawai Madhopur (ST)	42.16	42.04	6.69	15.91	Todabhim (52.46)	Khandar (SC) (34.56)
Tonk (SC)	39.13	39.05	3.11	7.97	Malpura (43.57)	Uniara (33.29)

Note: SD = standard deviation; CV = coefficient of variation.

Figure 4.2

Changing Patterns of Voter Turnout in North East Rajasthan (1991–93)

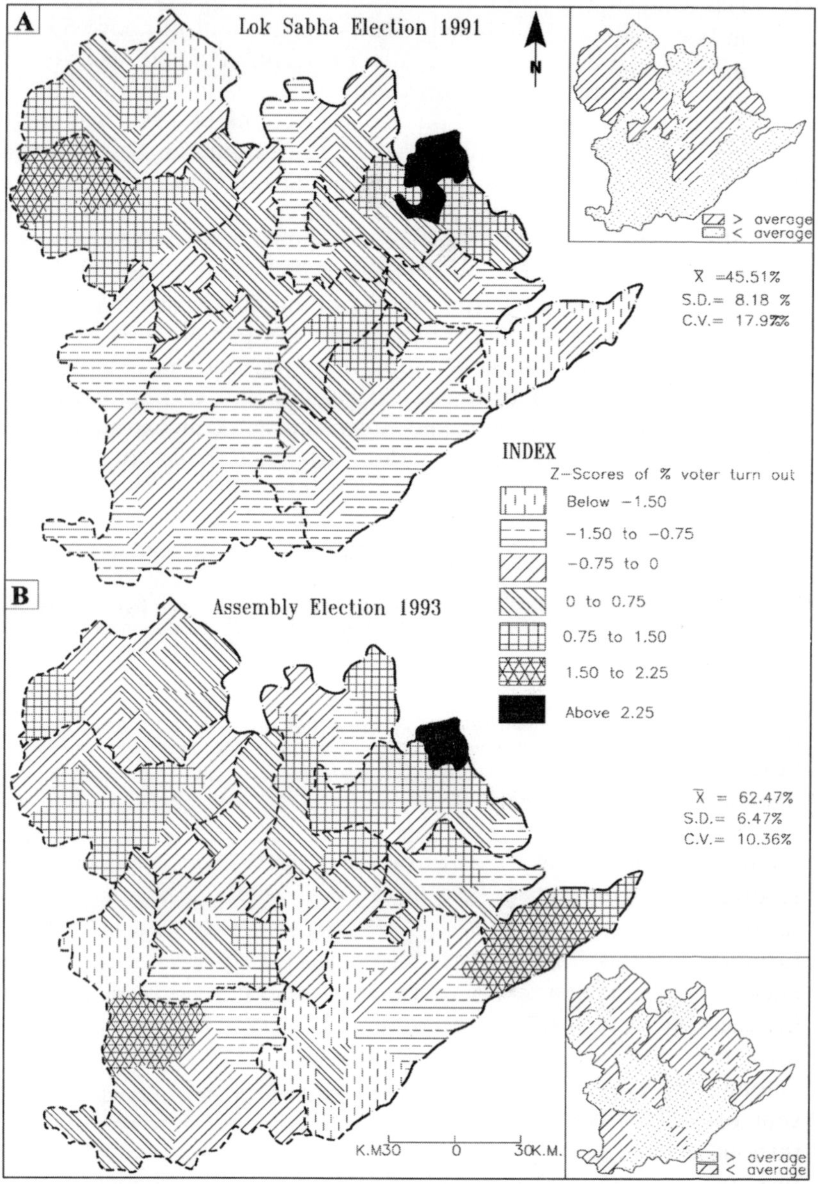

Some exceptional traits were also observed in some Assembly segments which can briefly be highlighted as under:

1. Hawa Mahal was the only segment to record a high voter turnout in Jaipur constituency whereas all other segments recorded low to moderately low turnout.
2. Chomu was the only segment to record a low rate of turnout in Sikar constituency whereas the remaining segments of the constituency registered high to very high turnout rates.
3. Bharatpur was the only constituency to have a high voter turnout in all constituent segments. As a result it also registered the highest mean turnout of 54.71 per cent among all the constituencies (Table 4.5).
4. Tonk constituency registered the lowest mean turnout (39.13%). All the constituent Assembly segments of Tonk polled below average.
5. The turnout in Assembly segments of the reserved constituencies, i.e. Bayana and Tonk which are reserved for SCs and Sawai Madhopur reserved for STs was generally low. Approximately 83 per cent of Assembly segments of the reserved constituencies registered low to very low voter turnout. Todabhim (ST) of Sawai Madhopur recorded the highest turnout of 52.46 per cent among the segments of reserved constituencies.

Assembly Elections 1993

The mean per seat voter turnout in Assembly Elections 1993 was 62.47 per cent, ranging between 77.96 per cent in Kaman and 47.69 per cent in Khandar. It is noteworthy that the minimum turnout in Khandar in these elections was higher than the mean turnout (45.51%) during the Lok Sabha elections 1991. The coefficient of variation of turnout was 10.36 per cent, considerably lower than 1991 which is indicative of relative uniformity in the pattern of electoral participation as compared to the preceding Lok Sabha Elections (Table 4.3). The level of voter turnout was in general high. Approximately 98 per cent of the constituencies recorded more than 50 per cent turnout and in 69.44 per cent of the constituencies more than 60 per cent of the electorate exercised their franchise. There was an equal distribution of constituencies among the categories of above and below average turnout, i.e. 50 per cent of the constituencies registered a voter turnout above average turnout per seat and remaining 50 per cent recorded below average turnout (Table 4.4). The constituencies were mapped on the basis of distribution about the average in the inset of Figure 4.1B. It is clear from the map that the clear zonal demarcation evident in Lok Sabha

Elections 1991 is absent in Assembly Elections 1993 and a scattered pattern exists. Figure 4.1B illustrates the constituencywise level of electoral participation during the Assembly elections 1993. The map clearly reveals the overall increase in voter turnout as compared to the preceding Lok Sabha Elections 1991. Khandar was the only constituency to record a turnout below 50 per cent. All Assembly units except Bamanwas voted more enthusiastically in the Assembly elections and the turnout registered a marked increase. The western, northern, eastern and south western parts including Jhunjhunu (except Mandawa), Sikar, Alwar (except Khairthal and Alwar), Dholpur, major part of Jaipur, Bharatpur and Tonk districts witnessed an electoral participation of more than 60 per cent. Since the average polling was quite high during these elections, the actual spatial pattern of variation in turnout can be identified through an examination of the constituencywise Z-scores which have been depicted in Figure 4.2B. Constituencies located in eastern Jhunjhunu, major part of Sikar, Alwar, Bharatpur, Dholpur and western part of Tonk district recorded high to very high voter turnout. Among these Dholpur, Bari, Malpura and Kaman recorded exceptionally high rates of voter turnout in the entire region. The constituencies in which the level of voter participation was low to very low were mainly located in Sawai Madhopur, eastern Tonk, Dausa, Jaipur and western part of Jhunjhunu district. An interesting feature of the Assembly Elections 1993 was the low turnout in the urban constituencies. All four urban constituencies located in Jaipur district along with Alwar and Bharatpur constituencies polled moderately low to very low. In Hawa Mahal constituencies also the polling was low.

The reserved constituencies as in Lok Sabha election 1991, again witnessed a low turnout. In all reserved constituencies except Kekri (SC), Rajgarh (ST) and Surajgarh (SC) the level of electoral participation was low and very low. Two third of the reserved constituencies polled between 50 per cent to 60 per cent and the remaining one-third polled above 60 per cent. Rajgarh (ST) recorded the highest voter turnout of 67.53 per cent among the reserved constituencies.

Lok Sabha Elections 1998

In Lok Sabha Elections 1998, the voting turnout ranged from 43.81 per cent in Bari to 72.55 per cent in Sikrai. In these elections the average per seat turnout was 58.77 per cent, 13.26 per cent higher than Lok Sabha elections 1991. Out of the total 72 Assembly segments, 80.56 per cent segments recorded more than 50 per cent turnout, half of them recorded more than 60 per cent turnout and 2.78 per cent recorded more than 70

Figure 4.3

Spatial Pattern of Voter Turnout in North East Rajasthan (1998–98)

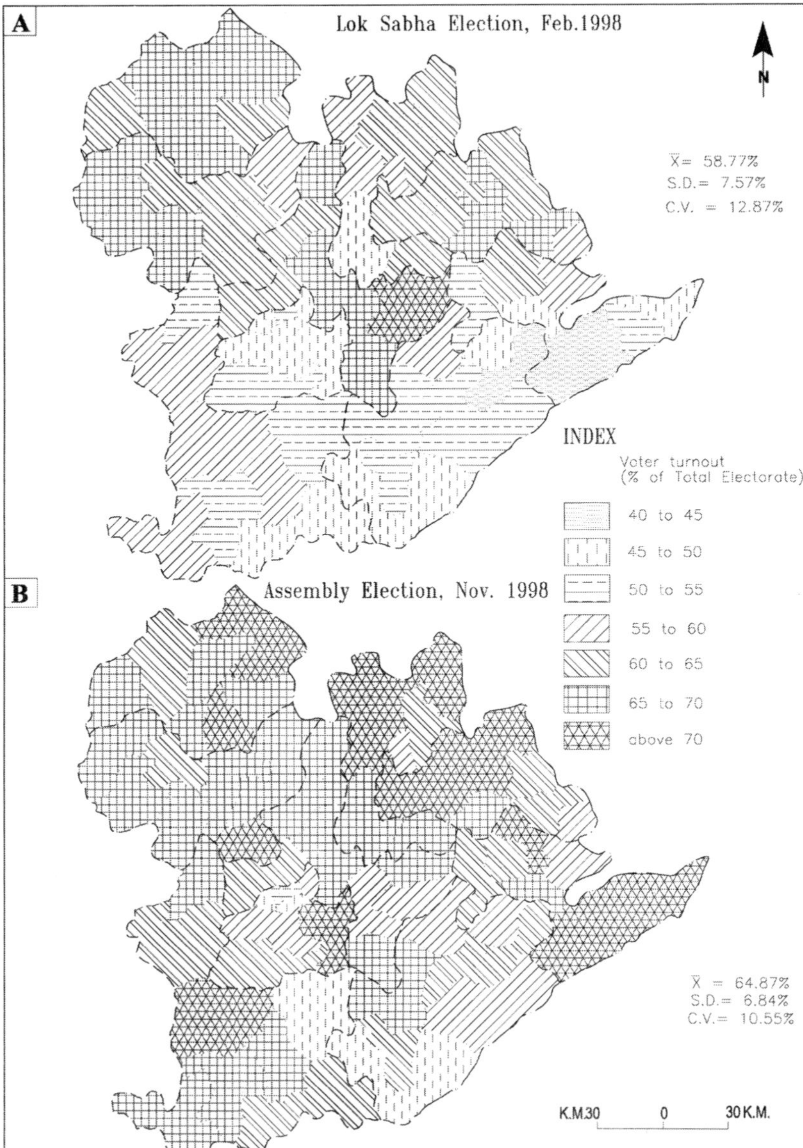

per cent turnout. The coefficient of variation of turnout was 12.87 per cent which was 5.1 per cent lower than Lok Sabha election 1991. Thus the spatial pattern of electoral participation was relatively more even in the Lok Sabha elections 1998 as compared to Lok Sabha elections 1991. The Assembly segmentwise level of voter turnout has been shown in Figure 4.3A. The map exhibits a clear two fold division of the study area into northern and southern parts wherein the northern half comprising Assembly segments of Jhunjhunu, Sikar, Dausa, Bharatpur and eastern part of Alwar constituencies polled above 60 per cent. Thanagazi recorded an exceptionally low turnout of 48.85 per cent in this region whereas the turnout in Behror, Bansur, Alwar and Neem-ka-Thana was also relatively low as compared to the surrounding areas.

The southern half of the study area comprising Tonk, Jaipur, Sawai Madhopur and Bayana constituencies recorded low rates of turnout below 60 per cent in general. In Bari and Karauli the rates of electoral participation were exceptionally low, i.e. 43.81 per cent and 44.31 per cent respectively.

Similar pattern has emerged when the Assembly units are mapped on the basis of Z-scores of percentage voter turnout (Figure 4.4A). Two distinct regions may be identified – northern region of high to very high turnout and southern region of low to very low turnout. Constituencywise variations in levels of voter turnout during Lok Sabha elections 1998 have been summarized in Table 4.6.

Table 4.6 *Lok Sabha Constituencywise Variations in Voter Turnout 1998*

LS Constituency	*Voting Turnout (%)*	*Mean Turnout (%)*	*SD*	*CV (%)*	*Highest*	*Lowest*
Jhunjhunu	67.08	66.84	2.66	3.98	Gudha (69.6)	Khetri (62.2)
Sikar	64.07	64.03	3.47	5.41	Dhod (69.59)	Neem-ka-Thana (59.17)
Jaipur	49.30	49.80	2.46	4.94	Hawa Mahal (54.8)	Jaipur Rural (47.69)
Dausa	66.85	66.95	3.06	4.57	Sikrai (72.55)	Amer (63.29)
Alwar	58.55	58.47	4.83	8.26	Mandawar (63.47)	Thanagazi (48.85)
Bharatpur	64.07	64.35	2.89	4.50	Kumher (68.03)	Bharatpur (59.44)
Bayana	53.13	53.65	6.74	12.57	Weir (64.03)	Bari (43.81)
Sawai Madhopur	50.40	50.34	4.09	8.12	Todabhim (56.76)	Karauli (44.31)
Tonk	54.48	54.50	3.19	5.86	Dudu (58.49)	Uniara (48.08)

Figure 4.4

Changing Pattern of Voter Turnout in North East Rajasthan (1988–98)

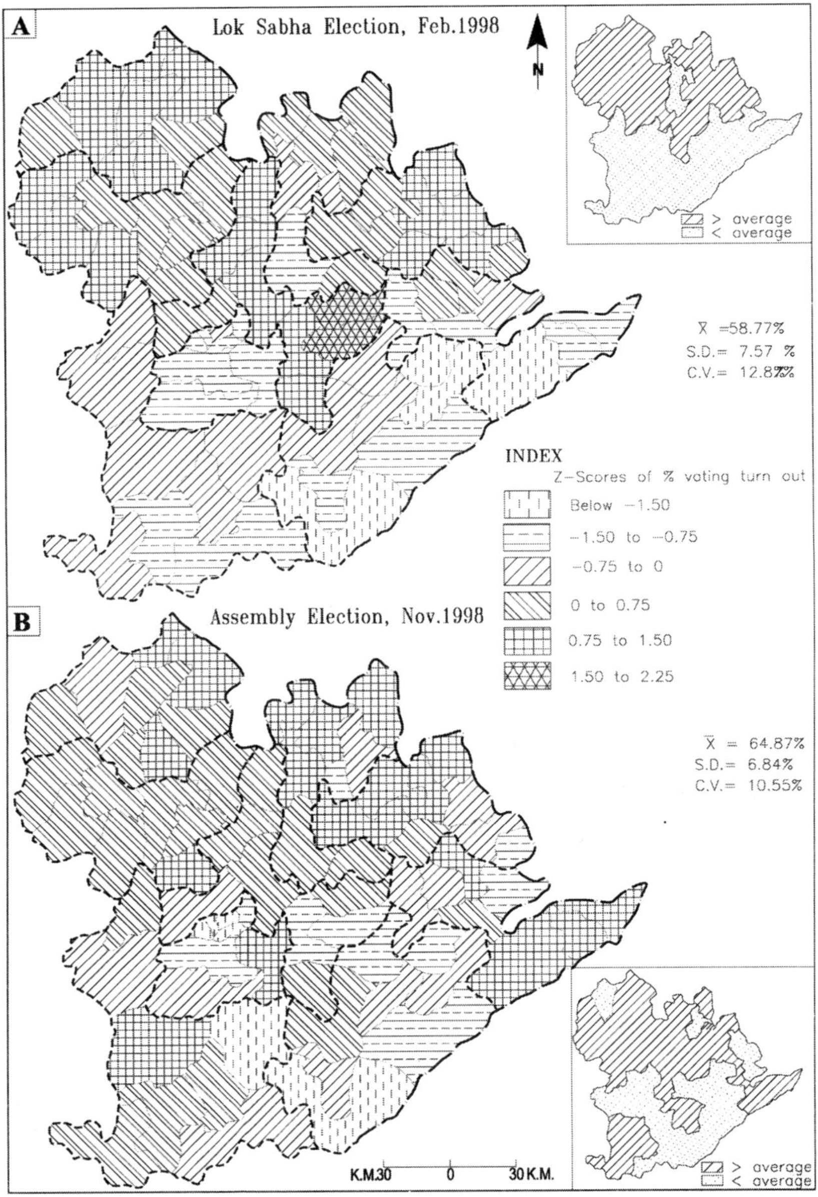

The salient features of voter turnout in Lok Sabha elections 1998 may be identified as under:

1. Jhunjhunu constituency recorded the highest rate of voter turnout where 67.08 per cent of the voters went to poll (Table 4.6). Intra constituency variation in turnout was also lowest in Jhunjhunu with a coefficient of variation at 3.98 per cent. All segments of Jhunjhunu constituency recorded moderately high turnout.
2. Dausa constituency also recorded a high turnout in which all segments polled high to very high. Bandikui and Sikrai (ST) recorded the highest turnout in the region where more than 70 per cent of the electors went to poll.
3. Jaipur constituency recorded the lowest turnout in the region where the absolute turnout was 49.30 per cent and the mean turnout of its constituent Assembly segments was 49.80 per cent.
4. None of the segments of Tonk, Jaipur and Sawai Madhopur constituencies polled above the regional average.
5. The level of electoral participation was low to very low in all the segments of reserved constituencies, i.e. Tonk (SC), Bayana (SC) and Sawai Madhopur (ST) except Weir and Nadbai segments of Bayana.
6. The urban Assembly units also polled low in general. Only Bharatpur (59.44%) polled above average but that too was on the margin.

Assembly Elections 1998

The mean voter turnout was 64.87 per cent during Assembly elections 1998 which was higher than the turnout recorded in the preceding Assembly elections of 1993 and Lok Sabha elections of 1991 and 1998. The turnout ranged from 46.89 per cent in Niwai (SC) to 74.32 per cent in Ramgarh. The coefficient of variation of constituencywise voter turnout was 10.55 per cent which is indicative of relative uniformity in the pattern of electoral participation as compared to Lok Sabha elections 1998. In only four (5.56%) constituencies the level of voter turnout was below 50 per cent; 94.44 per cent constituencies polled above 50 per cent; 77.78 per cent constituencies polled above 60 per cent; and 25 per cent of the constituencies polled above 70 per cent. These polling figures clearly reveal the high level of electoral participation in the study area. In all, 40.28 per cent constituencies polled below average and 59.72 per cent constituencies polled above average. The percentage frequency distribution of constituencies among various vote categories shown in Table 4.3 clearly indicates that majority of the constituencies were concentrated towards the higher end of the scale. Thus it may be inferred that the Assembly elections 1998 witnessed an active voter participation, resulting in high levels of turnout in most of the constituencies with an even spatial distribution pattern.

Figure 4.3B illustrates the constituencywise level of voter turnout during Assembly elections 1998. It is evident that majority of the constituencies of the northern, eastern, south western parts of the study area polled over 60 per cent which included constituencies located in districts of Jhunjhunu, Sikar, Alwar (except Alwar constituency), Bharatpur (except Bharatpur and Rupbas), Dholpur, Tonk (except Niwai) and major part of Jaipur. Among these, in eastern parts of Jhunjhunu district, northern part of Alwar (except Alwar and Khairthal), Kaman, Nagar and Nadbai constituencies of Bharatpur, entire Dholpur district, Chomu and Bassi constituencies in Jaipur and Malpura in Tonk, the voter turnout was 'very high', above 70 per cent. The constituencies lying in districts of Sawai Madhopur (except Bamanwas), Karauli, Dausa (except Bandikui and Lalsot), southern half of Jaipur and eastern Bharatpur polled low to very low. Niwai and Uniara in Tonk district also polled below average (Figure 4.4B).

The level of turnout was low in the urban constituencies of Jaipur district wherein all the four urban constituencies recorded 'very low' turnout. The turnout in Alwar and Bharatpur constituencies was also 'moderately low'. Therefore in all the urban constituencies, the level of voter participation was disappointing.

About 70 per cent of the SC reserved constituencies and 60 per cent of ST reserved constituencies polled below average. Among the SCs constituencies, Kekri, Kathumar, Lachhmangarh polled 'high' and Surajgarh polled 'moderately high' with a turnout of 72.46 per cent. Among ST constituencies the voter turnout was 'high' in Lalsot and Rajgarh. In Rajgarh 69.9 per cent of the electorate cast their votes. Thus the overall electoral participation in reserved constituencies was low. The Z-scores of percentage votes polled during Assembly Elections 1998 have been illustrated in Figure 4.4B.

Changing Patterns of Voter Turnout

To examine the consistency in rates of electoral participation in various Assembly units, the difference in the level of voter turnout between successive Lok Sabha and Vidhan Sabha elections were calculated. The Assembly units of the study area were broadly classified into two categories on the basis of temporal variation in the rate of voter turnout at the two levels of electoral contest.

1. Assembly units with consistent voting levels.
2. Assembly units with fluctuating voting levels.

The Assembly units where the difference in rates of voter turnout during a set of Lok Sabha and Assembly elections amounted to less than 10 per cent were regarded as having a consistent level of voting and those in which the turnout recorded a change (positive or negative) of more than 10 per cent were considered as having fluctuating voting levels.

Lok Sabha 1991 and Assembly Elections 1993

A comparative study of the spatial pattern of voter turnout in 1991 and 1993 reveals that the electorate of the study area voted more enthusiastically in 1993 elections than 1991. The per seat average turnout registered a marked increase of 16.96 per cent in 1993 as compared to 1991. The average turnout in 1993 was 62.47 per cent and the coefficient of variation was 10.36 per cent which was 7.61 per cent lower than 1991. Therefore it may be inferred that in 1993 elections, the level of electoral participation was relatively high as well as more uniformly spread. While in Lok Sabha election of 1991, only 2.78 per cent of the Assembly units recorded a turnout more than 60 per cent, in Assembly elections of 1993 the corresponding figure rose to 69.44 per cent. The

Figure 4.5

Frequency Distribution of Voting Turnout

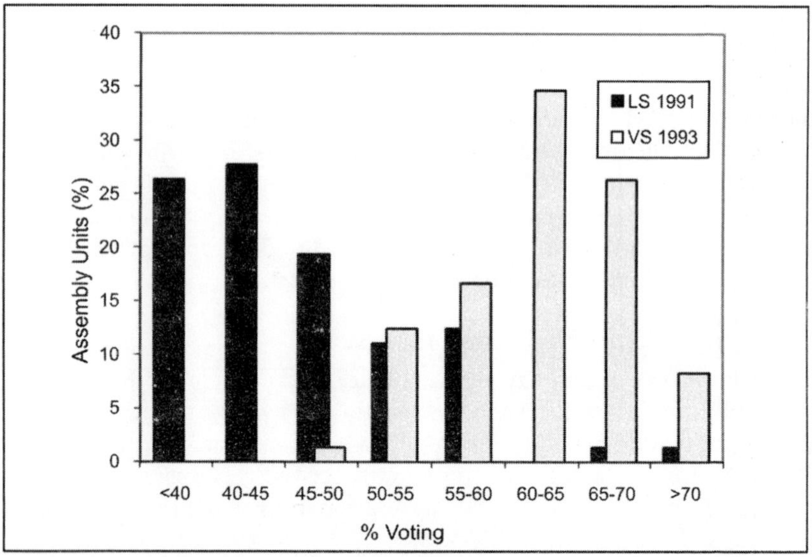

relative rise in the level of electoral participation is also underlined by the fact that during 1991 elections 73.61 per cent of the Assembly units polled below 50 per cent whereas during Assembly elections 1993 only Khandar recorded a turnout below 50 per cent. The distribution of Assembly units among various turnout categories during 1991 and 1993 has been compared in Figure 4.5.

Areas of Consistent Levels of Voting

During 1991–1993, in 14 Assembly units the difference in level of voter turnout between the two elections was less than 10 per cent. Bamanwas was the only Assembly unit where the turnout registered a negative change although the change was insignificant. Another notable Assembly unit in this category was Kaman which polled above 70 per cent in both elections, difference being 7.23 per cent in favour of Assembly elections. Figure 4.6A illustrates the Assembly unitwise change in voter turnout during 1991 and 1993 elections.

Areas of Fluctuating Levels of Voting

In 58 Assembly units, the voter turnout during Assembly elections 1993 was more than 10 per cent higher than the preceding Lok Sabha elections 1991. The difference ranged between 10.47 per cent in Banipark and 35.43 per cent in Rajakhera. It is interesting to note that in all three Assembly units of Dholpur district – Dholpur, Bari and Rajakhera – the turnout recorded a marked increase of more than 35 per cent during the Assembly elections. Malpura, Bassi, Bansur and Surajgarh (SC) were other Assembly units which recorded substantial increase of more than 30 per cent in 1993.

A detailed comparison of the spatial patterns of electoral participation during 1991 and 1993 elections brought forth the following trends of voter participation:

- Kaman was the only Assembly unit to poll 'extremely high' in both the elections.
- Assembly segments of Bharatpur, Sikar and Dausa Lok Sabha constituencies participated enthusiastically in 1991 Lok Sabha elections. The Assembly units of Bharatpur and Sikar polled high in Assembly elections also. Bharatpur, Lachhmangarh (SC) and Chomu were exceptions which, despite an increase in turnout, polled less than average in Assembly elections.
- Assembly segments of Dausa Lok Sabha constituency polled relatively low as compared to other Assembly segments in the region during the Assembly election. Although polling percentage registered a positive change over Lok Sabha election 1991 but

Figure 4.6

Difference in Level of Voter Turnout During Lok Sabha and Assembly Elections

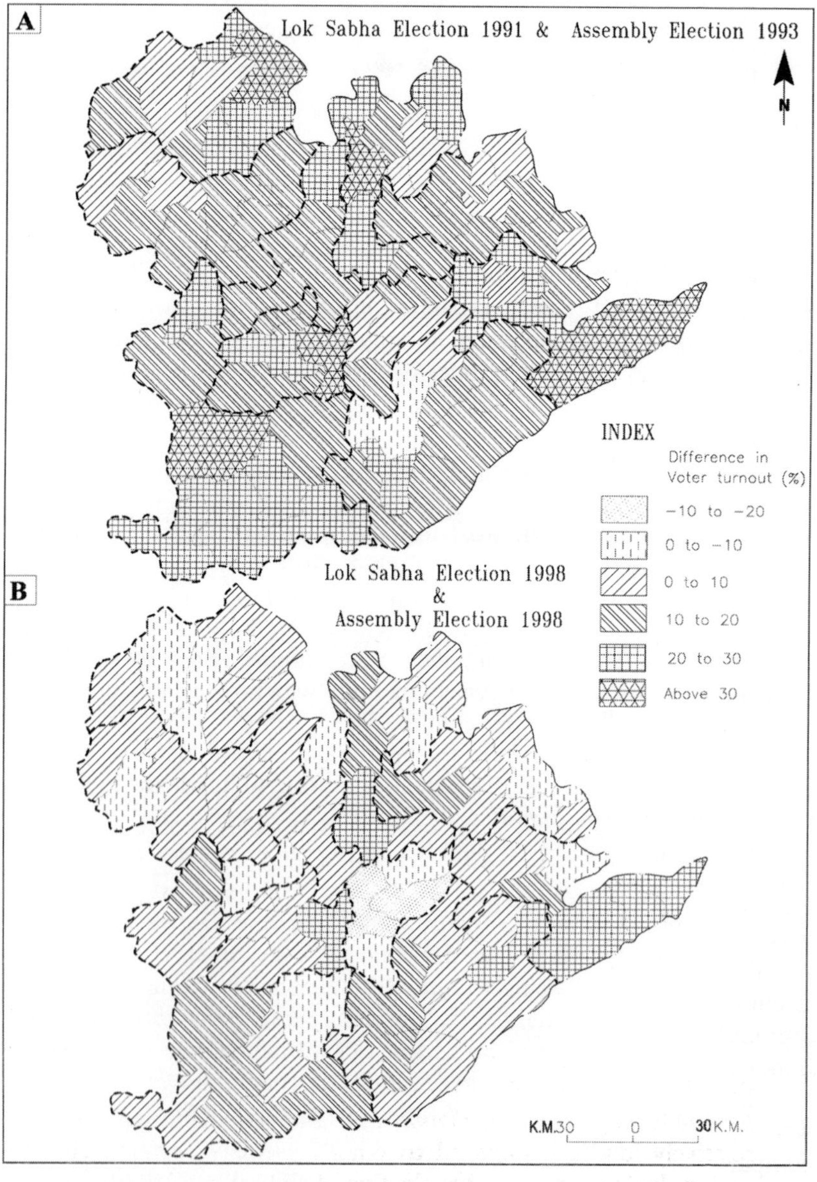

since the overall turnout in the study area was quite high in 1993 as compared to 1991, the apparent decline in rates of electoral participation in these Assembly units was due to the fact that the voter turnout in these areas did not increase at par with the remaining areas in the study region (Figure 4.6A).

- Sawai Madhopur and eastern Tonk (particularly Niwai, Tonk and Uniara) districts and Jaipur Lok Sabha constituency are areas of low electoral participation. In both elections, the Assembly units located in these districts have polled below average. Hawa Mahal polled above average in Lok Sabha elections, nevertheless the four urban constituencies of Jaipur recorded the lowest levels of turnout in the region. South western part of Tonk, including Malpura, Toda Rai Singh and Kekri polled below average in 1991 but polled high to very high in 1993.
- In Jhunjhunu Lok Sabha constituency, Fatehpur and Jhunjhunu segments polled relatively high in both the elections. Mandawa polled relatively low in both the elections. Pilani registered an increase of 20.61 per cent in 1993 over the election of 1991. The remaining segments also polled low to very low in Lok Sabha elections whereas the turnout was considerably higher in the Assembly elections.
  - Dudu, Phagi, Rupbas, Jaipur Rural and Dausa are also areas of low level of voter participation in general.
  - All segments of Alwar Lok Sabha constituency registered a significant positive change in voting turnout in 1993. Tizara, with an increase of 27.86 per cent polled above 70 per cent in 1993. In Ramgarh, the level of voter turnout was quite high in both the elections. Khairthal and Alwar segments recorded a relatively lower turnout as compared to the remaining segments of the constituency.

In general, all Assembly units reserved for SC/ST candidates recorded an increase in turnout in Assembly elections except Bamanwas where the rate of poll was almost constant. The increase was exceptionally high in Kekri (24.95%) and Surajgarh (32.50%). In remaining segments the difference ranged between 2.69 per cent in Lachhmangarh and 17.16 per cent in Phagi among SC reserved segments and from 2.58 per cent in Todabhim to 19.64 per cent in Sapotra among ST reserved constituencies.

It can safely be concluded that the voter turnout was higher as well as more uniformly spread during Assembly elections 1993 as compared to Lok Sabha elections 1991. Except Bamanwas, there was an increase in the level of turnout in all Assembly units, though to varying degrees, during Assembly elections. The low level of electoral participation in urban electoral units indicates the relative indifference of urban voters towards their political privileges and duties.

Lok Sabha Elections 1998 and Assembly Elections 1998

The average per seat voter turnout in Assembly elections 1998 was 6.1 per cent higher than Lok Sabha elections 1998. The average turnout in 1998 Assembly elections was 64.87 per cent which was the highest among all the four elections under consideration. The turnout was also more uniformly spread in Assembly elections, with a coefficient of variation of 10.55 per cent, which was 2.32 per cent lower than preceding Lok Sabha elections 1998. While in Lok Sabha elections 50 per cent of the Assembly segments polled above 60 per cent of total electorate, in Assembly elections more than three fourths (77.78%) of the Assembly units recorded more than 60 per cent voter turnout. The fact that one fourth of the total Assembly units polled above 70 per cent in Assembly elections also manifests the high level of electoral participation in the region during these elections. The corresponding figure was 2.78 per cent in Lok Sabha elections. The relative distribution of units among various vote categories during Lok Sabha 1998 and Assembly elections 1998 has been compared in Figure 4.7.

Figure 4.7

Frequency Distribution of Voting Turnout
(Lok Sabha 1998 and Assembly Elections 1998)

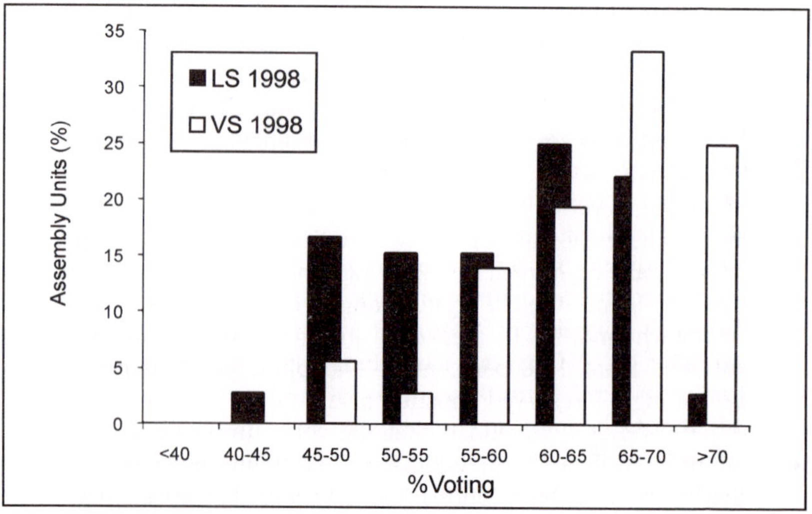

As indicated by the Figure 4.7 and the foregoing discussion, the level of voter turnout was relatively high with a clear shift in frequencies towards categories of higher turnout, as well as more evenly spread during Assembly elections as compared to the Lok Sabha ones.

Areas of Consistent Levels of Voting

In 14 Assembly units, there was a decline in turnout of less than 10 per cent (Figure 4.6B); 40 Assembly units registered an increase in turnout by less than 10 per cent.

Areas of Fluctuating Levels of Voting

Sixteen Assembly units recorded an increase of more than 10 per cent during the Assembly elections. The Assembly segments located in Dholpur district again polled quite low in Lok Sabha elections 1998 and recorded a marked rise, by more than 20 per cent, during Assembly elections 1998. Bassi voted 24.22 per cent higher in Assembly elections as compared to Lok Sabha elections. Only two Assembly units, Sikrai and Dausa recorded a negative change of more than 10 per cent, in voter turnout during the Assembly elections over the Lok Sabha election.

A close examination of spatial patterns of voter turnout during Lok Sabha and Assembly elections reveals the following trends:

- Tonk, Jaipur, Sawai Madhopur and Bayana (except Weir and Nadbai) Lok Sabha constituencies were areas of low voter turnout in Lok Sabha elections. During Lok Sabha elections, the study area was clearly divided into two divisions, northern region of high voter turnout (with few exceptions like Thanagazi, Alwar and Rupbas) and southern region of low voter turnout (Figure 4.4A). The pattern was relatively scattered in Assembly elections with an increased turnout in south western part of Tonk, Kekri, parts of Sawai Madhopur, entire Dholpur district and Bassi.
- All urban Assembly units invariably polled low in both the elections.
- Malpura, Bassi, Chomu, Thanagazi, Bari, Dholpur, Rajakhera and Bayana polled quite low in Lok Sabha elections but recorded sharp increase in turnout during Assembly elections and polled above 70 per cent.
- Assembly segments of Dausa Lok Sabha Constituency exhibited an opposite trend. The level of voter turnout was very high during the Lok Sabha elections but it declined remarkably in the consecutive Assembly elections particularly in Bandikui, Sikrai and Dausa.
- Niwai, Khandar, Sapotra, Todabhim, Rupbas, Jaipur Rural and Sanganer recorded a low turnout in both the elections.

- Assembly segments of Jhunjhunu, Sikar, Alwar and Bharatpur Lok Sabha constituencies participated enthusiastically in both the elections.
- Six of the total 19 reserved Assembly units recorded a decline in voter turnout during Assembly elections. The decline was maximum in Sikrai followed by Dausa. The increase in turnout in the remaining Assembly units was of low order except for Bamanwas which polled 12.97 per cent higher in Assembly elections.

Thus it may be concluded that the level of voter participation in the study area was higher as well as more evenly spread during Assembly elections as compared to the Lok Sabha ones. But at the same time, substantial number of Assembly units recorded a decline in voter turnout during Assembly elections, although the magnitude of decline was small in most of them. The northern part of the study area polled high in both the elections in general, whereas the Assembly units located in the southern part of the study area participated less actively in the Lok Sabha elections but were more active in Assembly elections. Assembly units of Dholpur and south western part of Tonk district exhibited marked variation in level of electoral participation at the two levels of electoral contest. The urban Assembly units were areas of low voter turnout at both levels of elections.

The foregoing analysis of spatial patterns of voter turnout during the four consecutive elections reveals the following common trends and patterns of electoral participation during the two sets of elections:

- The level of electoral participation is higher and relatively more uniformly spread during Assembly elections than the Lok Sabha ones.
- The rate of voter participation is invariably low in the urban Assembly units at both the levels of electoral contest.
- During Lok Sabha elections, Assembly segments of Alwar, Bharatpur, Dausa, Jhunjhunu and Sikar are regions of high voter turnout in general. Contrastingly, the reserved Lok Sabha constituencies – Tonk, Bayana and Sawai Madhopur record low rates of voter turnout. This is a fact which requires further investigation of whether the low turnout is resultant of disinterest of general category of voters to vote for a SC/ST candidate or it is due to low level of political awareness among reserved category of voters.
- Assembly segments of Jaipur Lok Sabha constituency record very low levels of polling at both levels of elections. Bassi is an exception where a marked increase in voter turnout occurs during Assembly elections.

- Assembly units located in south-western part of Tonk district, viz. Malpura, Toda Rai Singh, Uniara; Assembly segments of Dholpur district; Bayana, Phulera and Sawai Madhopur assembly units recorded substantial increase in level of electoral participation during Assembly elections while the same areas recorded very low levels of turnout during Lok Sabha elections. It is notable that all these segments form part of reserved Lok Sabha constituencies during Lok Sabha elections and are otherwise general seats in Assembly elections. This underlines the vital role of class bias and degree of voter identification of the contestants in determining the level of turnout in an area.
- The electorate of Dausa Lok Sabha constituency voted more enthusiastically during Lok Sabha elections perhaps due to the mass based popularity of Late Rajesh Pilot, INC candidate.
- The level of voter turnout is generally low in reserved Assembly units. Niwai, Rupbas and Khandar, reserved for SC during Assembly elections, recorded low levels of voter turnout in all the four elections. Nevertheless no specific patterns and trends could be discerned common to all the reserved electoral units. The turnout, in general, registers an increase during Assembly elections. Majority of reserved electoral units undergo a change in their nature (reserved or non-reserved) at different levels of electoral contest. This change, viz. a reserved electoral unit in Lok Sabha elections getting converted to a general seat in Assembly ones (e.g. Malpura, Uniara, Bari, Dholpur, Rajakhera) or vice versa (e.g. Lalsot, Surajgarh, Rajgarh, Kathumar, Lachhmangarh in Sikar, etc.) or an ST electoral unit getting converted into an SC seat in Assembly elections (e.g. Hindaun) or vice versa, along with closer identification of voters with the contestants during Assembly elections is mainly responsible for the variations in level of turnout at the two levels of elections.

Ecological Analysis of Voter Turnout

Impact of Polling Booth Accessibility on Voter Turnout

'Turnout in a way is the output of election arrangements' (Chandidas, 1972, p. 1,366). To examine the impact of election arrangements on voter turnout, the correlation between polling booth accessibility and voter turnout has been determined at the Assembly unit level. Two parameters of polling booth accessibility have been employed:

1. Ratio of polling stations to total number of villages in an Assembly unit (N_PS).
2. Proportion of small villages with a population size less than 900 persons, (N_SV).

For each Assembly unit in the study area the degree of accessibility of polling booths was ascertained in terms of the above two parameters. The analysis was restricted to the rural areas only, since owing to greater density of population and adequate transport facilities access to polling booths is not a significant factor affecting voter participation in urban areas. The four Assembly units located in Jaipur city, viz. Hawa Mahal, Johari Bazaar, Kishanpole and Banipark, which are entirely of urban nature, have been excluded from the analysis. For the remaining Assembly units, the polling booths located in municipal wards were deducted from the total number polling stations to derive the number of polling booths located in villages. Accordingly the ratio of polling booths per village has been determined for each Assembly unit, employing the following formula:

$$N\_PS_j = \frac{PS_{tj} - PS_{mj}}{N\_V_j}$$

where, PS_{tj} = total number of polling booths in an Assembly unit j

PS_{mj} = no. of polling booths located in municipal wards in assembly unit j

N_V_j = total no. of villages in Assembly unit j

The ratio of polling booth per village for the study area varied between 0.45 in Nagar and 2.04 in Nawalgarh. A low ratio indicates larger number of small villages clubbed together and attached to one polling booth, thus lesser polling booth accessibility. A higher ratio suggests larger number of villages of large population size, having polling booths located within themselves, thus higher degree of polling booth accessibility.

To determine the proportion of small villages in each Assembly unit, the total number of villages with a population less than 900 persons has been divided by the total number of villages. This proportion so obtained ranged between a minimum of 20 per cent in Pilani and 78.55 per cent in Phagi.

A low proportion indicates majority of large sized villages whereas a high proportion indicates dominance of small villages. Thus this proportion is inversely related to polling booth accessibility.

The correlation of Assembly unitwise voter turnout in each election with the ratio of polling booths per village and proportion of small villages yielded the following results (Table 4.7):

Table 4.7 *Relationship Between Voter Turnout and Polling Booth Accessibility (Pearson's Correlation Coefficients)*

Election Year	*N_PS*		*N_SV*	
	R	R^2	*R*	R^2
LS 1991	0.092	0.008	–0.119	0.014
VS 1993	0.100	0.01	–0.0173	0.029
LS 1998	0.337**	0.11	–0.391**	0.152
VS 1998	0.228	0.05	–0.270*	0.073

Note: R = Pearson's correlation Coefficient, R^2 = coefficient of determination

* Significant at 0.05 level (two tailed), **Significant at 0.01 level (two tailed)

The Pearson's correlation coefficient between the voter turnout and ratio of polling booths per village were found positive in all the elections. Although the magnitude of correlation coefficient was not very large or significant in Lok Sabha elections 1991 and Assembly elections 1993 and 1998, the value of 'R' was 0.337, significant at 0.01 level in Lok Sabha elections 1998. In terms of magnitude, during 1991 and 1993 the relationship was very weak but during both elections held in 1998, the relationship became relatively stronger. The ratio of polling booths accounted for 11 per cent of the variation in voter turnout during Lok Sabha elections 1998. Nevertheless, it may be inferred that a positive relationship obtains between the ratio of polling booths per village and voting turnout. The influence of this factor increased in later years as indicated by increasing value of 'R' in case of both Lok Sabha and Assembly elections.

Table 4.7 clearly reveals that the voter turnout in the study area is inversely related to the proportion of small villages to total villages in an Assembly unit. There existed a negative correlation (although not very high) between Assembly unitwise rates of voter turnout and percentage of small villages in all the elections. The magnitude of Pearson's correlation coefficient was of low order, –0.119 in 1991 and –0.173 in 1993 but it was relatively higher and significant, –0.391 in Lok Sabha elections 1998 and –0.270 in Assembly elections 1998. The proportion of small villages explained 15 per cent and 7 per cent of the variation in voter turnout in Lok Sabha 1998 and Assembly elections 1998 respectively. Thus it may be inferred that higher the number of small villages in an Assembly unit, more villages are attached to one polling booth thereby requiring the electors to travel a longer distance to polling booth, making them less enthusiastic towards exercising their franchise. The influence of this factor was higher in 1998 elections than the former set of elections.

The rate of voter participation was essentially positively related to the degree of polling booth accessibility. Although this factor did not exercise much influence on the voting behaviour of the electorate in 1991 and 1993 elections, during 1998 elections it significantly influenced the rate of voter turnout which is clearly indicated by the higher values of coefficient of determination. The role of electoral arrangements in determining the level of voter participation progressively became more important in successive elections of both Assembly and Lok Sabha.

Impact of Inter Party Competition on Voter Turnout

To investigate the impact of party competition on voter turnout, a bivalent analysis of distribution of Assembly units on the basis of per cent electors voting and the margin of victory in an electoral contest was carried out. Margin of victory (M_V) is described as the difference in the percentage of votes polled by the winning candidate/party and the runner up candidate/party. As competitive parties tend to produce a close vote (Milbrath, 1965, p. 22), the margin of victory or the 'closeness of the vote' can effectively be adopted as a measure of the degree of electoral competition. The patterns and trends of voter turnout during the various election years have already been described in detail in the previous sections of this chapter. The average margin of victory has varied from a maximum of 15.38 per cent in 1991 elections to a minimum of 10.75 per cent in 1998 Lok Sabha elections. In Assembly elections 1993, the average per seat margin of victory was 11.53 per cent which increased slightly to 12.50 per cent in Assembly elections 1998. These figures indicate that the party competition was the lowest during Lok Sabha elections 1991and was the highest during Lok Sabha elections 1998. It is noteworthy that the 1991 elections recorded the lowest per Assembly unit average turnout. During the remaining three elections the average turnout was considerably higher as compared to 1991 and the average margin of victory during these three elections was relatively lower. Therefore the correspondence between the degree of party competition and level of electoral participation is evident (Table 4.8).

Table 4.8 *Parameters of Margin of Victory*

Election	*LS 1991*	*VS 1993*	*LS 1998*	*VS 1998*
Average	15.38	11.53	10.75	12.50
Std. Dev	9.96	9.53	8.20	10.76
Min.	1.64	0.15	0.40	0.15
Max.	48.41	45.21	47.00	41.70
C.V. (%)	64.78	82.70	76.27	86.11
M_V less than 10%	30.55%	45.83%	52.77%	50.00%
M_V less than 20%	65.27%	84.72%	91.65%	80.56%

Note: Relative frequencies indicate cumulative percentage frequency of Assembly units in respective margin categories

The magnitude of coefficient of variation of margin of victory during various election years indicates that extremely high degree of spatial variation in the level of interparty competition prevailed in the study area. In all elections, the C.V. of Assembly segmentwise margin of victory was above 60 per cent, being minimum at 64.78 per cent in 1991 and maximum at 86.11 per cent in Assembly elections 1998.

For further investigation of the relationship between degree of party competition and electoral participation, the distribution of Assembly units among various levels of margin of victory at various levels of voter turnout has been studied. For each election year, the Assembly units comprising various turnout categories were further classified on the basis of margin of victory. It was observed that among the Assembly units recording higher levels of voter turnout, majority of the Assembly units were won by small margin of votes, i.e. they were more concentrated towards the lower end of the scale. On the contrary, the Assembly units comprising low turnout categories were relatively more evenly spread over various categories of margin of victory (Table 4.9A to D).

In Lok Sabha elections 1991, the Assembly segmentwise average voter turnout was 45.51 per cent with a coefficient of variation of 17.97 per cent. The voter turnout ranged from 29.06 per cent to 70.73 per cent. Almost 84.72 per cent Assembly segments recorded a turnout less than 55 per cent; therefore these elections witnessed a low level of voter participation. The average margin of victory at the level of Assembly segment was 15.38 per cent which ranged from a minimum of 1.64 per cent in Niwai to 48.41 per cent in Hawa Mahal. Out of 72, 30.55 per cent (22) Assembly segments were won by a margin of less than 10 per cent, 34.72 per cent (25) segments were won by margin of 10 to 20 per cent and 34.72 per cent (25) segments, the margin of victory was more than 20 per cent (Table 4.9A). Five segments recorded a turnout as low as below 35 per cent and all of them were won by margins of less than 20 per cent. Out of 34 segments in which the polling was 35 to 45 per cent, 73.53 per cent (25) segments were won by a margin of less than 20 per cent and nearly one third (11) by a margin of less than 10 per cent. The segments falling in turnout categories of 45 to 55 per cent turnout were more evenly distributed over various levels of margin of victory. Out of 22 segments comprising this category, only 22.73 per cent (5) were won by a margin of less than 10 per cent and an equal number were won by a margin of 10 to 20 per cent. In 22.73 per cent (5) segments margin of victory was 20 to 30 per cent, in 18.18 per cent (4) segments the margin of was 30 to 40 per cent and the remaining seats of this category were won by margins of 40 to 50 per cent. The segments falling in the turnout category of 55 to 65 per cent were distributed as 22.22 per cent, 33.33 per cent, 22.22 per cent, 11.11 per cent and 11.11 per cent in the same order of margin of victory. Only two segments recorded turnout above 65 per cent, of which one was won by a margin of less than 10 per cent and the other by 10 to 20 per cent margin. Although the foregoing distribution of Assembly segments over margins of victory and turnout intervals does not conform to our hypothesis and no specific pattern of association has been discerned but the larger proportion of Assembly segments in classes of wider margins can certainly be associated with the overall low level and high degree of variability in spatial distribution of turnout in the region in these elections.

During 1993 Assembly elections, the average voter turnout was 62.47 per cent with a coefficient of variation of 10.36 per cent. Only 13.89 per cent Assembly constituencies recorded a turnout below 55 per cent and nearly one third of the constituencies recorded a turnout above 65 per cent. Thus the spatial pattern of voter turnout was markedly different from 1991, with a higher level and more uniform distribution of voter turnout. The spatial pattern of party competition also underwent a marked change and there was an increase in the concentration of constituencies at lower end of the scale of margin of victory.

In 1993, the average margin of victory was 11.53 per cent with a C.V. of 82.70 per cent. The margin of victory varied between 0.15 per cent in Sikar and 45.21 per cent in Hawa Mahal. About 45 per cent of the Assembly constituencies witnessed a close electoral contest and were won by a margin of less than 10 per cent. In 38.89 per cent

Table 4.9 *Bivalent Analysis of Voter Turnout and Margin of Victory (1991, 1993, 1998)*

	(A)						*(B)*					
Voter Turnout	*M_V (Lok Sabha Election 1991)*						*M_V (Assembly Election 1993)*					
	0–10	*10–20*	*20–30*	*30–40*	*40–50*	*N*	*0–10*	*10–20*	*20–30*	*30–40*	*40–50*	*N*
25–35	3	2				5						
% f	(60)	(40)				(6.94)						
35–45	11	14	9			34						
% f	(32.35)	(41.18)	(26.47)			(47.2)						
45–55	5	5	5	4	3	22	6	1	2	1		10
% f	(22.73)	(22.73)	(22.73)	(18.18)	(13.64)	(30.6)	(60.00)	(10.00)	(20.00)	(10.00)		(13.9)
55–65	2	3	2	1	1	9	19	14	3		1	37
% f	(22.22)	(33.33)	(22.22)	(11.11)	(11.11)	(12.5)	(51.35)	(37.84)	(8.11)		(2.70)	(51.4)
65–75	1	1				2	8	12	3		1	24
% f	(50)	(50)				(2.78)	(33.33)	(50)	(12.5)		(4.17)	(33.3)
								1				1
Above 75								(100)				(1.39)
Total	22	25	16	5	4	72	33	28	8	1	2	72
% f	(30.55)	(34.72)	(22.22)	(6.94)	(5.56)	(100)	(45.83)	(38.89)	(11.11)	(1.39)	(2.78)	(100)

Cont'd...

...Cont'd

Voter Turnout	(C) M_V (Lok Sabha Election 1998)						(D) M_V (Assembly Election 1998)					
	0–10	*10 to 20*	*20–30*	*30–40*	*40–50*	*N*	*0–10*	*10 to 20*	*20–30*	*30–40*	*40–50*	*N*
25–35												
% f												
35–45	2					2						
% f	(100.00)					(2.77)						
45–55	8	11	2	1	1	23	2	2	1	1		6
% f	(34.78)	(47.83)	(8.70)	(4.35)	(4.35)	(31.9)	(33.33)	(33.33)	(16.67)	(16.67)		(8.33)
55–65	15	13	1			29	10	7	4	2	1	24
% f	(51.72)	(44.83)	(3.45)			(40.3)	(41.67)	(29.17)	(16.67)	(8.33)	(4.17)	(33.3)
65–75	13	4	1			18	24	13	2	3		42
% f	(72.22)	(22.22)	(5.56)			(25)	(57.14)	(30.95)	(4.76)	(7.14)		(58.3)
Above 75												
Total	38	28	4	1	1	72	36	22	7	6	1	72
% f	(52.77)	(38.88)	(5.56)	(1.38)	(1.38)	(100)	(50.00)	(30.56)	(9.72)	(8.33)	(1.39)	(100)

Note: N denotes frequency and relative frequency of Assembly units in each category of voter turnout. Figures in parentheses denote percentages of total Assembly units in each turnout category.

constituencies, the margin was 10 to 20 per cent and the proportion of constituencies which were won by a margin of more than 20 per cent decreased to 15.28 per cent. Thus increase in the degree of electoral contest was accompanied by rise in the level of electoral participation. In 1993, the voter turnout ranged between 47.69 per cent and 77.96 per cent. Out of 72, 13.69 per cent Assembly constituencies recorded a voter turnout between 45 and 55 per cent. Out of these 60 per cent of the constituencies were won by a margin of less than 10 per cent (Table 4.9B); 10 per cent were won by a margin of 10 to 20 per cent; and 20 per cent by a margin of 30 to 40 per cent. In the category of 55 to 65 per cent voter turnout, 51.35 per cent constituencies were won by a margin of less than 10 per cent and 37.84 per cent were won by margin of 10 to 20 per cent. In the turnout category of 65 to 75 per cent, one third were won by a margin of less than 10 per cent and a half were won by a margin of 10 to 20 per cent. Kaman, the only constituency which recorded a turnout above 75 per cent, was won by a margin of 12.73 per cent.

Thus in 1993 elections, as the number of constituencies recording low margins of victory increased indicating a keen party competition, the number of constituencies recording higher levels of voter turnout also increased.

During both the elections held in 1998, there was a close correspondence between degree of party competition and rate of voter turnout.

During Lok Sabha elections 1998, the average voter turnout was 58.77 per cent with a coefficient of variation of 12.87 per cent. One fourth of the Assembly segments recorded a voter turnout more than 65 per cent. The average margin of victory in the region, at the level of Assembly segments, was 10.75 per cent which indicates close interparty contest during these elections. The coefficient of variation of Assembly unitwise margin of victory was 76.27 per cent and it ranged from a minimum of 0.40 per cent in Kekri to a maximum of 47 per cent in Hawa Mahal. The high degree of electoral competition during these elections is also revealed by the fact that 52.77 per cent of the Assembly segments were won by a close margin of less than 10 per cent and only 8.32 per cent of the segments were won by a margin of more than 20 per cent (Table 4.9C).

In all categories of voter turnout, which ranged from 43.81 per cent to 72.55 per cent, there was a clear clustering of segments in classes of low margins. The Assembly segments of 45–55 per cent vote category spread over all the classes of margin of victory (Table 4.9C). Out of the segments comprising the 55–65 per cent vote category

(40.27% of total Assembly segments), 51.72 per cent were won by margin of less than 10 per cent and 44.83 per cent were won by margin of 10 to 20 per cent. In the 65 to 75 per cent vote category, 72.22 per cent of the segments witnessed a close victory by a margin of less than 10 per cent and 22.22 per cent were won by 10 to 20 per cent margin of votes. Thus an intense electoral contest was followed by a high level of voter participation.

Similarly, during Assembly elections 1998 the level of electoral participation was considerably high. The average per seat voter turnout was 64.87 per cent with a coefficient of variation of 10.55 per cent. At the level of Assembly constituencies the turnout ranged between 46.89 per cent and 74.32 per cent. The high degree of voter participation during these elections is evident from the fact that nearly 60 per cent of the constituencies recorded a turnout above 65 per cent. The average margin of victory was 12.50 per cent which varied between a minimum of 0.15 per cent in Deeg and a maximum of 41.70 per cent in Todabhim. The coefficient of variation of margin of victory was 86.11 per cent which was higher than all the other elections under consideration. The dispersion of constituencies over margins of victory and turnout intervals suggests a strong positive relationship between party competition and voter turnout.

Half of the constituencies were won with a close margin of less than 10 per cent, whereas nearly 80 per cent of the constituencies were won with a margin upto 20 per cent. In each turnout category, the constituencies show clear concentration in close margin categories, 0–10 per cent and 10–20 per cent. About 66 per cent of the constituencies of the turnout category of 45–55 per cent, nearly 70 per cent of the constituencies of the turnout category of 55 to 65 per cent and 88 per cent of the constituencies of the turnout group of 65 to 75 per cent fall in the margin classes of upto 20 per cent (Table 4.9D). The proportion of constituencies in the closest margin category, 0–10 per cent, also increased with increasing turnout, being 33.33 per cent, 41.67 per cent and 57.14 per cent in 45–55, 55–65 and 65–75 per cent turnout categories respectively. This clearly shows that in Assembly elections 1998, the degree of party competition and level of electoral participation were closely linked and keen electoral contest stimulated larger number of voters to exercise their franchise.

The foregoing analysis clearly manifests the impact of interparty competition on levels of voter turnout. The close examination of the distribution of Assembly units among various turnout and margin categories for each election year reveal a close positive relationship between degree of interparty competition and voter turnout. Although, the low turnout categories demonstrated a somewhat erratic behaviour, nonetheless the congruence between the two phenomena was quite strong in the high turnout categories. Degree of electoral contest did not seem to influence the voter outcome to any significant extent during 1991 elections but in the remaining three elections, more specifically in 1998 elections, the close positive correspondence between the two phenomena was clearly evident.

Effect of Socio-Economic Variables on Voter Turnout

The preliminary nature of bivariate relationships between each selected socio-economic variable and voter turnout, at the Assembly unit level was determined by calculating the Pearson's product moment correlation coefficient. The correlation coefficients thus obtained are given in Table 4.10.

Table 4.10 *Correlation Matrix Showing Bivariate Correlations between Selected Socio-Economic Variables and Voter Turnout*

S. No.	*Variable*	*LS 1991*	*VS 1993*	*VS 1998*	*LS 1998*
1.	D_E	–0.050	–0.251*	–0.462**	–0.246*
2.	U_P	0.016	–0.243*	–0.485**	–0.234*
3.	L_R	0.043	–0.187	–0.387**	–0.002
4.	W_P	–0.284*	–0.106	–0.175	–0.320**
5.	W_OS	0.030	–0.245*	–0.476**	–0.154
6.	AG_L	0.114	0.182	0.361**	0.242*
7.	AG_W	0.113	0.330**	0.514**	0.245*
8.	S_R_EL	0.030	–0.013	0.183	0.375**
9.	SC_EL	–0.294*	–0.109	–0.053	–0.168
10.	ST_EL	–0.162	–0.244*	–0.194	–0.243*

Note: *Correlation is significant at 0.05 level (2 tailed)
**Correlation is significant at 0.01 level (2 tailed)

The above correlation coefficients point towards the following relationships between individual selected variables and rate of voter turnout in the study area.

- In all the elections, the density of electorate was negatively associated with turnout. Except 1991, the correlation was statistically significant in the remaining three elections. Thus the rate of voter turnout is low in the more densely populated areas of the study area. Although the overall turnout increased considerably during 1993 and 1998 elections, it registered a decline in more densely populated areas. Assembly elections 1998 recorded the highest average turnout but the level of voter participation was markedly low in densely populated areas, as indicated by the correlation coefficient of –0.462, significant at 1 per cent level of significance. The relationship holds good for both Lok Sabha and Assembly elections.

- Except in 1991 when the relationship between proportion of urban population and voter turnout was positive but very weak and insignificant, significant negative relationship obtained between the two in 1993 and both elections held in 1998. Although there had been an increase in the overall turnout rate in 1993 and 1998 elections, the rate of voter participation was relatively low in more urbanized areas. The relationship was strongest in 1998 Assembly elections, the correlation coefficient being –0.485 significant at 1 per cent level of significance.
- The relationship between voter turnout and proportion of literate population has also followed a similar trend. Very weak but positive in 1991, the trend reversed ever since although the relationship was significant only during 1998 Assembly elections. The relationship was very weak and inconsistent during Lok Sabha elections but was relatively strong during Assembly elections. Thus the rate of voter participation was generally low in those areas where literacy rate is high, more conspicuously during Assembly elections.
- Similar trend obtained in the relationship between voter turnout and proportion of workers engaged in other services. In 1991, the association between the two was weakly positive. In 1993, the nature of relationship reversed and the correlation became negative as well as stronger, significant at 5 per cent level of significance. In Assembly elections 1998, the relationship was even stronger with R = –0.476 significant at 1 per cent level. In Lok Sabha elections 1998, although the relationship remained negative but the correlation coefficient was quite weak and insignificant. Thus it may be inferred that the voter turnout was low in areas where the proportion of population engaged in other services was high. Although the relationship was inconsistent and less marked during Lok Sabha elections, during Assembly elections, such areas invariably polled low.
- Density of electorate, proportion of urban population, literacy rate and proportion of workers engaged in other services are

mutually highly interrelated. All these variables exhibit strong positive intercorrelation in the study area which has been illustrated in the following correlation matrix for the year 1991:

Table 4.11 *Correlation Matrix for Developmental Variables*

S. No.	*Variable*	*I*	*II*	*III*	*IV*
I	D_E	1.00	0.711**	0.654**	0.650**
II	U_P		1.00	0.822**	0.844**
III	L_R			1.00	0.828**
IV	W_OS				1.00

Note: ** Significant at 0.01 level of significance (two tailed)

All these four variables are measures of level of socio-economic development of an area. The correlations between all four developmental variables viewed together and voter turnout reveals that during Lok Sabha elections the more developed areas of the study area manifest an inconsistent behaviour. In 1991, the developmental factor did not exercise a significant influence on level of voter turnout. Despite exceptionally low overall turnout rate during these elections, all developmental indices (except density of electorate) manifested a weak positive relationship with turnout. The relationship reversed in Lok Sabha elections 1998 when all development indices showed a negative relationship with turnout, although not of very high order.

Contrastingly all developmental factors invariably exhibited a negative association with rates of voter turnout during both the Assembly elections. The relationship was markedly strong during 1998 Assembly elections. Therefore, it may be inferred that during Assembly elections, the more developed and urbanized areas record considerably low rates of voter turnout. In recent years, this trend has further intensified.

During Lok Sabha elections, the degree of poll participation in urbanized areas has been found relatively higher as compared to the Assembly ones, but still it is markedly lower than the rural counterparts. It is noteworthy that in all elections, both Assembly and Lok Sabha elections, the average voting turnout in the six urban constituencies of the study area was markedly lower than the average turnout of the whole region (Table 4.12).

The difference is greater in the Assembly elections as compared to the Lok Sabha Elections, being maximum at 11.91 per cent in 1998 Assembly elections and minimum at 0.77 per cent in 1991 Lok Sabha elections. This further testifies that whereas the developmental factor did not exercise much influence on the level of electoral participation in

1991, in 1998 Assembly elections, despite of high overall rate of participation, the developed and urbanized areas registered markedly low voter turnout. This indicates the rising disenchantment of the educated voter with the electoral process since the impression has been gaining ground that the elections make little difference to the actual nature and complexion of governments. The entrenched capitalist interests have to a great extent succeeded in organizing society and control mechanism in its own best interests so that the political process of elections has become of only minor importance in the distribution of real power (Miliband, 1969).

Table 4.12 *Voter Turnout in Urban Constituencies (1991, 1993, 1998)*

(Figures in per cent)

	LS 1991	*VS 1993*	*LS 1998*	*VS 1998*
Bharatpur	46.30	53.79	59.44	59.44
Alwar	48.54	56.78	55.70	56.33
Banipark	40.96	51.43	48.15	48.54
Hawa Mahal	50.79	62.08	54.80	53.93
Kishanpole	39.67	51.45	49.25	50.35
Johari Bazaar	42.19	56.65	48.39	49.16
Average	44.74	55.36	52.62	52.96
Regional Average	45.51	62.47	58.77	64.87
Difference	0.77	7.11	6.15	11.91

The relationship between proportion of working population and voter turnout has also been negative in nature in all the elections. The correlation of voter turnout with proportion of working population was stronger in Lok Sabha elections as compared to Assembly elections. In 1991, the correlation was –0.284 which was statistically significant. The association became weaker in Assembly elections 1993 and 1998 but the nature of relationship remained negative. In Lok Sabha 1998, the correlation between voter turnout and proportion of working population was highest at –0.320, significant at 0.01 level. Thus the level of voter participation in north east Rajasthan is lower in areas where the rate of employment is higher.

In sharp contrast to the developed areas, the rural areas of the study region demonstrate relatively high level of political awareness. The relationship between voter turnout and proportion of agricultural labourers and agricultural workers has been positive in all the elections. In both the elections held in 1998, the correlation between voter turnout and proportion of agricultural labourers was significant. In Assembly elections 1998, the correlation was the highest at 0.361, significant at 0.01 level.

The proportion of agricultural workers significantly influenced the level of voter turnout. A positive relationship has been obtained between voter turnout and proportion of agricultural workers during all elections. In 1991, the correlation was positive but not too significant. But in successive elections, the association became stronger. The correlation coefficient increased sharply to 0.330, significant at 0.01 level in 1993. In Assembly elections 1998, it further increased to 0.514, significant at 0.01 level. In Lok Sabha elections 1998, the relationship was relatively weaker as compared to both Assembly elections but the correlation coefficient was positive and statistically significant. It may also be noted that the proportion of agricultural workers played a more crucial role in determining the voter turnout in Assembly elections than Lok Sabha elections, as indicated by the relatively high values of correlation coefficients.

Thus the pattern of correlation between proportion of agricultural workers and agricultural labourers to total working population and voter turnout indicates that the level of turnout was higher in rural areas than the urban areas and the agricultural segment of the population has displayed increased political awareness in recent elections. The rise in the level of average turnout in the region since 1993 may be associated with the higher level of political consciousness in the rural areas of the study area; manifested in higher levels of voter turnout among the agricultural class of voters. The pattern of correlation between voter turnout and proportion of agricultural workers and the pattern of fluctuation of average turnout in the region exhibit perfect congruence. This indicates that the class of agricultural workers in north east Rajasthan exercises a decisive influence in determining the level of voting turnout in the region.

The rate of voting turnout has all through remained negatively associated with the size of electorate belonging to SCs and STs. The relationship between voter turnout and proportion of SC electorate was significant in 1991 elections (R = -0.294), but ever since it has weakened considerably. The association has been relatively strong in Lok Sabha elections, nevertheless, it has been negative.

The association between proportion of ST electorate and voter turnout has also been negative in all the elections. Although the relationship was weaker in Lok Sabha 1991 and Assembly elections 1998, in Assembly elections 1993 and Lok Sabha elections 1998, the correlation between size of ST population and voter turnout was significantly negative. Thus it may be concluded that the rate of voter turnout is relatively low in areas where the ratio of population belonging to reserved categories is high. We have earlier observed that the reserved constituencies are generally areas of low voter turnout. This statistical inference from grouped data, however, does not provide a conclusive proof that the turnout rate among SC/ST voters has been lower than in case of general class of electorate. The low level of turnout in the areas with high concentration of reserved sections of population may be due to abstention on the part of non-reserved class of voters to vote for a candidate belonging to a reserved class and vice-versa.

The relationship of voter turnout with sex-ratio of electorate was weakly positive in 1991. In 1993, the situation reversed and a very weak negative correlation existed between the two. The nature of relationship reverted to positive in Lok Sabha elections 1998 and significant moderate correlation (R = 0.375) was obtained. During Assembly elections 1998, the relationship weakened but was positive. These results reveal that proportion of female population did not have a significant and consistent relationship with voter turnout. The political participation has been relatively higher in areas with higher sex-ratio in 1998 elections. Particularly during Lok Sabha elections 1998, these areas recorded markedly high levels of voter turnout.

Results obtained by Multiple Correlation and Stepwise Regression

The foregoing analysis of the bivariate correlations between selected socio-economic variables and voter turnout provides us with a preliminary idea of the nature of relationship of various socio-economic determinants with voter turnout levels in the study area during various elections. But care must be taken while drawing any conclusions from simple bivariate relations, as in such an analysis, the influence of other variables is not considered which coexists and simultaneously influences the phenomena under consideration. In reality we do not live in a bivariate world.

The voter turnout in the region is the combined outcome of a multitude of interrelated factors. Thus an investigation of the proportion of total variation of voter turnout which can be attributed to the selected socio-economic variables taken together has been made, using multiple correlation technique. The multiple coefficient of determination 'R^2' provided the combined explanatory strength of all the selected variables, thus indicating the proportion of variance in voter turnout accounted for by all the selected socio-economic variables together. Stepwise Regression was carried out to assort those variables which were practically more important in explaining the voter turnout in each election. 'R^2' values of stepwise regression indicate the combined explanatory strength of these assorted significant variables in the final equation. The multiple correlation coefficients 'R' and 'R^2' values obtained by multiple regression and stepwise regression exercises yielded the results as contained in Table 4.13.

Table 4.13 *Results of Multiple Regression and Stepwise Regression of Voter Turnout on Socio-Economic Variables*

	Lok Sabha Elections		*Assembly Elections*	
	1991	*1998*	*1993*	*1998*
Multiple Regression				
R	0.46	0.67	0.51	0.71
R^2	0.21	0.45	0.26	0.50
Stepwise Regression				
R	0.39	0.66	0.46	0.68
R^2	0.16	0.44	0.21	0.46

The 'R^2' values obtained through Multiple Regression in Table 4.12 reveal that the influence of socio-economic context in determining the levels of voter participation in the study area has progressively increased. In 1991, the total explanatory power of the socio-economic variables was 21 per cent which increased to 26 per cent in 1993. During Lok Sabha elections 1998, the selected set of variables accounted for 45 per cent of the variance in voter turnout in the region which further increased to 50 per cent in the consecutive Assembly elections. In both sets of elections, 'R^2' values for Assembly elections were higher than those for Lok Sabha ones indicating that socio-economic factors exercise a greater influence on voter turnout during Assembly elections than the Lok Sabha ones.

The multiple correlation coefficients and 'R^2' values do not reveal the relative importance of individual variables. For this purpose, the partial correlation coefficients were examined which provided a measure of correlation between voter turnout and each individual socio-economic variable in a multivariate situation, after the correlation of remaining variables was also taken into account. The partial correlation coefficients of the selected socio-economic variables and voter turnout for various elections are stated in Table 4.14.

Table 4.14 *Partial Correlation Coefficients of Voter Turnout and Selected Socio-Economic Variables (Stepwise Regression)*

Variable	*Lok Sabha Elections*		*Assembly Elections*	
	1991	*1998*	*1993*	*1998*
D_E	–0.103	–0.048	–0.077	*–0.338
U_P	0.054	*–0.294	–0.025	–0.191
L_R	0.079	*0.415	–0.029	–0.077
W_OS	0.103	0.010	–0.013	–0.227
W_P	–0.124	*0.366	0.041	0.07
AG_L	0.124	0.055	–0.027	0.082
AG_W	*0.273	*0.231	*0.403	*0.451
SC_EL	*–0.379	–0.124	–0.159	*–0.325
ST_EL	–0.022	–0.036	*–0.341	*–0.202
S_R_EL	–0.026	*0.445	0.056	0.046
R	0.393	0.66	0.461	0.679
†R^2	0.155	0.436	0.212	0.46

Note: * Variables included in the final regression equation
† Overall explanatory power of the significant variables obtained through stepwise regression

In stepwise regression, variables are added to the regression equation in accordance with their relative importance, on the basis of their contribution to explanation of the remaining variance in the dependent variable. Variables which do not contribute significantly to the explanation of the variance of the dependent variable are excluded in the final equation.

The stepwise regression analysis of voter turnout with the selected socio-economic variables assorted the variables which imparted decisive influence on the spatial variation in voter turnout for each election. In 1991, two variables, proportion of SC electorate and proportion of agricultural workers explained 16 per cent of the variance of voter turnout in the study area. The level of voter turnout in the region was positively related to the proportion of agricultural workers whereas inverse relationship obtained between proportion of SC population and voter turnout. The remaining variables showed weak associations and were not significant in explaining the variation in voter turnout. The total explanatory strength of all the variables together was also of low order (21%).

In Assembly elections 1993, the total variation in voter turnout accounted for by all the selected socio-economic variables together increased slightly to 26 per cent. Two variables, proportion of agricultural workers and proportion of ST electorate explained 21 per cent of the total variance in voter turnout. The proportion of agricultural workers showed moderate positive partial correlation of 0.403 with voter turnout. Proportion of ST electorate showed moderate negative association with voter turnout with a partial correlation of –0.341. The remaining variables were insignificant with very low order correlations.

During Assembly elections 1998, the influence of socio-economic variables increased remarkably and the R^2 value of all selected socio-economic variables increased to 0.50, almost twice of that in 1993. Proportion of agricultural workers, proportion of ST and SC electorate and density of electorate played crucial role in determining the level of voter turnout at constituency level. These four variables together explained 46 per cent of the variance in turnout. Proportion of agricultural workers was the most significant determinant followed by density of electorate, proportion of SC population and proportion of ST population in decreasing order of significance. The voter turnout was positively related to proportion of agricultural workers with a moderately high partial correlation coefficient 0.451. The association between density of electorate, proportion of SC and ST electorate and voter turnout was negative in nature with moderate partial correlation coefficients of –0.338, –0.325 and –0.202. The remaining variables were excluded from the final regression equation. Among these, proportion of working population, agricultural labourers and sex ratio had weak positive relationship with turnout whereas the correlations of proportion of urban population, literacy rate and workers in other services were negative. All developmental variables had negative correlations with voter turnout which indicates that the level of voter turnout was lower in urbanized areas than the rural areas.

The socio-economic variables accounted for 45 per cent of the total spatial variation in turnout during Lok Sabha elections 1998, at Assembly segment level. Forty four per cent of the variance of turnout was explained by sex-ratio of electorate, proportion of working population, proportion of agricultural workers, literacy rate and level of urbanization. It is interesting to note that significant positive correlations obtained between literacy rate, sex ratio of electorate and proportion of working population and voter turnout, which were of very low order in the other three elections. Proportion of urban population exhibited negative influence on voter turnout and emerged as a significant factor for the first time. Proportion of agricultural workers was positively related to voter turnout with partial correlation coefficient of 0.231. Out of the remaining variables, proportion of ST and SC electorate and density of electorate had very weak negative partial correlations whereas workers in other services and proportion of agricultural labourers had weak positive relationship with voter turnout but these variables were not significant regarding their explanatory strength.

A close scrutiny of the partial correlation coefficients indicating the relative importance of individual socio-economic variables in explaining the variation in voter turnout reveals the absence of any consistent relationship between voter turnout and the selected socio-economic factors, except that with proportion of agricultural workers. A brief statement of the relationship between each factor and voter turnout is given as under:

- Density of electorate had very weak partial negative correlation in three out of four elections; only in Assembly elections 1998 it exercised a significant negative influence on voter turnout.
- The proportion of urban population manifested weak negative relationship with voter turnout in Assembly elections. In 1991 Lok Sabha election the influence of this factor was positive but insignificant. The relationship reversed in Lok Sabha elections 1998 and it had significant negative relationship with voter turnout.
- The trend was more or less similar in regard to the literacy rate. During both the Assembly elections, literacy rate had very weak negative relationship with voter turnout. Contrastingly, in Lok Sabha elections, the relationship was positive, quite weak in 1991 but considerably significant in 1998.
- Proportion of working population was positively related to voter turnout during the Assembly elections but the relationship was very weak. In Lok Sabha elections 1991, the relationship was weak and negative but in Lok Sabha elections 1998, proportion of working population exercised significant positive influence on voter turnout.
- The proportion of population engaged in other services had weak positive relationship with voter turnout in Lok Sabha elections. During Assembly elections, the nature of relationship was negative. The explanatory value of the variable was of low order in all the elections.
- The partial correlation of proportion of agricultural labourers was weak and positive in three out of four elections. The variable exhibited a weak negative association in Assembly elections 1993.

- Proportion of agricultural workers was the only variable with significant explanatory power in all elections. In all elections, the partial correlation of this variable with voter turnout was positive and significant too. Higher correlation coefficients in Assembly elections vis-à-vis Lok Sabha ones indicate that the variable exercises greater influence in Assembly elections.
- The relationship between voter turnout and proportion of SC electorate lacked any definite pattern except that in all elections, the variable correlated negatively with voter turnout. Whereas in Lok Sabha 1991 and Assembly elections 1998, the explanatory power of the variable was significant, in Assembly 1993 and Lok Sabha elections 1998, the relationship was weak.
- While the proportion of ST electorate did not exercise any significant influence on voter turnout in both the Lok Sabha elections, it accounted for significant proportion of the variance in voter turnout in both Assembly elections. The explanatory value of this variable was the highest in Assembly elections 1993. Nevertheless, the relationship was negative in nature during all the elections.
- Male-female ratio of electorate in various Assembly units has lacked any consistent and significant relationship with voter turnout except for Lok Sabha elections 1998 when the partial correlation between sex-ratio of electorate and voter turnout was moderately high at 0.445.

Conclusion

The pattern of relationship of individual factors with intensity of voter turnout during various elections as indicated by the partial correlation coefficients does not reveal any consistent relationship between the socio-economic variables and intensity of voter turnout. Nevertheless, some significant trends may be identified. The significant positive relationship between proportion of agricultural workers and voter turnout underlines the fact that voting turnout is invariably higher in areas where the proportion of agricultural working population is high. The influence of this variable is higher in Assembly elections than the Lok Sabha ones. The urban development variables exercise a weak negative influence on the level of voting in Assembly elections, i.e. voter turnout is relatively low in urban areas, especially during Assembly elections. The total explanatory strength of the socio-economic variables was of low order in 1991 and 1993 whereas it markedly increased during both the elections held in 1998. Moreover the number of variables exercising significant influence on variation in level of electoral participation has also progressively increased. This clearly underlines the fact that in recent years, the influence of the socio-economic milieu of the study area in determining the level of electoral participation has progressively increased. In both pairs of Assembly and Lok Sabha elections, the amount of variance in voter turnout explained by the socio-economic factors, as indicated by values of 'R^2' derived from multiple regression as well as stepwise regression, was higher in Assembly elections as compared to its Lok Sabha counterpart. Thus it may be inferred that socio-economic determinants as a whole play a greater role in determining the pattern of voter turnout in Assembly elections vis-à-vis the Lok Sabha ones. Nevertheless, the individual segments of population lack consistency in their voting behaviour.

5 Social Issues and Political Parties

Elections in India have become highly competitive. Political parties contest every election on the basis of their ideologies and viewpoint towards the social issues contained in the manifestoes. An election manifesto is a charter of assurances and promises of a political party to the electorate on the basis of which it solicits votes. These are not comprehensive policy documents detailing out specific programmes but are indicative of broad goals for a large section of voters. Election manifestos are of great significance and purpose for the parties as well as the voters. For the parties they provide an opportunity periodically to articulate the loftiest hopes and the noblest aspirations. For the voters, they provide a means to compare various parties. Thus the voters' choice for a particular party is indeed conditioned by the promises made by the party during the elections. Many a times it is said that Election Manifestos are a verbal rhetoric of political parties and every party forgets its manifesto and election promises after the elections are over. It is true to hold that political parties to some extent win or lose elections on the basis of personality of their leaders, local acceptability of the party candidates and caste and community equations. Money also plays a crucial role during the elections not only for election campaign but to grease the palms of the voters and local influential leaders. The election campaigns have become very competitive and every political party mobilizes huge resources to reach and woo the voter. But this is only one side of the story. India is involved in the process of nation building through democratic process and the verdict of the voter is the pillar of legitimacy of the ruling party for governance. Every political party has to spell out its respective goals of governance and the parties have to compete by projecting their goals of nation building and the ways and means which would lead to achieve those goals. Thus party competition is to a significant extent centred around ideologies and goals of governance and nation building. Therefore, although many factors operate in conditioning an election outcome but the importance of contemporary issues, slogans, party manifestos and promises also demand due cognizance.

The Election Manifestos of the parties reflect the context of the Lok Sabha or the State Assembly elections. Every party manifesto lays down the party's goals and ideology which is linked with the social base of the party and offers a critique of the opposition parties.

Lok Sabha Elections 1991

Contemporary Issues

The ninth Lok Sabha was the most short lived in the history of Independent India. Many tumultuous political events occurred within the brief span of 15 months of its existence. The 'hung' Lok Sabha witnessed acute factionalism and splits within the Janata Dal and revealed utter incapability on the part of the centrist parties to form a coalition government. It was internally 'immobilized' because no party or a coalition of parties was able to provide a stable government. The impact of this political instability on the country was quite disastrous. The year 1990 was full of social disorders because of communal riots on Ram Janmabhoomi–Babri Masjid issue and anti Mandal riots arising out of opportunistic reservation policy announced by V.P. Singh. Secessionist and terrorist movements were raising their heads in Punjab, Jammu and Kashmir, Assam and Tamil Nadu because the Central government was intrinsically weak, unstable, faction ridden and it had no capacity to provide political and administrative direction to the country. During the ninth Lok Sabha, the country witnessed the fall of two governments. It also witnessed the collapse of governance because public policy making mechanisms were immobilized. The industrial policy, agricultural policy, foreign policy of India and Eighth Five Year Plan became serious victims of political instability. The consequences of instability were also reflected in the country's role in the Gulf War. The internal economy was crippled because of rising inflation and lack of policies to meet the challenges of economic crisis.

The tenth Lok Sabha elections were held in the context of these political developments. The major issues of national importance which formed the base of the policies and programmes of various political parties in fray were political instability in the country, the Mandir and the Mandal issues, containing the escalating spiralling prices, generation of employment, foreign exchange crisis, development and restoration of peace in Jammu and Kashmir, Punjab and Assam. The Congress party's main campaigning plank was political stability in the country. Janata Dal and V.P. Singh campaigned on the basis of social justice and equity for the backward classes and the minorities. The BJP defined its political programme on the basis of *'Ram and Roti'*, exposure of pseudo-secularism and replacement of the outdated Nehruvian model of economic and political development.

On the eve of elections new issues cropped up and many dormant demands, problems and questions re-emerged. Some local issues were also in the forefront with the national issues which were mainly concerned with regional development. Although national issues played a more important role in Lok Sabha elections but the voters choice was undoubtedly and significantly conditioned by the local development issues too. These issues not only manifested the expectations of the voters from the political contenders but also formed the basis of discontent and anguish of the electorate in form of anti-establishment wave during the next elections if not met with.

In Bharatpur constituency there was severe discontent among the people because of scarcity of drinking water and ineffective implementation of development projects. In Sawai Madhopur constituency there was a longstanding demand of forming Karauli as a district, construction of Hindaun Nallah, construction of anicut on the Gambhiri River and restarting the Sawai Madhopur Cement factory. The people also wanted an effective solution to the dacoit problem in the region, increased irrigation facilities from Panchna Dam and effective development plans for the district. In Tonk constituency there was a high degree of discontent among the voters because the district was not getting just share of the benefits from the Bisalpur project. Especially farmers of Tonk, Uniara, Niwai, Malpura, Toda Rai Singh bore severe anguish towards all political parties on this issue. The electorate also felt cheated on the issue of linking Kekri and Tonk with a railway line and channelizing industries to Tonk district as promised by the former Congress (I) and Janata Dal governments. In Dausa constituency the major demand in the Kotputli region was the formation of Kotputli district. In Jhunjhunu constituency the major demands were those of opening a Sainik School and Vigyan Kendra along with overall development of the district. In Bayana constituency also the electorate were dissatisfied over the low level of development in the region and held a series of demands related to installation of super thermal power station in Dholpur, college at Bari, an Industrial Training Institute at Weir and undertaking measures for industrial development in Dholpur district. In Sikar the voters were dissatisfied with Devi Lal as the constituency had not acquired the benefits it had expected from him who was heading the Union Agricultural Ministry. The promises made by Devi Lal regarding providing unemployment allowances and opening Saledipur fertilizer factory had also remained unfulfilled. The hike in the electricity connection charges and slow pace of agricultural development in the region had also added fuel to the fire.

Manifestoes of Various Political Parties

As stated earlier the 1991 Lok Sabha elections were held in a context of acute social and economic crisis. In their respective manifestoes, the various political parties laid down their approaches to deal with the crippling economy, disintegrating society and tumultuous polity.

Indian National Congress (INC)

The INC manifesto regarded the tenure of the National Front (NF) government as a complete failure and defined its rule as that of 'gross misrule and misgovernance' which severely impaired the country's economy, social integrity and international credibility, leading the economy in a distress with soaring prices, staggering development where all antipoverty and employment programmes had been rendered inoperative and ineffective. It blamed the NF government for jeopardizing the national unity by not taking any stringent stand to contain the mounting secessionist and terrorist activities in J&K, Punjab, Assam and Tamil Nadu. It also attacked the NF government on issues of reservations for backward classes and Ram Janmabhoomi–Babri Masjid. At the helm of affairs when the economy was in a mess with a slow rate of economic growth, declining investments, increasing unemployment, soaring prices, fiscal deficit, stagnant exports, uncontrolled imports, emptying foreign exchange reserves; the country virtually stood at a stage of bankruptcy. The party asserted that INC was the only party that could provide stability to the country and lead it on the road of progress and development. The manifesto also listed the achievements of INC government during 1984–89. It made several promises such as to restore the country's peace and integrity; curb inflation; arrest the spiralling prices; eradicate the poverty and unemployment by the end of the century. It promised resumption of growth, progress, justice, social and communal amity through stable governance. It also presented its vision of future and a detailed action plan to build a democratic, socialist, prosperous and forward looking India. The party expressed its commitment for fulfilment of its promises by putting forth a time bound programme in which the targets for the first 100, 365, 730 and 1,000 days of governance were clearly enlisted.

Bhartiya Janata Party (BJP)

In its 1991 party manifesto, for the first time BJP presented itself as an independent and complete alternative to INC and outlined a detailed plan of action on various issues facing the polity, economy and society of India. Expressing its commitment to nationalism, holism and integral humanism devoted to *swadesh* and *swa-dharma*, it expressed resolution to lead the country on the path of communal harmony, social security, economic growth, equitable regional development and technological progress along with strengthening its ties with the rich cultural heritage of the nation. It also enumerated sundry measures to reform the polity, rejuvenate the economy and restore internal peace in the country. It held the INC government responsible for terrorism in Punjab, Assam and Andhra Pradesh. It reiterated its commitment for construction of Ram Mandir, abrogation of Article 370 and promised for the formation of three new States of Uttaranchal, Vananchal and Delhi. The party manifesto provided an elaborate view of the party's stand and policies over a wide range of issues covering reforms in the field of law and constitution; strengthening Centre-State relations; ensuring fair elections; probity in public life; redressal of problems in North East, Punjab, Jammu and Kashmir and Ladakh, Telengana and Assam; dispensing quick, inexpensive and impartial justice and introduction of judicial reforms; decentralization of power; revival of economy; rural development; enhancing productivity in industrial sector keeping in line with the principles of self reliance, modernization, decentralization and *'daridra narayan sewa'*. In order to meet the increasing employment needs the party emphasized on promotion of the handicraft and village industries. It also presented a detailed account of the measures which would be taken to contain the fiscal imbalance, escalating prices and generation of employment. The manifesto also listed a host of welfare schemes for the labour sector, government employees, villagers, salaried people, senior citizens, soldiers, women, youth, scheduled castes and scheduled tribes, other backward classes, the destitute and the handicapped. Elaborative proposals for energy policy, transport policy, population policy, environment policy and foreign policy were also put forth in the manifesto. A noteworthy feature of the BJP manifesto was that it did not focus much on criticizing INC or other centrist parties. Instead it was a comprehensive document presenting a well defined strategy to combat the problems facing the nation in various fields and to bring about overall development of the country.

Assembly Elections 1993

Contemporary Issues

The November 1993 elections were crucial both for Congress and the BJP. INC had to displace the BJP in North Indian states and re-establish itself after its debacle in 1989 and 1991. For BJP, the elections were crucial because its political consolidation and existence as a political alternative to INC depended on its success in these elections. The traditional social groups which supported INC were the high castes, the SCs and the Muslims. The political development from 1989 to 1993 witnessed alienation of Muslims in North India from the Congress. This was because the Muslims felt that the various Janata Dals were better protectors of Muslims than the INC. The SC voter group which had traditionally been a very important social group supporting the INC during Nehru–Indira era, also drifted away from the INC because of the influence of Bahujan Samaj Party. Internal factionalism also posed a threat to INC. BJP had made efforts to broaden its support base from *'Brahmin–Bania* community' of towns and cities to rural areas in North India by taking up the issues of farmers. 'Temple' was the main agenda for the BJP, although it was extending its base by raising the issues which concerned the farmers.

The State Assembly elections of November 1993 were necessitated because the BJP led governments in Himachal Pradesh, Rajasthan, Madhya Pradesh and Uttar Pradesh were dismissed by the President of India in the wake of demolition of Babri Masjid on December 6, 1992; and serious communal divide generated following the demolition of the mosque by the Kar Sevaks who were led by the BJP leaders. In view of this context, the INC asked for voter's support for political stability, economic development and national unity. Its manifesto was directed against the communal, divisive and disruptive politics of the BJP in the states where BJP was the ruling party. Besides targeting the performance of BJP government in the four North Indian states, the main thrust of INC campaign was political mobilization against *Hindutva* and in favour of economic development and national building on the basis of secularism.

BJP had given the slogan of *'Onwards to Ramrajya'*. It issued a 'Statement of National Issues' and asked the voters to participate in a referendum on *Hindutva* and vote against the 'pseudo-secularists' who practised 'minoritysm'. BJP appealed to the voters to elect the BJP again for the construction of Ram Temple, the task left unaccomplished because of obstruction laid by the 'enemies of Ram Temple' especially the INC party. BJP also made an indictment of the performance of Narasimha Rao government at the Centre and also talked about *Swadeshi* economic programme. Its central theme was to promote religion based politics for building Hindu India.

The various Janata Dals merged on the eve of elections and launched its campaign on the slogan of 'Social Justice and Economic Equity'. The social constituency of Janata Dal was the intermediate peasantry and the backward castes thus Mandal and pro-peasant policies were the quintessence of Janata Dal electoral politics. Their programme focussed on caste politics, rural interests and Muslim voters.

The emotional issues such as Bofors, Mandir and Mandal were not preponderant and the mundane issues like image of the candidate, development record and above all caste considerations were dominant. Caste alignments were a determining factor in framing the electoral outcome. All parties played their cards according to the by-laws of *'sameekaran'* politics of individual constituencies.

The Jat community which traditionally voted for the Lok Dal or the Janata Dal thereafter had shifted its loyalty towards Congress. This was primarily due to the weak prospects of Janata Dal, the campaigning of Nathu Ram Mirdha in favour of Congress and the prospects of having a Jat Chief Minister in Rajasthan in the event of Congress victory.

Manifestoes of Political Parties

Indian National Congress Manifesto and Promises

In its manifesto for the Assembly elections 1993, INC asked for the voter's support for political stability, economic development and national unity. The manifesto targeted the BJP State government's non-performance while ruling over four North Indian states and also listed the achievements of the Narasimha Rao government at the Centre in 28 months of assuming office. It spelt out clearly the party's stand on various issues including Ayodhya, GATT proposals of Arthur Dunkel, welfare measures for farmers, scheduled castes, scheduled tribes and minorities, provisions of Mandal Commission, public sector, economy, prices, foreign affairs, religion and politics and panchayati raj. It pledged to protect the secular character of the country and warned that voting BJP and various versions of Janata Dal would lead to disaster. 'A vote for INC, is a vote for Development', the manifesto proclaimed.

Justifying the dismissal of BJP governments in the four states in the light of erstwhile circumstances, the party reiterated its commitment for an amicable solution to the temple – mosque issue and construction of both Temple and Mosque at Ayodhya in accordance with the directions of the Supreme Court. It altogether dismissed the possibility of any further debate on this issue as it hoped that voluntary offers in the formation of two separate trusts from purely religious persons for construction of Temple and Mosque would eventually come and issue would be resolved. INC regarded the BJP governance in Uttar Pradesh, Madhya Pradesh, Rajasthan and Himachal Pradesh as inefficient and incompetent which had put to halt the process of economic development and social welfare. Addressing the BJP government in the four states as 'anti-development, anti-women, anti-Scheduled Castes and anti-minorities', it criticized the BJP government in Rajasthan for dissolution of cooperative bodies, closure of 6,000 schools opened by INC government during 1988 and 1989 and held it responsible for the unprecedented communal riots in Jaipur. Similarly in the remaining states too, the BJP government had neither utilized the available funds for various welfare schemes and development projects nor took up any new projects.

The stand of INC on various issues was as under:

1. *Restoration of Peace:* INC counted its achievement regarding restoration of peace and holding of election as well as resumption of agricultural and industrial activities with accelerated pace in Punjab. It also emphasized the containment of the Bodo agitation by setting up of Development Council for Bodoland and settlement of the Jharkhand agitation, improvement of the law and order in Jammu and Kashmir.
2. *Economic Revival:* The manifesto provided an outline of the economic reform programme to be carried out with a view to strengthen the Indian industry, trade and business, increase in exports and ultimately increase in employment. The main features of the programme were:
    (i) *Boosting Foreign Investment:* Inviting foreign investment in vital areas of infrastructure like power, oil, telecommunications and steel so that domestic resources could be utilized for investing in education, health, agriculture and anti poverty programmes.
    (ii) *New Economic Policy:* New economic policy focussed on agricultural development and prosperity, providing equal status to industry and agriculture without taxes imposed on the latter. The achievements in the economic field till date were also emphasized which were mainly as under:
    - Rejuvenation of the economy, inflation checked and prices controlled.

- Ten times increase in foreign exchange reserves as compared to 1991 reserves, having reached a safe level.
- Providing a new environment to the business, trade and industry favourable for producing goods, creating wealth and generation of employment opportunities.
- Launching of Eighth Plan with focus on agriculture and rural development.
- Introduction of new Public Distribution System in 1752 most backward blocks in the country consisting of tribal, desert areas in order to ensure delivery of essential commodities to the poor and the needy.
- Resumption of development activities and projects in the four states of Uttar Pradesh, Madhya Pradesh, Himachal Pradesh and Rajasthan.
- Regarding public sector, INC expressed a need of restructuring of the public sector in view of declining efficiency and loss incurred by its enterprises while protecting the interests of the labour in the process.

(iii) *The Agricultural Sector:* For the benefit of farmers the following measures were proposed:

- Substantial increase in government allocations for agriculture in the Eighth Five Year Plan.
- Increasing support prices for paddy, wheat, oil seeds, gram and sugar cane.
- Introduction of Crop Insurance Scheme.
- Formulation of National Agricultural Policy for the first time.
- Abolition of Capital Gain Tax on all farm lands.
- Providing greater autonomy to cooperatives through new cooperative policy which was under way of being finalized.
- Facilitating unrestricted movement of agricultural product from state to state.

The manifesto provided a clear exposition on the misunderstanding prevailing regarding the Dunkel proposals, especially those relating the farmers and assured that no aspect of Dunkel text would in any case interfere with the national agricultural policies and programmes or adversely affect the interests of Indian farmers.

(iv) *Rural Development and Generation of Employment:* It further highlighted the efforts being made by the union government for rural development and generation of employment. The following commitments were made:

- Allocation of ₹ 30,000 crore for rural development in VIII five year plan.
- Increments in allocation for programmes like Jawahar Rozgar Yojana (JRY) in order to generate more employment opportunities in rural India.
- Introduction of Special Assured Employment Scheme in the poorest 1,752 blocks of the country.
- Launching of new 500 crore Rozgar Yojana for educated youth with an aim to provide 10 lakh jobs within three years.

Quick implementation of the recommendations of the Mandal Commission by way of negotiations and discussions unlike the approach adopted by NF government was also stressed. The commitment for settlement of the vexed issue of reservation of post in central government services for the members of other backward classes (OBC) as per directions of the Supreme Court was also emphasized. It also highlighted the establishment of Backward Classes Finance and Development Corporation for supporting the economy of the backward classes.

The INC also took merit in passing the Constitution Amendment Bills to strengthen Panchayats and Nagarpalikas, relating to regular elections and assured funding for local bodies as well as reservation for women, SCs and STs.

3. *Empowerment of Women and Weaker Sections:* It also listed the following schemes which had been taken up for the empowerment of women and weaker sections:
   - Passing a law to establish Statutory Commission for Safai Karamcharis which would take up the rehabilitation of the community.
   - Inclusion of weavers in rural development schemes like Integrated Rural Development Programme, Jawahar Rozgaar Yojana and Training of Rural Youth for Self Employment (TRYSEM).

- Implementation of New Textile Policy incepted by Rajiv Gandhi in 1985, relating to reserving 22 items for handloom industry.
- Mahila Samridhi Yojana for welfare of women with an aim to make rural women self-reliant and economically independent.
- Establishing National Commission on women to promote economic and social well being of women.
- Conferring powers of civil court on the National Commission on SCs and STs.

4. *Welfare of the Minorities:* INC reiterated its faith in being sensitive to the special needs and concerns for minority communities and listed the measures taken up by the union government to this end. They were:
    - Proposed formation of ₹ 500 crore National Minority Finance and Development Corporation to support projects and schemes that were meant to improve the economic well being of minorities.
    - Statutory status to Minorities Commission.
    - Amendment of Waqf Act to make it more effective.
    - Introduction of special schemes for improving educational status of minorities.
    - Enactment of 'Protection of Places of Worship Act'.
    - Constitution of 'Rapid Action Police Force' to quell communal riots quickly and effectively.
5. *Foreign Affairs:* The manifesto also mentioned the various successes of the Narasimha Rao government in the field of foreign affairs resulting in improved relation with China and Iran and its constructive role in resolving problems in South Africa and West Asia. It also underlined INC's foreign policy aimed at maintaining peaceful and amicable relations with all neighbours by way of constructive diplomacy and discussions.
6. *Law and Order:* It also expressed its resolution to foil the terrorist activities in Jammu & Kashmir and Punjab and to defend the internal unity and territorial integrity of the nation.

Promises of INC

The INC outlined the following tasks which were to be taken up on priority basis in the four states if elected to power.

1. Development
   - To restart all important schemes relating to agriculture, irrigation, building of roads and bridges, etc.
   - Energization of tube wells and clearing all pending applications in this regard within three months.
   - Linking all villages through *pucca* road within two to three years.
   - Opening new schools, colleges, polytechnics and universities.
   - Special employment plans for each state within six months. Generation of employment in rural areas through *Jawahar Rozgar Yojana* and launching special employment programmes for educated in urban areas.
2. Social Welfare
   - Social security schemes for workers in unorganized sector like weavers, *khet mazdoors, beedi* workers, rickshaw pullers and artisans.
   - Restarting and expanding schemes like *Indira Avaas Yojana*, the *Kutir Jyoti* scheme and *Jal Dhara* scheme for weaker sections.
   - Effective and speedy implementation of schemes like Special Deposit Scheme for women.
   - Involving ex-servicemen in development programmes like afforestation.
3. Agriculture and Farmers
   - Making necessary changes in the lending norms and requirements of financing agencies like NABARD to enable farmers to borrow more and more early from banks.
   - Increasing agro processing and food processing activities in rural areas to increase the income of farmers, augment employment opportunities and set up industries.
   - Launching *'Banjar Bhoomi Pariyojna'* to improve productivity of land holdings of small and marginal farmers.
4. Decentralization of Power
   - Elections to all local bodies in rural and urban areas within one year and transferring financial and administrative power to Zila Parishads and Nagar Palikas.
   - Elections to all cooperative societies and ensuring efficient and viable functioning of cooperative.

- Imparting greater autonomy to sub-regions within a state by way of creation of Jharkhand council, like the Gorkhaland Council and Bodo Council.

Along with the above, INC promised to establish fair price shops covering every village within three years, ensure speedy and inexpensive justice through expansion of free legal aid centre network in the four states, finding an expedient solution to the sales tax issue and setting up commissions for STs and STs at the state level too.

BJP Manifesto and Promises

The BJP manifesto primarily focussed on the 'non-performance' of the Narasimha Rao government. It also highlighted the party's stand on various issues and the achievements of its governments in the four States. Criticizing the Narasimha Rao government for its failure to provide political stability to the country and controlling prices and unemployment, it accused the government of being directionless and unconcerned towards national priorities. It asserted that the prices and unemployment had in fact increased after the INC government resumed power therefore the government was guilty of belieing its poll promises. The INC government was also attacked for patronizing Bofors conspirators and the people involved in securities scam. It held the government responsible for all percolating 'suitcase culture' of loot, bribery and corruption in public life. It expressed grave concern over the recent terrorist activities in Mumbai, Kolkata, Chennai and New Delhi and pointed towards the role of Pakistan behind them. In the wake of expanding terrorist network in the country and its political linkages, BJP stressed on an urgent need for taking up stringent measures to counter terrorism and exposing Pakistan and other Islamic bodies responsible for it. But it alleged that the INC government was shying away from evolving any effective anti-terrorist strategy for reasons grounded in its 'secular' face, thus jeopardiizng the security of the people.

BJP held the INC and Janata Dal governments responsible for the explosive state of affairs in Jammu and Kashmir and for not advocating the Kashmir problem adequately in international bodies. It also targeted the government for its insensitivity and indifference towards Kashmiri migrants, resignation of G.C. Saxena as a Governor and increasing interference of outside forces like Organisation of Islamic Conference and US in the issue. It emphasized on the need for abrogation of Article 370. The party also drew attention to the threat imposed by increasing number of Bangladeshi infiltrators and resolved to remove their names from the electoral rolls and ensure their expulsion. Criticizing the economic policies of Narasimha Rao government which as alleged had resulted into rising foreign debt and invasion of multinationals in undesired sectors, it branded INC as anti-farmer for accepting the Dunkel proposal and scrapping subsidies on fertilizers. It stressed on the need for a '*Swadeshi*' approach to liberalization and globalization thereby assisting Indian companies to establish abroad and harnessing ingenious talent of farmers, engineers and entrepreneurs instead of borrowing to meet the money constraints.

Regarding reservations, the party advocated reservations to the poor of all castes, 27 per cent reservations to Backward Classes while incorporating the creamy layer concept and 30 per cent reservation for women in Panchayats and other local bodies. To extend social justice it promised intensification of awareness campaigns against crime against women, dowry, female infanticide and gender based discrimination, Antyodaya and special privileges for SCs and STs.

BJP categorically repeated its commitment for construction of the Rama temple at Ayodhya and labelled the 'secularism' of INC, Janata Dal, Samajwadi Party and Communist Party as 'pseudo-secularism' which reflected repugnance for Hindus. It claimed that its performance in the four states had been commendable and the BJP governance had established a culture of 'administrative commitment, integrity and rectitude' in the states. The dismissal of BJP led governments in Himachal Pradesh, Madhya Pradesh, Rajasthan was unconstitutional, undemocratic and illegal. It defined its objective as *'Ram Rajya'* which epitomised a quest for happiness and glory of Indian people.

Lok Sabha Elections 1998

Contemporary Issues

Since 1989, the country had six governments with six different Prime Ministers and five of these were non-INC governments. Out of the six governments lasting eight years, five years were accounted for by an INC government. More than two years accounted for by three governments which were supported by INC from outside. Governments of V.P. Singh's for eleven months and Vajpayees' for 13 days were genuinely non-INC.

The eleventh Lok Sabha was dissolved owing to the withdrawal of support to the UF government by the INC within a period of less than two years. In it's brief tenure of 1 year 6 months and 19 days, it was headed by two Prime Ministers, H.D. Deve Gowda and I.K. Gujral. The lack of stability at the Centre had led the economy of the country lay in shambles. The country's internal integrity and international image had also suffered a setback. The twelfth Lok Sabha elections were entirely undesired and uncalled for, for the people as well as the political parties which were totally reluctant to face it. People were disappointed by the sudden dissolution of the government when they were looking forward to the passage of bills of Lokpal, Electoral Reforms, Prasar Bharti, Reservation for Women and formation of Uttarakhand, etc. These elections marked a crucial turn in the history of both the INC and the BJP. At the time of declaration of elections, the Congress party was in a mess. It did not have a strong leader and its veteran leaders were deserting the party. Subsequently, Sonia Gandhi agreed to lead the party which to some extent rejuvenated the party but the party still faced the challenge to refurbish its tarnished image of a decaying party ripped by infighting and factionalism and to restore its lost mass base. For BJP, these elections were a 'now or never battle of votes'. BJP shed its ideological rigidity and adopted a 'middle path' approach. Its sole aim was to acquire the seat of power by any means and therefore it changed its former policies and character drastically. For the first time BJP ran a personality oriented campaign projecting Atal Bihari Vajpayee as its prime ministerial candidate.

The United Front was also in a critical position. The party lacked unity of its constituent parties and consensus over crucial policies, ideology, leadership issue and seat distribution.

Stable government was the biggest issue in the Lok Sabha elections 1998. People had lost faith in the coalition experiments and wanted a stable government of one party at the Centre. The national economy was in a dismal state featured by escalating prices, rampant unemployment, low pace of development of crucial industries such as steel, cement and engineering, stagnation in agricultural production and insufficient supply of essential commodities. The Economic Reform Policy favouring disinvestment in public sector, globalization and liberalization also needed to be debated with respect to their expediency to the staggering economy of the nation.

The contest in Rajasthan was essentially between the INC and the BJP. A special feature of Rajasthan politics till date was that always no significant 'third force' had emerged in any Lok Sabha elections. The election was a referendum on the policies and programmes of the BJP government. Discontent prevailed against the government for increasing power tariff, water charges and bus fare. Employees were dissatisfied with the government for its failure to release the pay scales in time. Local issues dominated the election campaign and issue of the stability of Government did not cut much ice with the voters. These were primarily related to the all round development of the constituencies, viz. provision and expansion of basic facilities such as drinking water, electricity, health centres, schools, roads, unemployment, irrigation facilities, etc. The image of the candidate and caste equations were also important determinants of the voter behaviour.

Atal Bihari Vajpayee commanded great popu rity and wide acceptability among the voters as the prime ministerial candidate. People were sympathetic towards the way he was bereaved of the throne in 13 days in 1996. Sonia Gandhi had also cast great influence on the voters specially the women voters and had managed to generate a wave in favour of INC. The extent to which the seating members of Parliament had strived to fulfill their promises made in 1996 were also being considered by the voters. In Alwar constituency the demand for medical and engineering college in Alwar was longstanding and the seating MP Pt. Nawal Kishore Sharma (INC) had promised for the same but eventually made no sincere efforts for it. In Bharatpur and Bayana too regional development was the foremost demand of the people. The constituency faced paucity of basic amenities like roads, drinking water, schools, etc. The masses held a general view that BJP had performed relatively better in a short span of governance in the State as compared to the Congress. Although there was some discontent towards the ruling party for hike in roadways bus fare, water charges and slow pace of development of the region. In Jaipur constituency, national issues like stability, corruption, inflation and criminalization of politics were more in air in the urban parts of the constituency. Acquisition of drinking water from Bisalpur project, regularization of residential colonies located on agricultural land, upgradation of Sanganer airport to international airport and upgradation of University of Rajasthan to Central University were the prominent demands and issues in the capital region. In Jhunjhunu, the major demand of voters was generation of employment in the region through establishment of new industrial units. The constituency had witnessed substantial development during the preceding short tenure of Shish Ram Ola including some major projects like getting clearance for ₹ 2,000 crore neptha based power plant, solution to drinking water problem in Churu and Jhunjhunu districts by bringing water from the Yamuna, inclusion of Jhunjhunu district in the agricultural insurance scheme, etc. Owing to this, the voters in the area were highly satisfied with the performance of seating MP Shish Ram Ola (INC).

In Dausa the foremost demand was related to building infrastructure in the constituency to facilitate industrial development. Increasing unemployment, improper management of drinking water and development issues were also important. In Sawai Madhopur, major local issues were low level of development of Sawai Madhopur as well as Karauli district, resolution of Sawai Madhopur Cement factory problem, problems related to drinking water and electricity, rail link to Karauli, roadways depot in Sawai Madhopur, dismal state of roads, expansion of irrigation facilities and generation of employment through industrial development. But issue of stability of the union government surpassed all issues of local importance in this area.

In Sikar constituency there was widespread discontent among the farmers against the state government because of inadequate compensation received by the hail affected farmers. The demand for a broad gauge railway line in Sikar district, rural development, cheap and adequate power supply for farmers, employment to local manpower in Saledipur fertilizer factory, employment to retired soldiers and construction of an overbridge on Sikar city railway crossing were main demands in the region. The electorate held deep anguish against the seating MP Dr Hari Singh (INC) for neglecting the constituency during his tenure. In Tonk there was a strong anti-incumbency wave as there were seven MLAs of BJP in the State Assembly from the eight assembly segments of the constituency but the region had reaped no harvests from it. Regional development and rail connectivity in the district were longstanding issues in the region which were still unattended.

Manifestos of Political Parties

Indian National Congress (INC)

In Lok Sabha elections 1998 INC made the stability of the government as the bedrock of its campaign, signifying an outright rejection of coalition experiment. Stability, curbing corruption and secularism were the main election planks of the party. Other major issues were economic self-reliance and socio-economic justice. The party's main agenda was *'arthik swaraj'* and *'garibon ka raj'* (economic self-reliance and governance by the poor). The focus was on development with equity, eradication of poverty, education and healthcare for the masses. Thus the INC manifesto emphasized stability, integrity and progress. The most important feature of this was that it tendered an 'unreserved apology' for failing to prevent the Babri Masjid demolition. Besides several other promises were made in the agenda of the party:

- A quick budget with a short term blueprint and special focus on speedy employment generation. Ninth five year plan to follow with detailed action plan to boost employment. Annual job survey on job data, results to be made public .

- *'Desh ke liye ek saal'* a drive to pay jobless youth a monthly stipend in return for working in literacy programmes, family planning, social reform, afforestation, etc. Youth free to join or look for jobs on their own minus the stipend.
- Functional autonomy for CBI with its operations to be more transparent and time bound.
- All rural development funds with the Centre now around ₹ 8,000 crore, to be transferred to Zila Parishad and other local bodies.
- All Congress MPs and MLAs to declare assets on day of assuming office and quitting as well.
- Freedom of Information Act to end 'culture of secrecy' and minister's discretionary powers to be publicly scrutinized.
- Constitutional amendment to make free education up to 14 years a fundamental right.
- Privatization of insurance sector with Indian companies to hold majority equity, urban infrastructure projects to be opened for private Indian and foreign companies.
- Power distribution to be privatized, power transmission to be privatized, Power Transmission Bill to be enacted, independent tariff-fixing and regulatory bodies to be established.
- State funding of elections to be started. Election Commission to monitor funds to each party.
- Retirement age of the state government employees to be raised to 60.
- National Cadet Corps mandatory in all schools.
- New administrative reforms commission to be set up to prune union government.
- Separate National Commissions for STs and unorganized labour. Reservations to be legalized and put under Ninth Schedule of the Constitution.
- New ministry for Minorities and fresh high powered Commission to recommend measures for increasing minorities representation in the Union Public Service Commission.

Bhartiya Janata Party (BJP)

The 1998 elections were a crucial electoral battle for BJP. The party had realized that if the party could not acquire the power that time, it might never make it to the Centre. Thus BJP approached the electorate with the slogan 'give us a chance this time' in context of the United Front and INC failures in 1996–97. It was desperate to gain the seat of power by any means. For this purpose, it transformed itself dramatically. It shied away the areas of conflict that it had so strenuously developed for almost half a century. It promised not to reverse the 'economic reforms' but to provide them a 'human face'. It also shed its 'fundamentalist' character as reflected in the *Adyodhya* event and resorted to 'practical idealism'. Its image as an ideological party with a commitment to *Hindutva* was eroded. Vajpayee had made the party as a party with middle path character becoming quite pragmatic in its viewpoints. It adopted a 'purity to plurality' approach admitting anybody into its fold and aligning with whoever was willing irrespective of their background. To remove the stigma of being a *'Brahmin–Bania'* party, it made efforts to expand its base among backward castes and dalits. The effort was to project itself as a responsible, broad based and acceptable to all shades of society. Efforts were also made to negate the perception that BJP is anti-Muslim.

In Rajasthan, these elections assumed a special significance as the Vidhan Sabha elections were round the corner in December. In its campaign BJP was avoiding to raise local issues. Instead it highlighted the achievement of Bhairon Singh Shekhawat's seven years regime as a chief minister. The core content and ideological pillars of the Bhartiya Janata Party were a five fold concept of *Shuchita* (probity in public life), *Suraksha* (security), *Swadeshi* (economic nationalism), *Samajik Samrasta* (social harmony) and *Hindutva* (cultural nationalism). These principles were manifest in their commitments to national security, good governance, national unity and integration, democracy, genuine secularism, eradication of mass poverty, opportunity for economic advancement for all, social justice, gender injustice, harmonious Centre-State relations, probity in public life, revival of institutions, politics of consensus and cooperation as against confrontation and raising India's prestige, power and profile in international area. The party expressed its commitment to fulfil the unfinished agenda of *Swaraj* to *Su-raj* under the able leadership of Atal Bihari Vajpayee. Like the INC it had also pumped for the stability plank assuring the electorate of the party's commitment to 'resolve the prevailing chaos'. The party's manifesto covered a wide range of subjects from the BJP's vision to the concept of cultural nationalism. Electoral reforms were also a part of the manifesto. The manifesto presented a choice before the electorate between 'stability and another round of elections soon', between 'nationalism and foreign hand', between an 'Able Prime Minister and Prime Ministerial Pretenders'. It also focussed on future action plans and was issue specific. The party was action oriented on issues like economic policy, foreign policy and national security. The manifesto made the following promises to lead the country towards *'su-raj'*.

- Appointment of a Commission to review the Constitution of India.
- Taking necessary steps to prevent misuse of Article 356 of the Constitution.
- Abrogation of Article 370 of the Constitution.
- Introduction of a scheme of State funding of election.
- Rationalizing the number, structure, composition and role of paramilitary forces.
- Undertaking reforms in district administration and police.
- Appointment of a Lok Pal to inquire into allegations of corruption against holding public office, including the prime minister.
- Transparency in the functioning of government.
- Generation of employment.
- Promotion of non-conventional sources of energy.
- Housing, health and education for all. Provide shelter to all by the year 2010 and construct 20 lakh new houses each year and full literacy by the year 2010.
- Enforcement of land ceiling laws in all the states.
- Acceleration of total rural electrification programme.
- Give India a role and position in world affairs. Improve relations with China and Pakistan and other nations.
- A total ban on cow slaughter.
- Re-evaluation of the country's nuclear policy, development of the Agni missiles.
- Peace in Kashmir.
- High priority to North-East, to intercept illegal infiltrations.
- Welfare of SCs and STs by strengthening constitutional safeguards including reservations.
- Equal opportunity and prosperity to minorities.
- Protection of human rights of citizens.
- Protection of children's right to play, education, shelter and protection from sexual exploitation and abuse.
- Caring schemes for disabled and senior citizens.
- Introduction of a National Environmental Policy.
- Common Civil Code for women empowerment and 33 per cent reservation for women were very much on their agenda. It also

had a scheme to offer a special incentive in the form of a fixed deposit that would mature in 21 years for those couples with only a girl child or those who adopt a girl child under *'datak putri yojna'*. The party also offered free education upto 14 years.

The most striking feature of this manifesto was that the party was guided by a 10-year perspective to achieve all the aims set out in the manifesto so that India entered the 21st century with a head held high.

Assembly Elections 1998

Contemporary Issues

In Rajasthan the prestige of both the parties; the INC and the BJP was at stake during the Vidhan Sabha elections 1998. BJP was desperate to acquire power for the third time in the State. INC bereaved of power for eight years was desperate to resume the throne. Although other small parties, defectors and independents were also in the fray but main contest was between INC and BJP. The context of the elections was provided by the performance of BJP government at the centre which had been formed six months ago and eight years of BJP governance in the State since 1990. The party boasted of affecting a lot of development in the State which had been far greater than the development which INC had done in its 40 years of governance. Some main achievements enumerated by the party were:

- Reducing the percentage of poor from 38 to 26.
- Commendable progress in development activities in the field of poverty alleviation, agriculture and agro-production, watershed development, etc.
- Position of Rajasthan among top five states of the country ranked on the basis of development.
- Waiving off farmers' loans, providing subsidies.
- Distribution of 2.57 lakh electricity connections.
- Subsidies worth ₹ 8,000 crore in eight years.
- Multifold increase in plan expenditure.
- Construction of schools, hospitals, roads, etc.

Thus the main election plank of the BJP was the performance of the central government and development in eight years of BJP rule in the State. In the short term of six months there had been some sincere accomplishments to the credit of the central government like the nuclear test in Pokharan, solution of longstanding Kaveri water dispute and inclusion of prime minister in Lokpal legislation. But the government could not demonstrate similar efficiency in tackling the international reactions and consequences of the Pokharan test in the form of diplomatic and economic restrictions imposed on the country.

The context of Vidhan Sabha elections 1998 in the State was provided by two major burning issues, corruption and unprecedented hike in prices of basic food items such as onion, potatoes, edible oils and pulses. Due to non-seasonal rainfall, the crop of onion and potatoes had been spoiled and owing to lack of timely corrective measures from the government their prices had sky rocketed. The law and order situation in the State was also quite dismal, with increasing incidents of crime against women. The Shivani Jadeja case in Jaipur City and the J.C. Bose Hostel gang rape case in the University of Rajasthan had created a sharp wrath among the masses regarding the deteriorating law and order situation. The government had failed to provide adequate, timely and expeditious relief to draught stricken farmers. Farmers were facing a tough time because of drought, manifold increase in the prices of seeds and untimely rains which ruined the crops. This had generated a sharp rage among the farmers who accused the government of being insensitive and indifferent towards the problems faced by the farmers. Discontent also prevailed against the BJP government due to failure of government to generate employment for ever increasing unemployed youth force, all pervading corruption in the public system and excessively strong bureaucracy in governance. The people had huge expectations of 'good governance' from the BJP government which had not been met with. BJP had also failed to fulfil its promises regarding abolition of '*Chungi*' (toll), regularization of residential and *Kucchi* colonies and curbing corruption in public life. The government employees also held several grievances against the government. All the above factors accounted for an 'anti-incumbency' factor in the State against the party. In addition to this, 'development', i.e. demand for roads, schools, health centres, electricity, drinking water, irrigation facilities, etc. was the main issue in all the constituencies of the study area.

Manifestoes of Political Parties

Indian National Congress

Indian National Congress had a separate manifesto for Rajasthan. Besides the prominent national issues, the manifesto highlighted the failures of BJP government at the centre and also enlisted its promises and goals with respect to Rajasthan. In its manifesto Congress alleged that the misgovernance of the Vajpayee government had resulted in internal conflicts in the country, the inflation had doubled and the prices of all essential commodities including onion, pulses and potatoes had registered an unprecedented rise. The economy had stagnated. It also attacked the government's foreign policy that the central government had proved unable to tackle the political, economic and international consequences of nuclear test, the relations with China were strained, the Kashmir issue was internationalized. The development had also suffered a setback and the projects relating to basic infrastructure such as electricity, roads, highways and communication had been impeded. The party promised a *'samvedansheel, pardarshi aur jawabdeh shasan'* (sensitive, transparent and accountable governance) in the State and made the following commitments:

- Highest priority to agriculture, 65 per cent of budget expenditure to be incurred on rural development. Agriculture to be given a status of an industry and establishment of fodder banks for cattle.
- To encourage investment in order to strengthen basic infrastructure for industrial development.
- To achieve the target production of 5,000 megawatt of electricity in Ninth Plan period. Establishment of Nuclear Power plant, to abandon the Nursery Plan.
- All applications for electricity connections for agricultural activities received till 1998 were to be worked upon and connections be given within five years.
- Regularization of all urban slums which came into being till 15 August 1998.
- Reduction of retirement age of government employees to 58 years so as to generate employment opportunities for the unemployed youth.
- Establishment of Youth Board State Human Rights Commission.
- Minimum wages to be raised to ₹ 60.
- Right of information to the masses.
- Linking of all villages with population more than 1,000 with roads.
- Consideration of feasibility of formation of new districts.
- Commission to ensure transparency in public system and to check corruption and criminalization.
- Empowering Panchayati Raj institutions, administrative control of District Rural Development Authority by Zila Parishads.
- Formation of Minorities Commission, reviewal of all matters related to TADA, new Waqf Board, implementation of all investigation reports pertaining to communal riots and foging, legal

action against people responsible for communal riots, establishment of Minority Cells in Department of Home and Finance.

- Direct recruitments on vacant posts reserved for OBC. Inclusion of several castes like Jats, Vishnois, Sindhis, Kayamkhanis, Mevs, Bhomians, etc. in OBCs.

INC also held the State BJP government responsible for the all pervading corruption in public life. It criticized the eight years of BJP governance on the following grounds:

- Dismal state of law and order situation
- Increasing incidents of crime and violence against women
- Widespread Corruption
- Paucity of drinking water
- Anti-farmer policies
- Ineffective industrial policy
- Poor state of the economy
- No perceptible development in spite of ₹ 12,500 crore expenditure in Ninth Five Year Plan

BJP Manifesto

The Bhartiya Janata Party made 21 promises for the State as well as enumerated the achievements of eight years of its governance. It asserted that the development which had taken place in eight years of BJP governance was far greater than 40 years of Congress governance. It pledged to provide a committed *'swatchh, pardarshi* and *samvedansheel'* governance. There was no mention of the burning issues of corruption and prices. The promises made by the party were:

- Provision of grains to the BPL masses at ₹ 4 per kg.
- Keeping with the current reservation policy, reservations to the economically and socially backward classes on purely economic basis.
- Road links to all villages having a population of 500.
- Fifty per cent reservations in government recruitments to local tribal population in tribal regions.
- Special Desert Region status to Marwar region. Institution of Development Council.
- Additional provision of 5,000 megawatt power.
- Linking minimum wages with prices.
- Establishment of a women police station in every tehsil.
- Compulsory and free primary education to all.

- Farmers' Welfare Fund worth ₹ 500 crore. Kisan Jeevan Kalyan Yojna for serious ailments, Kisan Credit Card Yojna, etc.
- Abolition of taxes on land and buildings and repeal of Urban Land Ceiling Act.
- Employment to 1,00,000 unemployed youths under various schemes worth ₹ 100 crore including Khadi Board and Prime Minister Employment Scheme.
- Constitution of a commission for formation of new tehsils and districts.
- To provide 50,000 houses at cheap rates every year in rural and urban areas both.
- Residential schools and sports grounds in SCs and STs. Aids to minority schools as per rules.
- Schools in all villages with a population of less than 250.
- Right to information to all citizen.
- Women banks in every district, constitution of Women Rights Commission.
- Constitution of Youth Board.
- Status of international airport to Jaipur (Sanganer) Airport and airport facility at Ajmer.
- Drinking water supply to Jaipur from Bisalpur project.

BJP claimed that Rajasthan had witnessed a lot of development during its short tenure of eight years and had several achievements to its credit. Per capita investment which was ₹ 217 during Congress rule had increased five fold to ₹ 968 during BJP rule. There had been a four fold rise in food grain production. It waived off the rent on *barani bhoomi*, opened up 80 colleges, linked all Panchayat headquarters by roads, conducted elections in the cooperative and self governing bodies which hadn't taken place for last two decades, extended reservation benefits to the minorities and women and right of information to the masses. Thus BJP made its achievements and development the bedrock of its campaign.

6 Spatial Patterns of Party Performance

Politically Rajasthan has remained by and large, a relatively peaceful State since independence. Prior to independence Rajasthan was composed of several princely states and jagirs. After 1947, the process of uniting scattered states commenced from 1948 to 1956 when the States Reorganisation Act was promulgated. First came Matsya Union (1948) consisting of a fraction of princely states. Slowly and gradually other states merged with this Union. By 1949, major states like Bikaner, Jaipur, Jodhpur and Jaisalmer joined this Union making it United States of Greater Rajasthan. Ultimately by 1956 the present State of Rajasthan formally came into being with the merger of Ajmer State, Abu Road Taluka and Sunel Tappa in United States of Greater Rajasthan.

Composed of 21 former princely states, Rajasthan's history has been characterized more by competition and conflict than by cooperation. The feudal nature of the State created regional imbalances in its socio-economic development. After independence these imbalances and their feudal geneses have also influenced the choice of the electorate. Since it is not possible that all imbalances be redressed by a single political party, several parties have shot to prominence in a particular region. There are several areas where electoral behaviour displays great temporal variations. These volatile areas (floating vote regions) turnout to be crucial in deciding the ultimate winner of the election.

Caste tends to be of great significance and caste structure is exploited by political leaders in different elections. The Jats along with the Muslims, the Scheduled Castes (SCs), the Scheduled Tribes (STs) and Gujars had been a major electoral base for Congress. Bhartiya Janata Party (BJP) had commanded a base mostly in the urbanized areas and the upper castes.

Indian National Congress (INC) is the oldest political party not only in India but also in Asia. Being the party of the struggle for National freedom, the Congress party in India has remained part of the common man's political conscience for a long period. This historical legacy has made the Congress party a mass based aggregative party which draws electoral support from every caste, community and linguistic religious group – albeit in varying degrees at different places and times. Rajasthan is considered to have been one of the strongholds of the Congress.

Between the years 1952 and 1977 the INC could always secure or manage a majority to form the government. The post-Emergency Janata Party wave took the toll of the fortunes of INC in Rajasthan too as in other parts of northern India. The Janata Party secured 151 seats in the Assembly while Congress was reduced to only 41 seats. The Congress party recovered the lost ground in 1980 and retained the lead in 1985 elections also. But 1990 elections again displaced the Congress out of power. The BJP secured 85 seats and with the help of Janata Dal which had strength of 54 members, it could form a government that was eventually dismissed by the Centre on 15 December 1992 in the wake of Babri Masjid demolition issue.

In the Lok Sabha elections too except 1977 and 1989 INC had always fared well in Rajasthan. In 1977 Nathu Ram Mirdha was the only INC candidate who could secure a seat in the Parliament from the State. In 1989, INC faced a BJP–JD combined in all the 25 constituencies and it was a complete rout for INC. Despite having obtained 36.96 per cent of the polled votes it lost all the 25 seats.

Out of the nine Lok Sabha elections held till 1989, INC had won six times in Alwar, five times in Jhunjhunu, Bharatpur, Dausa and Sawai Madhopur and four times in Sikar and Tonk. In Bayana constituency which was formed in 1962 INC candidates were returned five times out of the seven elections.

BJP had never been a force to reckon with till 1985. In Rajasthan it was founded in 1980 Assembly elections. It was polled 6.35 per cent votes and gradually improved its tally to 25 per cent in 1990 when it won 85 seats, mainly because of an accord with the Janata Dal. In the political history of Lok Sabha constituencies BJP had registered only token presence when its candidates had returned from Jaipur, Sawai Madhopur and Dausa in 1989. BJP gained strength in Rajasthan in the wake of Ram Janmabhoomi movement in which a large number of Kar Sevaks had participated in the Ayodhya march and many of them became casualties. In fact the movement was mishandled by Mulayam Singh Government leading to political fallouts. In 1991, BJP had contested all 25 Lok Sabha seats for the first time.

Janata Party was founded in 1977 election by five non-Congress opposition parties as a result of constitutional emergency imposed by ruling INC party. The Anti-Congress wave rewarded 150 Assembly seats and 24 Lok Sabha seats to Janata Party. But in consecutive elections this performance sharply declined because of the division of the party into various splinter groups.

In 1991, the contest was four cornered in almost all the Lok Sabha constituencies. The main four parties in the fray were the INC, BJP, JD and SJP. The Samajwadi Janata Party (SJP) and JD had quite feeble presence in the election scene. SJP was a weak party without any grassroot organization. JD also faced a dilemma in the State as most of its 12 members in the dissolved Lok Sabha had deserted the party and joined the JD (Digvijay) group or INC. Thus the contest was mainly between INC and BJP.

Since INC and BJP were the only dominant parties with a State wide base and appeals in the election scenario in the State, the analysis in this chapter has been confined to the electoral performance of these two parties only.

Methodological Framework

This chapter attempts an ecological analysis of the areal patterns of political party support with respect to INC and BJP. The primary objective of this chapter is primarily to present a comparative analysis of differential electoral behaviour in the Assembly elections vis-à-vis the Lok Sabha elections. To achieve this objective the electoral performance of the two parties has been analysed by grouping the election into two pairs as under:

1. Lok Sabha 1991 and Assembly Elections 1993
2. Lok Sabha 1998 and Assembly Elections 1998

Electoral performance of each party for each of the two sets of electoral contests has been analysed with a view

- to identify main areas of party's electoral support;
- to assess to what extent the party's electoral support is regionally concentrated or uniformly spread;
- to determine temporal consistency or vote trends of spatial distribution of party support;
- to quantify the degree to which the selected socio-economic contexts explain the vote variance of each party.

The electoral support (or party performance) for each party is measured in terms of percentage of votes polled in favour of each party in relation to the total valid votes in each Assembly unit. The intensity of support for a party and uniformity of spatial distribution has been defined in terms of average, coefficient of variation of party support and Assembly unit wise percentage vote share. The pattern of spatial variation in intensity of electoral support for each party has been identified by using Z-score values of per cent votes polled by the party. The Z-score values have been interpreted as per following scheme:

Z-score Values	*Intensity of Party Support*	*Z-score Values*	*Intensity of Party Support*
Positive		**Negative**	
Above 2	Extremely high	0 to –1	Low
1 to 2	Very high	–1 to –2	Very low
0 to 1	High	Below –2	Extremely low

Vote trends refer to the ways in which the party votes have changed in the same Assembly units in each pair of elections. For this purpose, we have established three categories reflecting the general trends in party support that might conceivably occur. These categories are constancy, growth and decline. Constancy of performance is defined as variation of less than 5 per cent from the share of the vote received by the party as compared to the former of the elections in the pair. The basic idea of constancy is that the party has obtained the same general magnitude of support in a particular Assembly unit both the times. A party's vote trend in a given Assembly unit has been termed as 'growth' in support when there has been an increase of more than 5 per cent in the vote received by the party from the base election to the next one contested. The term 'decline' indicates a drop of more than 5 per cent from the first election to the next.

The 'strong' and 'weak' support areas for each party have also been delineated. For this purpose, Assembly units have been classified on the basis of level of 'floor support'. Floor support is defined as the lowest support a party has received in both the elections under study. By combining the Assembly unitwise vote trends for a party with the levels of floor support, 'support surfaces' for each party in the two sets of elections have been delineated. The support surfaces reflect a composite picture of intensity and continuity of support in favour of a party in an area.

North east Rajasthan represents a case of biparty region where INC and BJP are the only two dominating parties in the elections. Other parties do not possess a widespread voter base and are influential sporadically in only few and scattered pockets. In this biparty scenario and on the basis of empirical evidences, the lower and upper limits of categories of floor support have been determined as under:

Below 20 per cent of votes polled – Low floor support
20 to 40 per cent of votes polled – Medium floor support
Above 40 per cent of votes polled – High floor support

By combining these floor support categories with the categories of vote trends two broad types and three sub-types of support surfaces have been identified. The two major types of support surfaces are 'stable' and 'unstable' support surfaces. Stable support surfaces include those areas where the nature of support for the party in terms of magnitude and continuity (constancy, growth or decline) has not exhibited drastic changes during two successive elections.

The stable support surface have been further classified into three sub-types:

1. *Strong areas:* These include those Assembly units where the party has received substantial proportion of the total votes polled in each election irrespective of the 'waves' in favour of or against it. These areas form dependable support bases for the party where the prospects of the party's victory in each election are high. Three types of Assembly units have been included in this category:
   (i) Assembly units having constant support at high floor support level.
   (ii) Assembly units having declining support at high floor support level.
   (iii) Assembly units having growing support at high floor support level.
2. *Weak areas:* This category includes those Assembly units where the party's support level has been far below what is required to either earn it a victory or to even set forth substantial competition for the other parties in the fray. Three types of Assembly units have been included in this category:
   (i) Assembly units having constant support at low floor support (Below 20%).
   (ii) Assembly units having declining support but the party's vote share below 30 per cent in both elections.
   (iii) Assembly units having growing support but the party's vote share below 30 per cent in both elections.

3. *Marginal areas:* This category includes those Assembly units where the party has garnered a sizeable vote share in both the elections, large enough to be in tough competition with other contenders. But the level of support is on the margin of majority which may or may not translate into a seat or victory. Two types of Assembly units have been included in this category:
   (i) Assembly units having constant support at medium floor support level.
   (ii) Assembly units of growing or declining support at medium floor support level, with variation less than 10 per cent in vote share of the party between successive elections.

The Unstable Support Surface comprises of areas where the party support has witnessed drastic changes during successive elections. These areas are vulnerable to waves in favour of or against a particular party consequent upon current issues and political equations, hence also termed as 'Vulnerable or Fluctuating areas'. The Assembly units at all floor levels in which the vote share of a party has fluctuated by more than 10 per cent, be it growth or decline between two successive elections have been included in this category.

The distribution of Assembly units among the various categories of vote trends and stability of support outlined above also clearly highlight the areas which exhibit differential electoral behaviour in the two levels of electoral contest. The Assembly units ranking in growth, decline and the unstable support surfaces are the areas where the voter preferences exhibit marked shift in Assembly vis-à-vis Lok Sabha elections.

Lastly an attempt has been made to determine the extent to which the selected socio-economic characteristics of the region account for the distribution of each party's electoral support. The spatial patterns of support for each party have been analysed and explained in relation to 14 socio-economic variables (Table 6.1). These 14 variables were compressed into fewer and more manageable contextual dimensions of significantly interrelated variables by using the Principal Component method of factor analysis. Factors with eigen values higher than one were rotated to normal varimax position. This provided a set of three factors which explained 73.91 per cent of the variance in the data set. Factor scores for each of the three contexts were computed for all the 72 Assembly units separately.

Each of the variables has a loading on each of the factors. The loading is in the form of correlation coefficient which indicates the degree of association between the given variable and the relevant factor. Higher the loading, higher is the degree of association between the two. A negative loading, on the other hand, indicates inverse relationship between the variable and the relevant factor.

Table 6.1 *List of Socio-Economic Variables*

Variables	*Abbreviation*
Density of Population (per square km)	D_P
Urban Population (per cent of total population)	U_P
Literacy Rate (literate population as % of total population)	L_R
Working Population (% of total population)	W_P
Agricultural Labourers (% of W_P)	AG_L
Agricultural Workers (% of W_P)	AG_W
Workers Engaged in Trade and Commerce (% of W_P)	W _TR
Workers Engaged in Manufacturing – Household (% of W_P)	W_M(H)
Workers Engaged in Manufacturing – Other than household industry (% of W_P)	W_M(OH)
Workers engaged in transport and communication (% of W_P)	W_T_C
Workers engaged in other services (% of W_P)	W_OS
SC Population (% of total population)	SC_P
ST Population (% of total population)	ST_P
Sex-Ratio (females per 1000 males)	S_R

Factorial Ecology

The principal axes factor analysis yielded three rotated factors which together explained 73.91 per cent variation in the data set. Table 6.2 shows the rotated factor matrix for each of the 14 variables. The first factor has been named 'Urban Developmental Context'. It alone explains nearly half, i.e. 49.26 per cent variation in the data set. Urban population, literacy rate, workers engaged in trade and commerce, workers engaged in transport and communication, workers in other services and workers engaged in manufacturing (other than household industry) loaded very high (above +0.8) on this factor. Density of population also recorded considerably high loading of +0.77 on this factor. All these variables are indicators of socio-economic development and urbanization.

As contrasted to the above, the agricultural labourers and agricultural workers variables have recorded high negative values of –0.70 and –0.91 respectively. These variables are indicators of rurality.

Table 6.2 *Rotated Factor Matrix for the Selected Socio-Economic Variables*

Variable	*Factors*		
	I	*II*	*III*
D_P	0.77	0.01	–0.09
S_R	–0.12	–0.12	0.83
U_P	0.91	–0.15	–0.04
L_R	0.83	–0.26	–0.13
SC_P	–0.46	0.51	–0.32
ST_P	–0.03	0.81	–0.02
W_P	–0.07	0.83	–0.06
AG_L	–0.70	–0.04	–0.09
AG_W	–0.91	0.01	–0.16
W_TR	0.97	–0.09	0.03
W_T_C	0.81	–0.18	0.10
W_OS	0.92	–0.24	–0.02
W_M(H)	0.17	–0.02	0.87
W_M(OH)	0.87	0.02	0.18
Eigen Value	6.897	1.804	1.647
% variance explained	49.26	12.89	11.76
Cumulative %	49.26	62.15	73.91

Note: Extraction Method: Principal Component Analysis. Rotation Method: Varimax with Kaiser Normalization. Rotation converged in five iterations
Factor I: Urban Developmental Context
Factor II: Social Backwardness Context
Factor III: Gender Context

Figure 6.1A portrays the standardized (Z-score) values of the factor scores for this context. In this analysis the Z-score values have been interpreted as per scheme given as under:

Z-score Value of Factor Scores	*Intensity*
More than 0.75	Very high
0.00 to 0.75	High
0.00 to –0.75	Low
Less than –0.75	Very low

Figure 6.1

Factoral Ecology of Assembly Units of North East Rajasthan

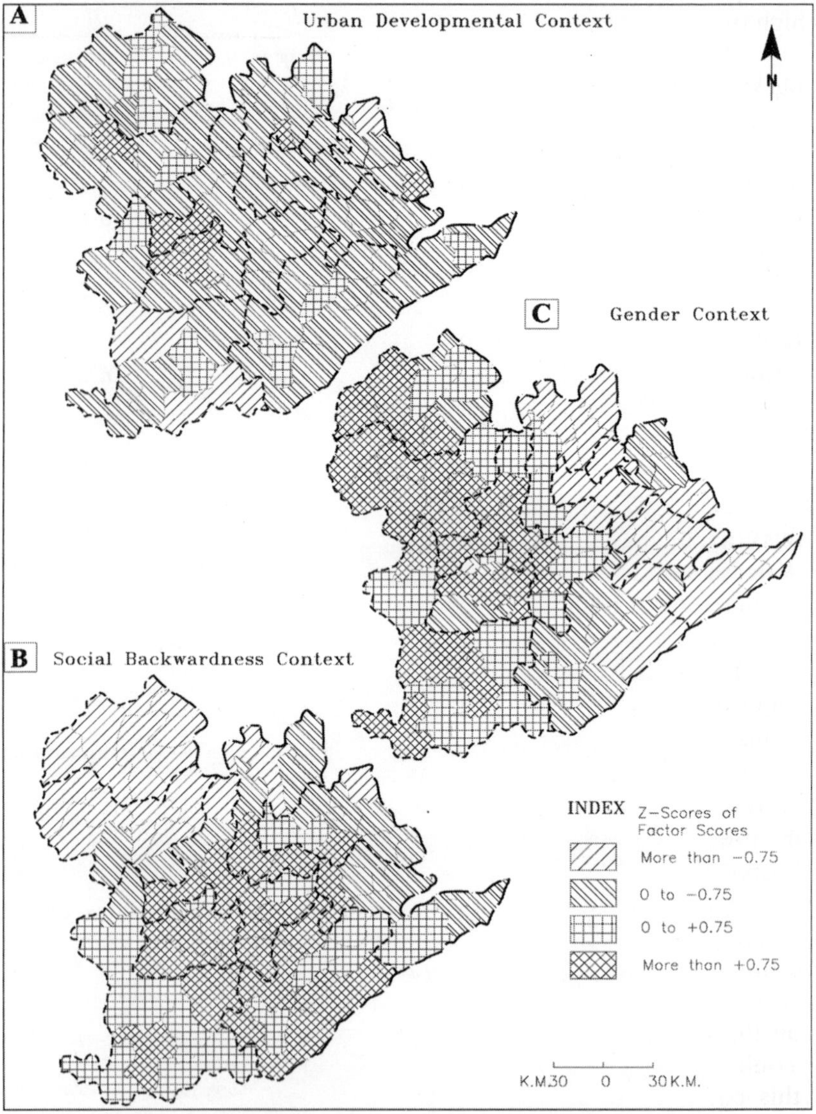

The urban and semi urban Assembly units record positive scores on this context whereas rural Assembly units generally record scores on the negative side. The map reveals that majority of the Assembly units in the study area are rural in nature whereas urban areas are very few and scattered. Assembly units comprising of district headquarters and region surrounding the capital city of Jaipur score high on this factor in general.

The second factor in Table 6.2 has been termed as 'Social Backwardness' context. This factor explains 12.89 per cent variation in our dataset. Percentage of working population and proportion of Scheduled Tribe (ST) population show very high positive loadings on this factor (above 0.8 in each case), while proportion of Scheduled Caste (SC) population also loaded fairly high (above 0.5) on this context. The positive scores of this context indicate substantial concentration of SCs and STs population and labour class of workers.

The Assembly unitwise Z-score values of factor scores for Social Backwardness context have been mapped in Figure 6.1B. It is interesting to note that there is clear two fold division of the study area into areas scoring positively and negatively on this context.

As expected all Assembly units reserved for ST and majority of those reserved for SCs during Assembly elections predominantly located in southern part of the study area, scored high to very high on this context. Lachhmangarh (Sikar), Suratgarh, Khairthal, Rupbas and Weir scored negatively despite having substantial strength of SC population. This may be attributed to the extremely small proportion of ST population in these areas.

The third factor termed as 'Gender Context' explained 11.76 per cent variance in the data. Two variables sex-ratio and workers engaged in manufacturing in household industry loaded significantly high on this context (above 0.8). It is noteworthy that both the variables have a fairly strong positive correlation of 0.5 with each other. This indicates the predominance of female workforce in household industrial sector. Proportion of SC population has a weak negative loading of –0.32 on this context.

Figure 6.1C shows the factor scores of this context. An interesting feature of the spatial distribution of this context is the marked east – west division of the study area into areas scoring high and low on this context. The western part spreading over Jhunjhunu, Sikar, Tonk and Dausa districts predominantly scored high to very high on this context which indicates relatively larger proportion of female population in the total population of these Assembly units. The eastern part of the study region comprising of major part of Alwar, Bharatpur, Dholpur, Karauli and Sawai Madhopur invariably recorded low to very low scores on this context.

Spatial Distribution of Congress and BJP Votes in Lok Sabha vis-à-vis Assembly Elections

This section examines the areal pattern of electoral support and degree of uniformity in spatial distribution of support for INC and BJP in the two pairs of elections. The section also highlights the differences in the spatial patterns of support at the two levels of electoral contests.

Lok Sabha 1991 vis-à-vis Assembly Elections 1993

In Lok Sabha elections of 1991 the main parties in the fray were INC, BJP, JD and JP. INC, BJP and JD contested all the seats of the study area. JP did not contest in Sikar. INC and BJP together secured more than 70 per cent of the total votes polled in each of the constituencies, securing the first two positions in terms of vote share. Bharatpur was an exception, where the contest was triangular and JP stood as the runner up party with 22.13 per cent of the total votes polled. In Bharatpur INC and BJP together polled 63.30 per cent of total votes.

Out of the nine Lok Sabha constituencies of the study area, BJP won in Alwar, Bayana, Bharatpur, Jaipur, Sawai Madhopur and Tonk. It polled 43.14 per cent of the total votes polled. The constituencywise results have been summarized in Table 6.3.

Table 6.3 *Lok Sabha Constituencywise Winning Party, Nearest Rival Party and Margin of Victory (Lok Sabha Elections 1991)*

Lok Sabha Constituency	*WP*	*Vote share*	*NRP*	*Vote share*	*Margin of Victory*
Jhunjhunu	INC	40.49%	BJP	36.66%	3.83%
Sikar	INC	52.30%	BJP	34.39%	17.91%
Jaipur	BJP	59.03%	INC	36.21%	22.83%
Dausa	INC	50.63%	BJP	37.42%	13.21%
Alwar	BJP	48.30%	INC	23.50%	24.79%
Bharatpur	BJP	42.15%	JP	22.13%	20.02%
Bayana(sc)	BJP	42.74%	INC	33.10%	9.64%
Sawai Madhopur(ST)	BJP	43.70%	INC	39.64%	4.06%
Tonk(SC)	BJP	45.94%	INC	42.55%	3.39%

WP – Winning Party, NRP – Nearest Rival Party

As evident from Table 6.3 in individual constituencies the vote share of BJP ranged from 34.39 per cent in Sikar to 59.03 per cent in Jaipur. It faced a tough contest in Tonk by INC and won the seat by a bare margin of 3.39 per cent of valid votes. The road to success was a quite smooth in Alwar and Bharatpur where BJP won with wide margins of more than 20 per cent. The margin of victory was maximum in Alwar in favour of BJP.

INC could secure a majority in only three constituencies, i.e. Dausa, Jhunjhunu and Sikar. It secured 38.43 per cent of the total votes, with a maximum of 52.30 per cent in Sikar and minimum of 21.14 per cent in Bharatpur. The margin of victory in favour of INC was the lowest (3.83%) in Jhunjhunu and the highest (17.91%) in Sikar.

JD and JP secured 10.87 per cent and 4.54 per cent vote share respectively. None of the two parties could secure any seat in the study region.

In Assembly election 1993, INC contested all the seats and won 30 of them securing 36.63 per cent of the total votes. BJP contested 71 seats, all except Deeg and registered a victory in 29 constituencies, receiving 34.40 per cent of the total votes. Two seats were bagged by JD and one, i.e. Dhod by CPI(M).

Assembly Unitwise Presence and Performance of INC Lok Sabha Elections 1991

In 1991 the average vote share of INC per segment was 37.58 per cent. In individual segments the vote share ranged between 7.75 per cent in Kaman and 65.39 per cent in Khandela. The standard deviation of party votes was 12.29 and coefficient of variation was 32.7 per cent which indicates considerable disparity in areal distribution of electoral support for INC. In 38 (52.77%) Assembly segments it polled more than its average vote share per seat. Table 6.4 displays the level of success and parameters of distribution of Congress votes in all the four elections under consideration.

Table 6.4 *Performance of the Congress in North East Rajasthan (1991, 1993, 1998)*

Election	*Seats Contested*		*Seats Won*		*% Votes*	*Average Votes (%) per Assembly Seat*	*SD*	*CV (%)*	*Min.*	*Max.*
	A	*B*	*A*	*B*						
Lok Sabha 1991	9	72	3	24	38.43	37.58	12.29	32.7	7.75 (Kaman)	65.39 (Khandela)
Assembly 1993	72	—	30	—	36.63	36.64	10.71	29.23	5.81 (Nagar)	65.88 (Nadbai)
Lok Sabha 1998	9	72	5	37	37.81	38.38	13.06	34.03	7.41 (Surajgarh)	58.52 (Niwai)
Assembly 1998	72	—	54	—	41.70	41.54	13.25	31.90	13.37 (Malpura)	66.52 (Chomu)

Note: A = number of constituencies, B = number of Assembly segments

Of the 72 Assembly segments comprising the nine Lok Sabha constituencies in the study region, INC registered a victory in 24 Assembly segments. These segments mainly belonged to western Jhunjhunu, Sikar and Dausa constituencies. A few segments of Sawai Madhopur and Tonk constituencies and Mahuwa were also won by INC but the overall result in these constituencies was in favour of BJP. The Assembly segmentwise winning party has been depicted in Figure 6.2A.

Table 6.5 and Figure 6.3 display the frequency distribution of Assembly segments on the basis of votes polled to INC. In 1991, the party polled less than 30 per cent votes in 20 Assembly segments. In only 11 Assembly segments it received a thumping majority with more than 50 per cent votes. The performance of the party was poorest in Kaman where its vote share could not touch the mark of even 10 per cent. In four Assembly segments its vote share was 10 to 20 per cent; in 15 Assembly segments it ranged between 20 to 30 per cent; in 20 Assembly segments it was between 30 to 40 per cent; 40 to 50 per cent votes in 21 and 50 to 60 per cent votes in nine Assembly segments. Khandela and Todabhim rendered a whole hearted support to the party and it received more than 60 per cent votes in these segments.

Table 6.5 *Categorization of Assembly Units on the Basis of Per Cent Votes Polled to INC (1991–93)*

% votes polled	*INC*			
	1991		*1993*	
	f	*%f*	*f*	*%f*
0 to 10	1	1.39	1	1.39
10 to 20	4	5.56	2	2.78
20 to 30	15	20.83	17	23.61
30 to 40	20	27.78	24	33.33
40 to 50	21	29.17	21	29.17
50 to 60	9	12.50	6	8.33
60 to 70	2	2.78	1	1.39
70 to 80	—	—	—	—

Note: % votes refer to votes polled by the party as percentage of total votes polled in the Assembly unit.
f = frequency, %f = relative frequency in per cent

Figure 6.2

Spatial Pattern of Partywise Election Results in North East Rajasthan (1991–93)

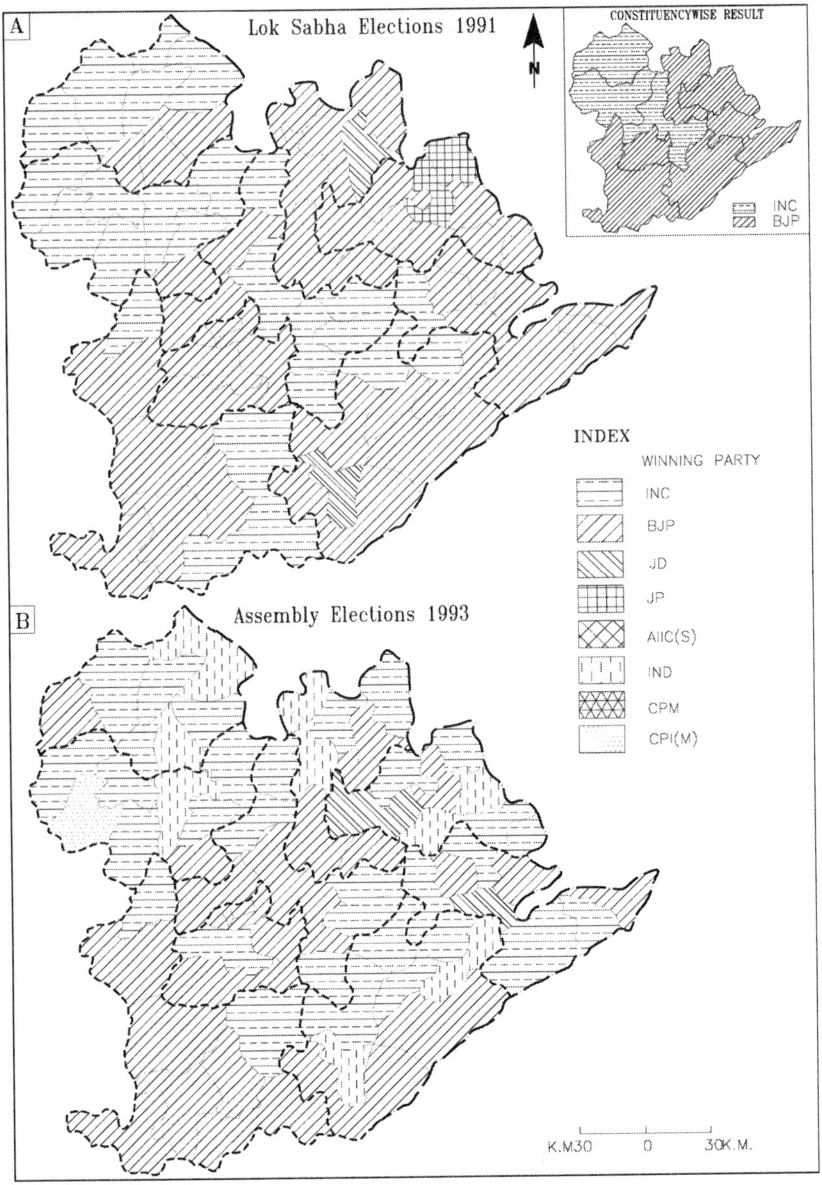

Figure 6.3

Frequency Distribution of Vote Percentage of INC (Lok Sabha 1991 vis-à-vis Assembly Elections 1993)

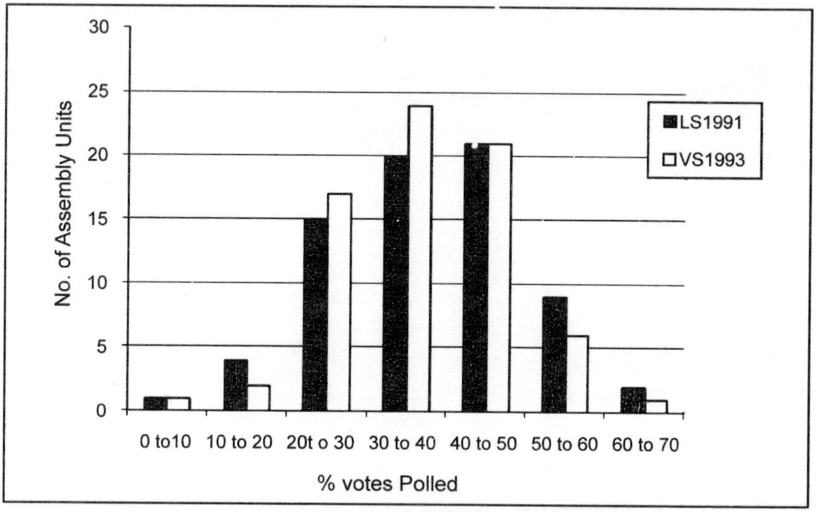

Figure 6.4A portrays the spatial pattern of electoral performance of INC during Lok Sabha Elections 1991. The areal pattern of support for INC as revealed by mapping the Z-score values of party's vote share (Figure 6.5A) in various Assembly segments reveals that the areas of very high support for the party were predominantly concentrated in central part of the study area, comprising Dausa, some part of Sikar constituency, Todabhim and Mahuwa. High support was recorded in western parts of Jhunjhunu, Sikar, eastern part of Sawai Madhopur, major part of Tonk and peripheral part of Jaipur constituency. The northern part of Alwar and Bharatpur constituencies recorded very low support. Areas of low support included southern part of Alwar and Bharatpur, Bayana, western Sawai Madhopur, urban part of Jaipur (except Johari Bazaar and Jaipur Rural) and some areas in eastern part of Jhunjhunu constituency. There was a complete rout for the party in Alwar, Bharatpur and Bayana districts.

The party was polled below average in all the urban constituencies except Johari Bazaar. The reserved constituencies on the whole, were hit by the anti Congress wave.

Assembly Elections 1993

In 1993, INC had fielded its candidates in all the 72 Assembly constituencies of the study area. Although it suffered a slight loss in terms of

Figure 6.4

Electoral Performance of INC in 1991 Lok Sabha and 1993 Assembly Elections

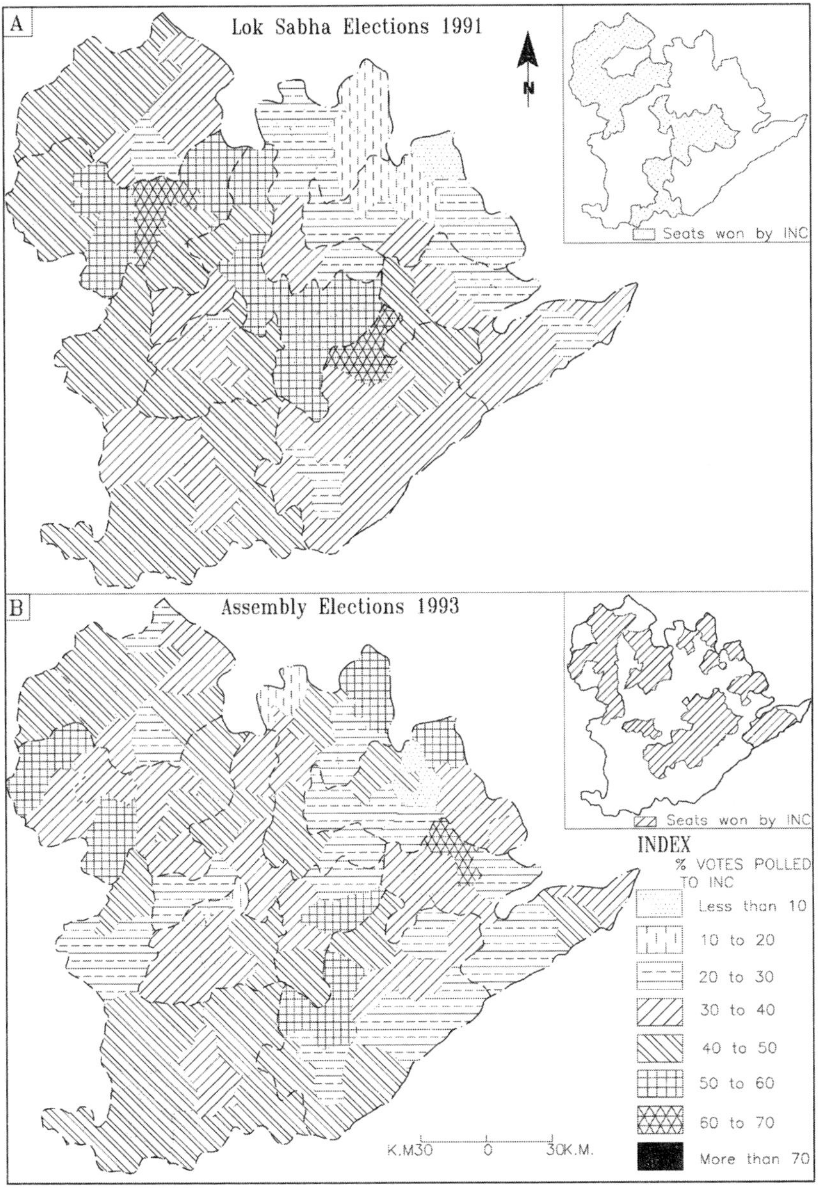

Figure 6.5

Spatial Variation in Intensity of Support for INC in North East Rajasthan

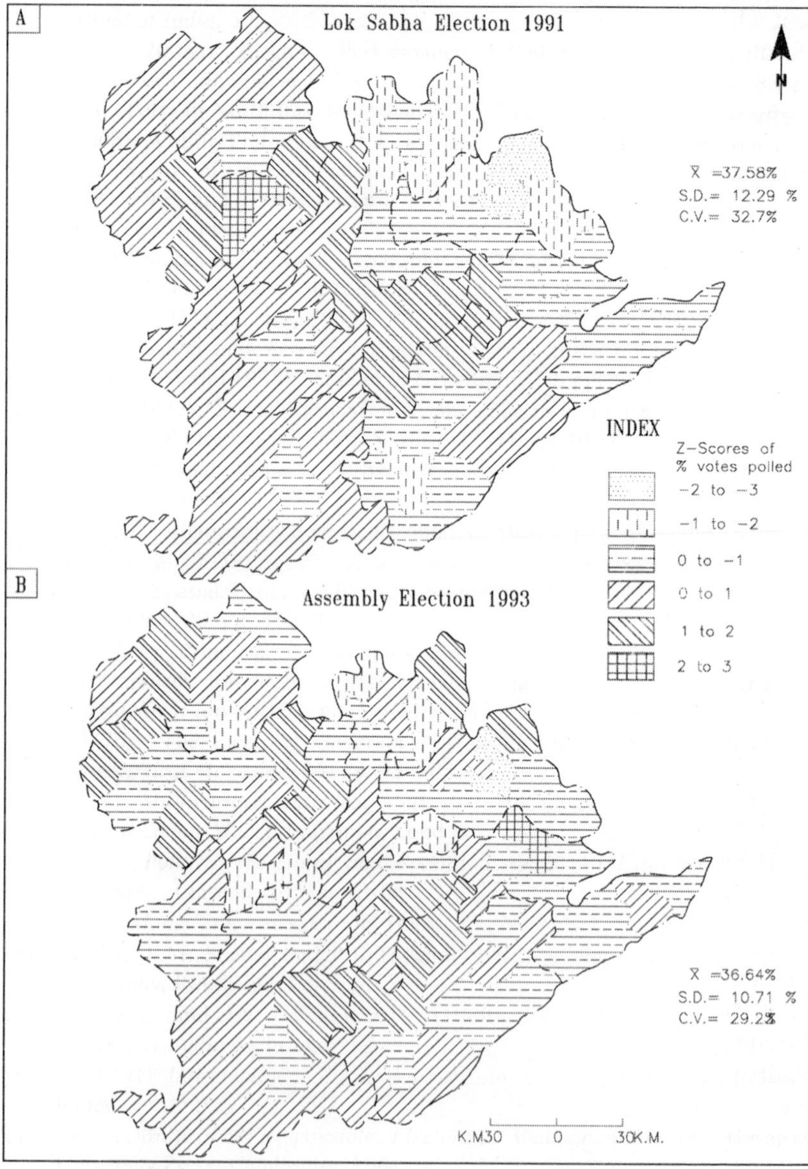

total vote share and average vote share per seat but it gained in terms of magnitude of victories. The total vote share dropped by 1.8 per cent as compared to 1991. The average vote share per seat was also 36.64 per cent which registered a small decline of 0.94 per cent. The percentage of votes polled in its favour ranged from 5.81 per cent in Nagar to 65.88 per cent in Nadbai (Table 6.4). A drop of 3.47 per cent in the coefficient of variation of party's vote indicates increased uniformity in the distribution of party support as compared to the preceding election. Nevertheless, the standard deviation was 10.71 and coefficient of variation of party votes was 29.23 per cent which indicate considerable variation in level of support for the party. It secured more than average vote share per seat in half of the constituencies.

INC candidates returned in 30 constituencies. A comparative view of Figure 6.2A and B reveals that the party retained majority of the areas in Sikar, Jhunjhunu and Dausa and made a marked presence in the eastern part of the study area too where it had been completely bereft of any success in the preceding elections. The spatial pattern of the success of the party reveals considerable variation from 1991.

In Nadbai, Kaman and Tizara, INC won with substantial margins of more than 10 per cent whereas it had lost in all these segments in 1991. In Nadbai, the margin of victory was 40.91 per cent. Likewise Bari, Bharatpur, Kumher, Ramgarh, Dholpur, Mandawar and Bairath were also lost in 1991 and won in 1993. Khandela, Pilani, Dhod, Jamwa Ramgarh, Dausa and Hindaun which were won by INC in 1991 were lost in 1993. It is noteworthy that the party had secured highest vote share in Khandela in Lok Sabha elections recording a victory by 41.40 per cent votes.

The frequency distribution of party votes as shown in Table 6.5 and Figure 6.3 clearly indicate that there was an increase in the number of Assembly units recording a vote share between 20 to 40 per cent in favour of the Congress. The party received less than 30 per cent votes in 20 Assembly units and in seven Assembly units it polled above 50 per cent votes. Nagar was the only Assembly unit where it polled below 10 per cent votes. It polled 10 to 20 per cent votes in two Assembly units; 20 to 30 per cent votes in 17 Assembly units; 30 to 40 per cent in 24 Assembly units and 40 to 50 per cent votes in 21 Assembly units. Nadbai was the only Assembly unit where it polled above 60 per cent votes. Figure 6.4B portrays the level of electoral support for INC in Assembly elections 1993.

The areal pattern of party support changed substantially as compared to 1991. The areas of high support for the party which were quite well defined in the preceding elections became scattered. Figure

6.5B portrays the spatial variation in intensity of support for INC during 1993 election. Nadbai rendered 'extremely high' support to the party which was in striking contrast to 1991 when it had received low support in the area. Areas of high to very high support were scattered including major part of Tonk, Dausa, Sawai Madhopur, peripheral part of Jaipur district and scattered pockets in Alwar, Bharatpur, Dholpur, Jhunjhunu and Sikar. Areas of low support were mainly concentrated in Dholpur, Bharatpur, Alwar, eastern Jhunjhunu and central part of Sikar district. Urbanized belt of Jaipur district predominantly rendered very low support to the party. Johari Bazaar was an exception where the party polled high. The extremely low support for the party in Nagar was a common feature of both the elections.

A comparative examination of Figure 6.5A and B clearly reveals that some areas exhibit striking contrast in their preference for INC at the two levels of electoral contest. Assembly segments like Khandela, Tizara, Kaman, Nadbai, Hindaun, Kotputli, Dudu, Bamanwas, Khandela, etc. may be included in this category. Contrastingly, areas like Assembly units of Tonk and Dausa districts, Mahuwa, Nagar and urban areas exhibit more or less consistent nature of support towards the party. The urban constituencies (except Johari Bazaar) invariably rendered low support to the party in both the elections.

Assembly Unitwise Presence and Performance of BJP
Lok Sabha Elections 1991

Table 6.6 reveals that in 1991 the average per segment vote share of BJP was 43.40 per cent. The percentage of votes polled by the party in various Assembly segments ranged from 22.23 per cent in Lachhmangarh to 72.90 per cent in Hawa Mahal. The standard deviation of party votes was 10.07 and coefficient of variation was 23.21 per cent which was 9.49 per cent lower than that for INC. Thus BJP had a relatively more uniform support base in the study area as compared to INC.

The party received votes more than its average vote share per segment in 52.78 per cent of the Assembly segments and registered a victory in all Assembly segments where its vote share exceeded 44.7 per cent. The party secured a majority in 44 Assembly segments. The spatial distribution of these segments has been illustrated in Figure 6.2A. BJP dominated the entire eastern and south western part of the study area. It won in all the segments of Jaipur, Alwar and Bayana constituencies (except Khairthal and Mahuwa); all segments of Bharatpur constituency except Kaman and Nagar; major part of Tonk and Sawai Madhopur and some part of eastern Jhunjhunu. All the urban constituencies were bagged by BJP. Its performance was magnificent in Alwar and Hawa Mahal where it won with a lead of 36.92 per cent and 48.91 per cent respectively.

Table 6.6 *Performance of BJP in North East Rajasthan (1991, 93, 98)*

Election Year	*Seats Contested*		*Seats Won*		*% Votes*	*Average votes (%) per Assembly Seat*	*SD*	*CV (%)*	*Min.*	*Max.*
	A	*B*	*A*	*B*						
Lok Sabha 1991	9	72	6	44	43.14	43.40	10.07	23.21	22.23 (Lachhmangarh-SC)	72.90 (Hawa Mahal)
Assembly 1993	71	—	29	—	34.30	34.99	14.27	40.78	4.89 (Kaman)	70.19 (Hawa Mahal)
Lok Sabha 1998	9	72	3	24	39.64	39.18	10.1	25.78	18.11 (Rajgarh-ST)	72.25 (Hawa Mahal)
Assembly 1998	71	—	8	—	28.91	28.53	11.53	40.43	4.04 (Nagar)	48.69 (Hawa Mahal)

Note: A = number of constituencies
B = number of Assembly segments

The frequency distribution of Assembly units on the basis of votes polled by BJP has been shown in Table 6.7.

Table 6.7 *Frequency Distribution of Assembly Units on the Basis of Votes Polled to BJP (1991–93)*

% votes polled	*1991*		*1993*	
	f	*%f*	*f*	*%f*
0 to 10	—	—	3	4.23
10 to 20	—	—	9	12.68
20 to 30	5	6.94	15	21.13
30 to 40	24	33.33	17	23.94
40 to 50	27	37.50	16	22.54
50 to 60	13	18.06	10	14.08
60 to 70	2	2.78	—	—
70 to 80	1	1.39	1	1.41

Note: % votes polled refer to votes polled by the party as percentage of total votes polled in the Assembly unit.
f = frequency, %f = relative frequency in per cent

It is evident from the table that the level of support for BJP was more towards higher side in majority of the constituencies (Figure 6.6) which indicates high degree of electoral support for the party in the study area in 1991. The poll percentage of BJP was below 30 per cent in five Assembly units whereas in 16 Assembly segments it polled above 50 per cent votes. In 24 Assembly segments the vote percentage of the party was between 30 to 40 per cent; in 27 segments it polled between 40 to 50 per cent; in 13 segments it polled 50 to 60 per cent votes and in two Assembly segments it polled 60 to 70 per cent votes. The party received highest level of support in the urban constituencies of Jaipur. Figure 6.7A illustrates spatial pattern of intensity of support for the party in the study area.

Figure 6.6

Frequency Distribution of Vote Percentage of BJP (Lok Sabha 1991 and Assembly Elections 1993)

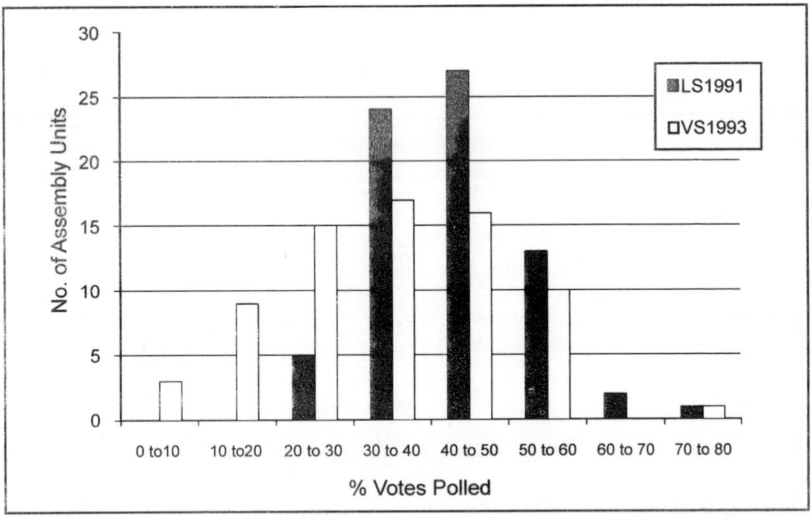

The areal pattern of performance of BJP as revealed by Z-scores of Assembly segmentwise vote share of the party (Figure 6.8A) clearly indicates the stronghold of the party in the urbanized areas. In Hawa Mahal the intensity of support for the party was of extremely high order. The urban and semi urban areas of Jaipur and Alwar constituencies, Rajgarh and Bamanwas recorded very high support for the party. Areas of high support included major part of Tonk and Sawai Madhopur, eastern parts of Sikar and Bharatpur constituencies along with Bayana, Dholpur, Behror, Bansur, Khetri and Bairath. The party polled above average votes in all the urban constituencies.

Figure 6.7

Electoral Performance of BJP in 1991 Lok Sabha and 1993 Assembly Elections

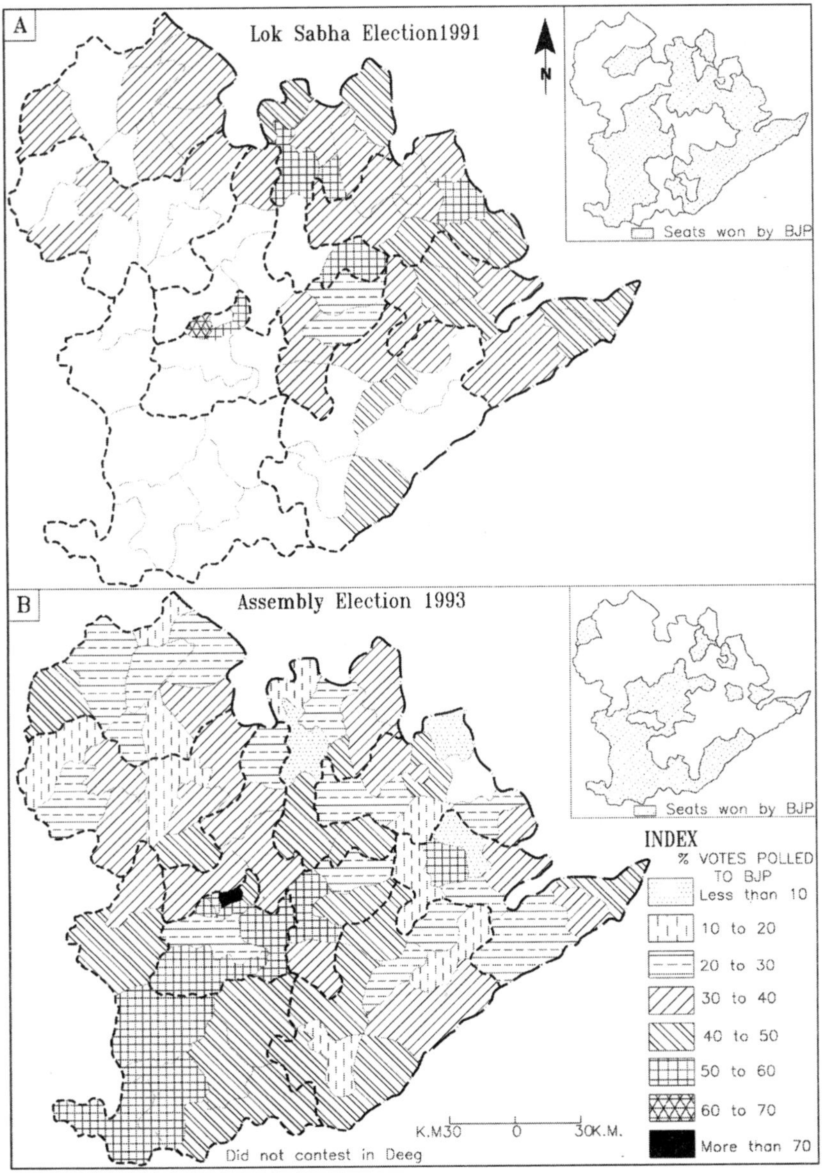

Figure 6.8

Spatial Variation in Intensity of Support for BJP in North East Rajasthan (Lok Sabha 1991 and Assembly Elections 1993)

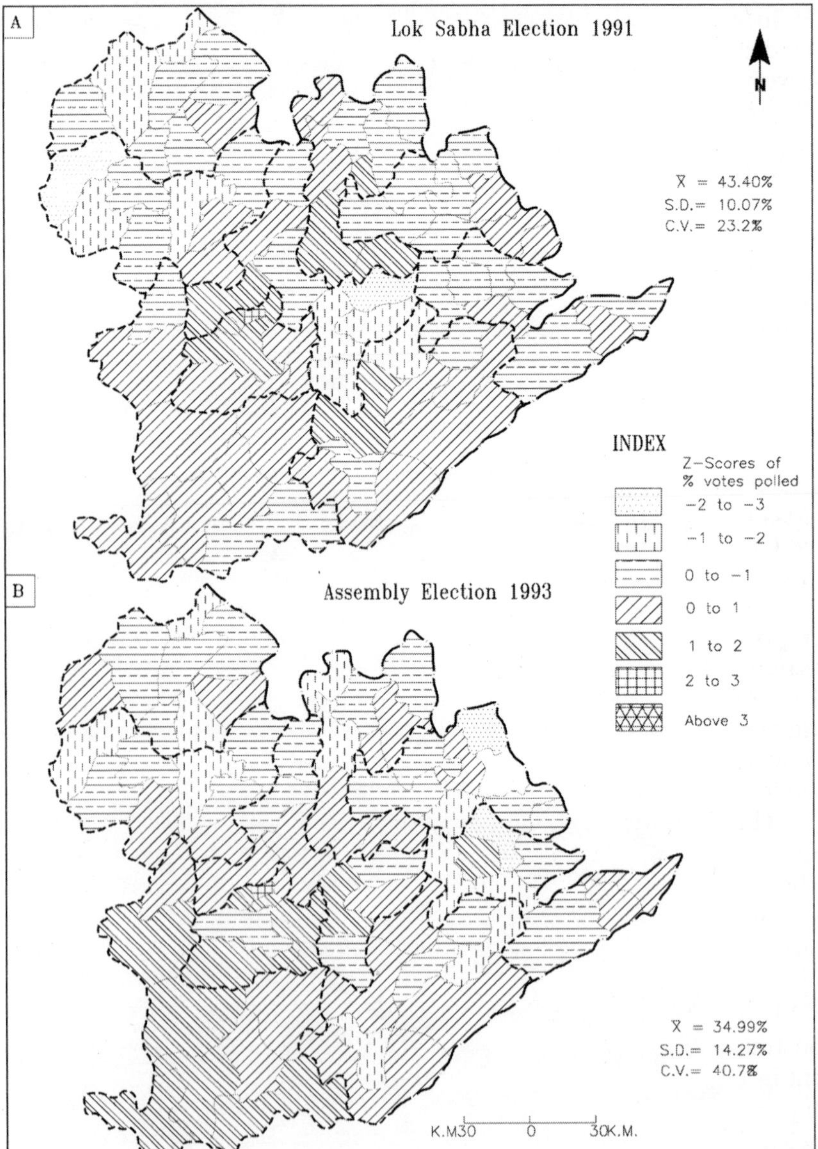

The areas which recorded low support for the party were north eastern part of Alwar, western part of Bharatpur, Bayana and scattered parts of Jhunjhunu and Sikar constituencies. Phulera, Uniara, Sawai Madhopur, Jamwa Ramgarh and Kotputli also extended low support to BJP. In western parts of Jhunjhunu, eastern part of Dausa, Dhod and Khandela segments of Sikar constituencies the support for the party was very low. Areas of extremely low support included Lachhmangarh in Sikar constituency and Bandikui.

Assembly Elections 1993

In Assembly elections 1993 BJP contested in 71 constituencies. In Deeg, it supported independent contestant Arun Singh. Its average per seat vote share was 34.99 per cent which was 8.41 per cent less than the preceding Lok Sabha elections. In individual constituencies its vote share ranged between 4.89 per cent in Kaman to 70.19 per cent in Hawa Mahal. The standard deviation of distribution of party votes was 14.27 per cent and coefficient of variation was 40.78 per cent which was 17.57 per cent higher than 1991. Thus, the variability of party support in the study area increased considerably (Table 6.6). In 35 constituencies, the vote share of the party was above its average per seat.

Out of the 71 seats contested by the party, it registered a success in 29 constituencies. The seats won by the party have been illustrated in Figure 6.2B. In the central and southern part of the study region comprising of constituencies of Jaipur, Tonk and Sawai Madhopur districts; and Alwar district the balance was conspicuously in favour of BJP. Contrastingly, in the northern, western and eastern parts of the study region the party could not bag much seats except some scattered few as Fatehpur, Khairthal, Nagar, Rupbas and Rajakhera. The party won in all the urban constituencies except Bharatpur.

The frequency distribution of constituencies over various categories of percentage votes polled by BJP has been summarized in Table 6.7 and Figure 6.6. In 1993, the proportion of constituencies in low vote categories increased markedly. Twenty seven Assembly units recorded a support of below 30 per cent votes for BJP whereas the number of seats where it received more than 50 per cent votes drooped to 11. The vote share of the party was below 10 per cent in three constituencies; 10 to 20 per cent in nine constituencies; 20 to 30 per cent in 15 constituencies; 30 to 40 per cent in 17 constituencies; 40 to 50 per cent in 16 constituencies and 50 to 60 per cent in 10 constituencies. Hawa Mahal again polled above 70 per cent in favour of BJP. The spatial distribution of constituencies comprising the above categories has been illustrated in Figure 6.7B.

The areal pattern of intensity of support for BJP as portrayed in Figure 6.8B reveals that the areas of high support for the party were mainly concentrated in the southern and central part of the study area. The performance of the party was weak in the northern and eastern region except for a few scattered pockets of high support. The support for the party was again extremely high in Hawa Mahal. Areas of very high support included southern and western part of Tonk district along with Kekri, southern part of Jaipur district including the urban constituencies of the region, Dausa and Weir constituencies. Eastern Tonk, central part of Jaipur, southern part of Alwar, eastern part of Dholpur district, reserved constituencies of Sawai Madhopur district, Fatehpur, Khetri, Danta Ramgarh and Nagar extended high support to the party. In all urban constituencies except Bharatpur, it received high degree of support. It garnered substantial support in most of the reserved Assembly constituencies also especially in Alwar, Dausa, Sawai Madhopur, Tonk and Jaipur districts. The areas of low to very low support for the party included major part of Jhunjhunu, Sikar, northern part of Jaipur, northern and eastern part of Alwar, eastern Sawai Madhopur, western part of Dholpur and major part of Bharatpur districts. Sanganer, Lalsot, Bandikui, Mahuwa and Sawai Madhopur constituencies also extended low support to the party. In Kaman and Nadbai, the percentage of party votes was extremely low.

Several areas exhibited markedly different attitude towards the party in the two levels of electoral contest. Behror, Bansur, Bairath, Bayana, Sri Madhopur, Bharatpur, Kumher, Gangapur and Karauli extended high support to the party in 1991 but polled relatively low in its favour in 1993. Contrastingly, in Fatehpur, Phulera, Uniara, Jamwa Ramgarh, Khairthal, Weir, Dausa, Sikrai, Todabhim, Rajakhera and Danta Ramgarh, the party improved considerably in Assembly elections.

A comparison of Figure 6.7A and B, 6.8A and B clearly highlights the fact that the spatial pattern and intensity of electoral support for the party has varied considerably during the two elections.

Lok Sabha 1998 vis-à-vis Assembly Elections 1998

In Lok Sabha elections 1998 several parties and numerous independent candidates were in the fray, yet the major contest was between INC and BJP. INC, BJP and BSP contested on all the seats of the study area, AIIC(S) contested only in Jhunjhunu; CPM contested only in Sikar; CPI had fielded its candidates in Jaipur and Bharatpur; SAP contested in Jhunjhunu, Jaipur and Bharatpur; and JD was in the fray in all constituencies except Jhunjhunu and Sikar. INC and BJP dominated the electoral battle and together claimed more than 80 per cent of the votes in Bayana, Dausa, Jaipur, Sawai Madhopur and Tonk

(Table 6.8). In Alwar, Bharatpur, Jhunjhunu and Sikar the contest was triangular. In Alwar Mahendra Kumari, an independent candidate posed a strong challenge especially before BJP as she had filed as an independent after being denied a ticket by BJP. In Bharatpur BSP was quite strong. In Jhunjhunu, AIIC(S) candidate Ram Ola held a strong base in the region owing to his immense popularity for his efforts for the development of the constituency in his short tenure in the Eleventh Lok Sabha. CPM was the main threat before INC and BJP in Sikar. In these constituencies also, INC and BJP claimed 50 to 70 per cent of the total votes polled.

INC bagged five seats which were Alwar, Bharatpur, Dausa, Sawai Madhopur and Tonk. The party's total vote share was 37.81 per cent. The vote share in individual constituencies ranged between 12.34 per cent in Jhunjhunu to 52.46 per cent in Tonk. In Alwar it faced a tough competition and could win the seat with a bare margin of 0.39 per cent. Its margin of victory was highest (10.63%) in Sawai Madhopur. In terms of percentage vote share, BJP exceeded INC and garnered 39.64 per cent of the total votes. In spite of it, the party lagged in terms of seats and could register a victory in only three constituencies, i.e. Bayana, Jaipur and Sikar. In Bayana, the contest was intense and the margin of victory was 0.82 per cent in favour of BJP. Jaipur, the party's bastion, earned the party a sweeping success with a lead of 17.6 per cent (Table 6.8).

Table 6.8 *Lok Sabha Constituencywise Winning Party, Nearest Rival Party and Margin of Victory in Lok Sabha Elections 1998*

1	*2*	*3*	*4*	*5*	*6*	*7*	*8*
Constituency	*WP*	*Votes (%)*	*NRP*	*Votes (%)*	*Margin of Victory*	*Others*	*BJP+ INC*
Jhunjhunu	AIIC (S)	44.25	BJP	39.3	4.95	48.37	51.63
Sikar	BJP	37.24	INC	32	5.24	30.76	69.24
Jaipur	BJP	56.43	INC	38.83	17.6	4.73	95.27
Dausa	INC	51.37	BJP	43.81	7.56	4.82	95.18
Alwar	INC	31.26	IND	30.87	0.39	41.57	58.43
Bharatpur	INC	38.52	BJP	28.08	10.44	33.40	66.60
Bayana(sc)	BJP	40.83	INC	40.01	0.82	19.16	80.84
Sawai Madhopur (ST)	INC	48.17	BJP	37.54	10.63	14.30	85.70
Tonk(SC)	INC	52.46	BJP	42.81	9.65	4.73	95.27

Note: Column No. 2. Winning Party; Column No.3. Votes polled by Winning Party; Column No. 4. Nearest Rival Party; Column No. 5. Votes polled by Nearest Rival Party as % of total Voting Turnout of Constituency; Column No. 7. Votes polled by other parties including independents (excluding INC and BJP).

Jhunjhunu was the only seat which was won by a party other than INC and BJP. AIIC(S) won the seat with a margin of 4.95 per cent votes.

Assembly elections 1998 witnessed an impressive pro-Congress swing in the study area. INC had contested on all the seats in the region and with 41.70 per cent votes share, 3.89 per cent higher than preceding Lok Sabha elections, it bagged three-fourth of them. BJP received a sound drub and its share reduced to a token success in eight seats. Its vote share also declined to 28.91 per cent. The rout may be attributed to the strong anti-incumbency wave against the party after its eight years of continuous rule in the State.

Dhod went to CPM, Tizara to RJD and Bansur and Nagar to BSP (Figure 6.9B).

Presence and Performance of INC

Lok Sabha Elections 1998

The average per segment vote share of INC was 38.83 per cent in Lok Sabha elections 1998. The percentage votes polled by the party ranged from 7.41 per cent in Surajgarh to 58.52 per cent in Niwai. The standard deviation of distribution of party votes was 13.06 and coefficient of variation was 34.03 per cent which indicated considerable disparity in areal distribution of party support (Table 6.4). In 55.55 per cent of the Assembly units, the vote share of the party exceeded its average per segment share.

INC won in 37 Assembly segments covering almost all Assembly segments of Tonk, Sawai Madhopur, Dausa, Bharatpur, southern part of Alwar, eastern part of Sikar and western part of Bayana constituencies. The party faced a complete debacle in Jhunjhunu where it couldn't win a majority in any of the segments. In Jaipur, Bayana, Sikar and northern part of Alwar constituencies the party lost in majority of the segments (Figure 6.9A).

As evident from Figure 6.10 and Table 6.9, in Lok Sabha 1998 elections INC secured 30 to 60 per cent votes in most of the Assembly segments. The vote percentage of the party was below 30 per cent in 16 Assembly segments whereas in 14 segments it polled above 50 per cent. Surajgarh was the only segment where the party's vote share was below 10 per cent. Its vote share was between 10 to 20 per cent in eight segments seen; between 20 to 30 per cent in seven segments; between 30 to 40 per cent in 21 segments and 40 to 50 per cent in another 21 segments. Figure 6.11A illustrates the Assembly segmentwise performance of the party.

Figure 6.9

Spatial Pattern of Partywise Election Results in North East Rajasthan (1998–98)

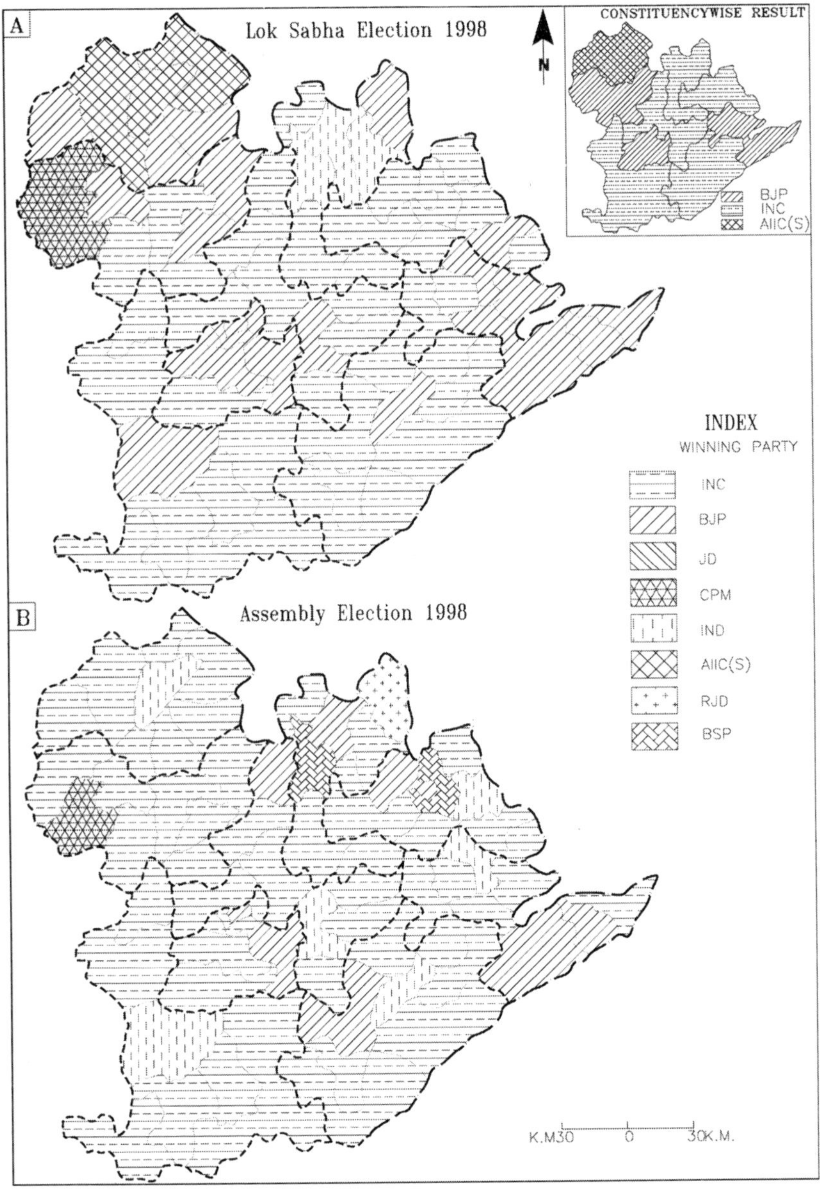

Table 6.9 *Categorization of Assembly Units on the Basis of Per cent Votes Polled to INC 1998*

% votes polled	*INC*			
	LS 1998		*VS 1998*	
	f	*%f*	*f*	*%f*
0 to 10	1	1.39	—	—
10 to 20	8	11.11	5	6.94
20 to 30	7	9.72	10	13.89
30 to 40	21	29.17	17	23.61
40 to 50	21	29.17	18	25.00
50 to 60	14	19.44	19	26.39
60 to 70	—	—	3	4.17
70 to 80	—	—	—	—

Note: % votes polled refer to votes polled by the party as percentage of total votes polled in the Assembly unit.
f = frequency, %f = relative frequency in per cent

Figure 6.10

Frequency Distribution of Vote Percentage of INC (Lok Sabha 1998 and Assembly Elections 1998)

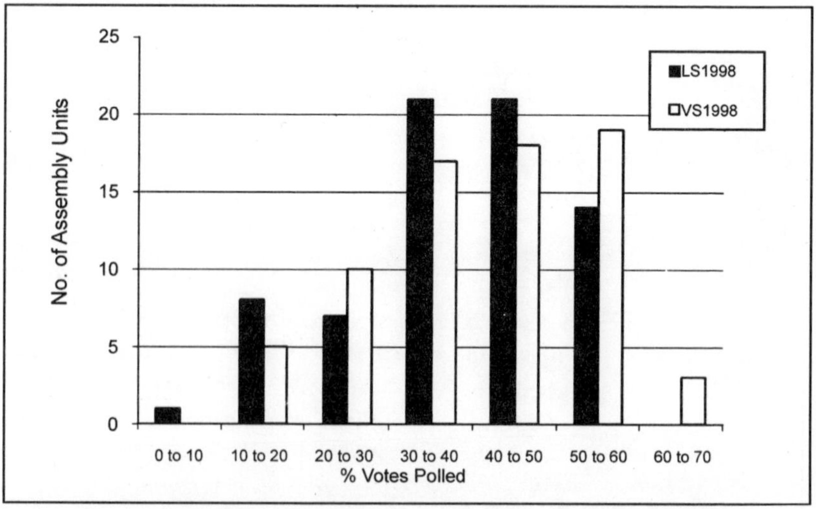

The spatial pattern of intensity of party support as indicated by Z-score of values reveals that southern part of the study region extended high degree of support to the party whereas barring a few exceptions, it acquired a low support in northern part of the study area.

Figure 6.11

Electoral Performance of INC in Lok Sabha 1998 and Assembly Elections 1998

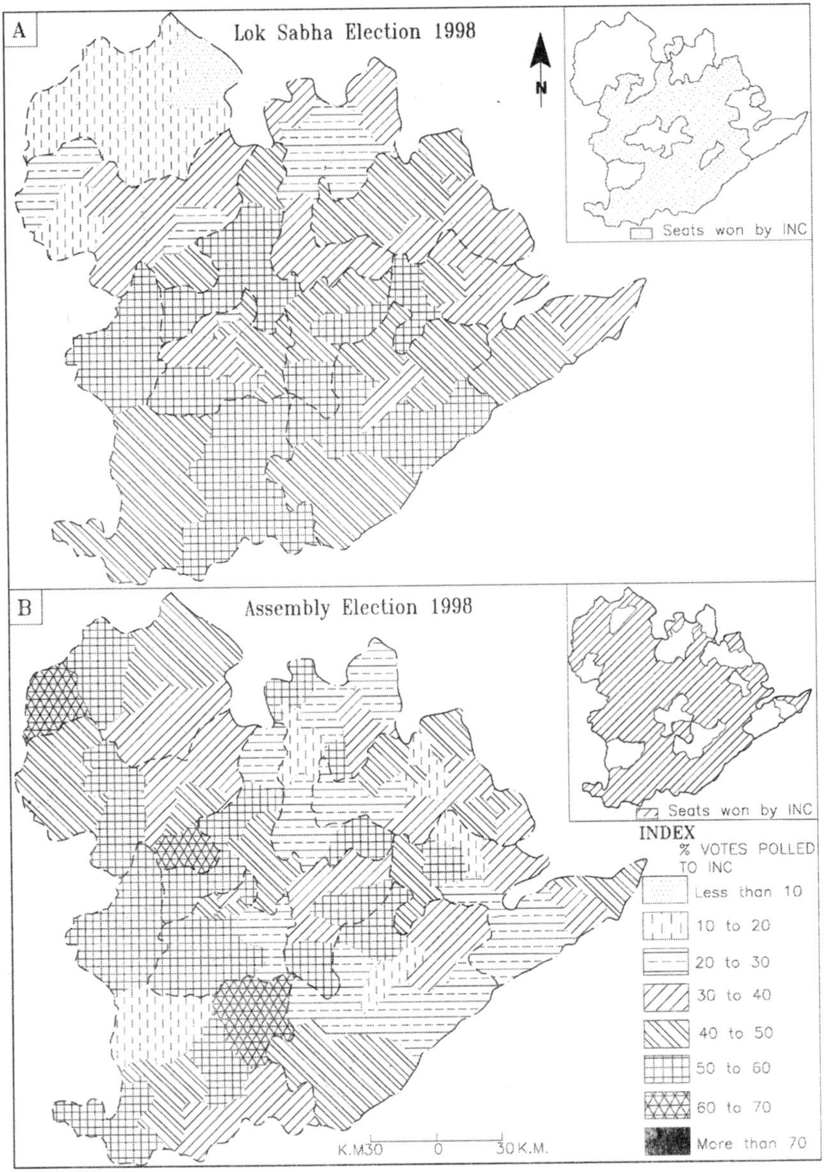

Areas of very high support included northern and eastern part of Tonk, central part of Sawai Madhopur, northern and southern part of Dausa constituency and Mahuwa. Areas of high support included western part of Tonk, southern and north eastern parts of Sawai Madhopur, Jaipur, eastern part of Dausa constituencies alongwith scattered areas in Bayana, western Bharatpur and eastern part of Sikar constituencies (Figure 6.12A). The party received extremely low support in segments located in eastern part of Jhunjhunu constituency. Very low support was recorded in western part of Jhunjhunu and Sikar constituencies. Eastern part of Sikar, entire Alwar, eastern part of Bharatpur and Bayana constituencies recorded low support for the party.

INC intruded in the BJP bastion, i.e. Jaipur Lok Sabha constituency. Except Hawa Mahal and Banipark, the party acquired high support.

Assembly Elections 1998

The performance of INC was highly impressive in Assembly elections 1998. There was marked increase in both the magnitude and territorial extent of support for the party. The average per seat vote share of the party increased to 41.54 per cent which was 3.16 per cent higher than the preceding Lok Sabha elections. This modest increment in vote share translated into 28.61 per cent increase in the number of Assembly units won by the party. It won in 54 Assembly constituencies (Figure 6.9B).

The vote percentage of INC in individual constituencies varied between 13.37 per cent in Malpura to 66.52 per cent in Chomu. The standard deviation of party votes was 13.25 and coefficient of variation was 31.90 per cent, 2.13 per cent lower than the preceding Lok Sabha elections (Table 6.4).

The party made a clean sweep covering majority of the constituencies in Jhunjhunu, Sikar, Tonk, Karauli, southern part of Sawai Madhopur, Jaipur, Dausa, southern part of Bharatpur, southern and central part of Alwar districts. The party won all the urban constituencies too, except Hawa Mahal. Another conspicuous feature of these elections was INC's success in Jaipur region, the traditional stronghold of BJP. In Jhunjhunu, Malpura, Dausa and Kotputli, the party's rebels who were denied tickets became the major cause of its debacle as the defectors filed as independents.

The frequency distribution of constituencies into various categories of votes polled by INC has been displayed in Table 6.9 and Figure 6.10. There was a marked shift of Assembly units from the lower end towards the higher end of the scale. The interclass variation

Figure 6.12

Spatial Variation in Intensity of Support for INC in North East Rajasthan (Lok Sabha 1998 and Assembly Elections 1998)

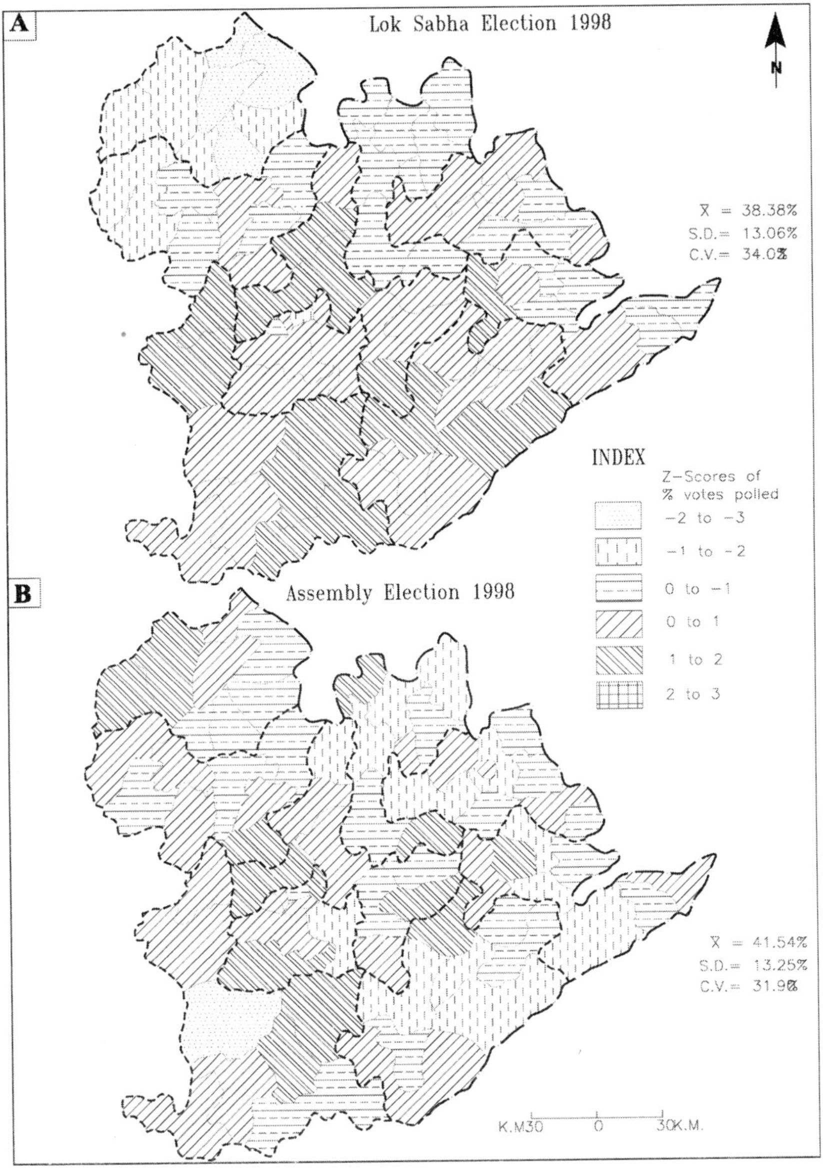

in frequency was also reduced as is evident from Figure 6.10. The vote percentage of the party was below 30 per cent in 15 constituencies whereas the number of constituencies where it polled above 50 per cent votes increased to 22. The vote share of INC was 10 to 20 per cent in five; 20 to 30 per cent in 10; 30 to 40 per cent in 17; 40 to 50 per cent in 18; 50 to 60 per cent in 19 and above 60 per cent in three constituencies. The areal distribution of constituencies comprising the above classes has been illustrated in Figure 6.11B.

The areal pattern of intensity of party support was drastically different from the preceding elections. Areas in western Jhunjhunu and central parts of Sikar district which had provided low level of support during Lok Sabha elections provided high to very high support during Assembly elections. Northern part of Sawai Madhopur, Karauli, western part of Dholpur, western part of Bharatpur districts, Dausa, Bandikui, Malpura and Uniara constituencies were low support areas during the latter whereas the same areas had rendered high support to the party during the former. The well-defined areal pattern of high and low support areas which existed in Lok Sabha elections was replaced by a scattered one during Assembly elections.

Presence and Performance of BJP

Lok Sabha Elections 1998

In Lok Sabha Elections 1998 the average per segment vote share of BJP was 39.18 per cent. In individual Assembly segments the vote percentage of the party ranged from 18.11 per cent in Rajgarh to 72.25 per cent in Hawa Mahal. The standard deviation of inter segment party vote share was 10.1 and coefficient of variation was 25.78 per cent. The party polled above its average per segment vote share in 51.38 per cent of the Assembly segments.

Although the drop in average vote share of the party was not very high in terms of magnitude but there was drastic contraction in the spatial extent of its victory as compared to 1991. The party won in 24 Assembly segments, a figure which was 44 in 1991. The segments in which it received a majority included all segments of Bayana except Weir and Mahuwa; all segments of Jaipur constituency excluding Phagi, Khetri, Gudha and Fatehpur in Jhunjhunu constituency; Sikar, Sri Madhopur and Neem-ka-Thana in Sikar constituency; Malpura, Dausa, Gangapur, Tizara and Kumher (Figure 6.9A).

The vote share of the party in individual segments was more concentrated in categories of 30 to 50 per cent votes. It polled less than 30 per cent votes in 13 Assembly segments whereas in seven Assembly

Figure 6.13

Electoral Performance of BJP in Lok Sabha 1998 and Assembly Elections 1998

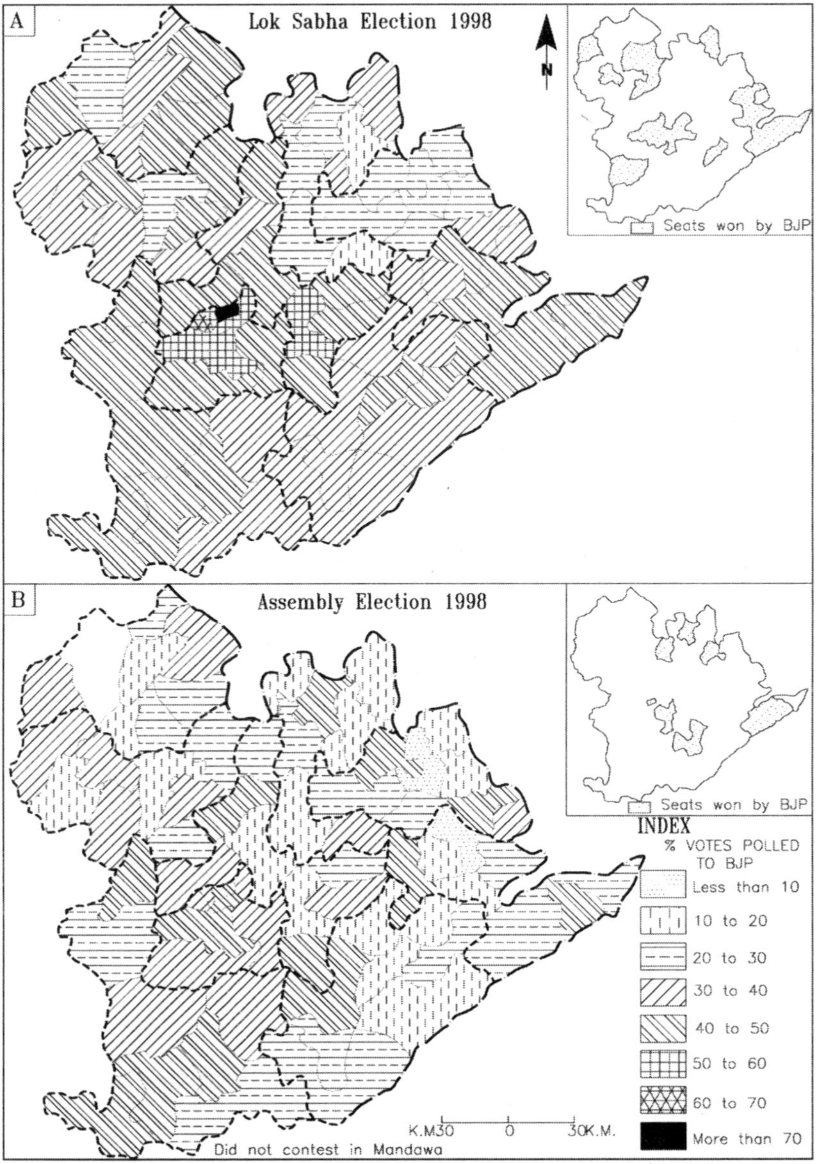

segments its vote share was more than 50 per cent. Highest polling in favour of BJP occurred in urban and semi urban segments of Jaipur constituency (Figure 6.13A). The frequency distribution of Assembly segments according to the levels of voting in favour of BJP has been displayed in Table 6.10 and Figure 6.14.

Table 6.10 *Categorization of Assembly Units on the Basis of Per cent Votes Polled to BJP 1998*

% votes polled	*BJP*			
	LS 1998		*VS 1998*	
	f	*%f*	*f*	*%f*
0 to 10	—	—	2	2.82
10 to 20	2	2.78	19	26.76
20 to 30	11	15.28	18	25.35
30 to 40	23	31.94	17	23.94
40 to 50	29	40.28	15	21.13
50 to 60	5	6.94	—	—
60 to 70	1	1.39	—	—
70 to 80	1	1.39	—	—

Note: % votes polled refer to votes polled by the party as percentage of total votes polled in the Assembly unit.
f = frequency, %f = relative frequency in per cent

The vote share of the party was 10 to 20 per cent in two Assembly segments; 20 to 30 per cent in 11 Assembly segments; 30 to 40 per cent in 23 Assembly segments; 40 to 50 per cent in 29 Assembly segments; 50 to 60 per cent in five and above 60 per cent in two Assembly segments.

The areal pattern of intensity of support for the party has been illustrated in Figure 6.15A. The regions of above average support were more or less well defined which included south western, central, eastern and some area in north western part of the study area. In Hawa Mahal and Banipark the support for the party was extremely high. In the surrounding region comprising segments of Jaipur constituency and Dausa, the support was of very high order. Areas of high support included entire Tonk constituency except Niwai, eastern part of Jhunjhunu, entire Bayana except some area in the west, major part of Dausa except Bairath and some parts of Sikar constituency. In Gangapur and Karauli also, the party received high level of support. On the whole, Alwar, Bharatpur, Sawai Madhopur, Western Jhunjhunu and southern part of Sikar constituency recorded below average support for BJP. Nagar and Rajgarh recorded extremely low

Figure 6.14

Frequency Distribution of Vote Percentage of BJP (Lok Sabha 1998 and Assembly Elections 1998)

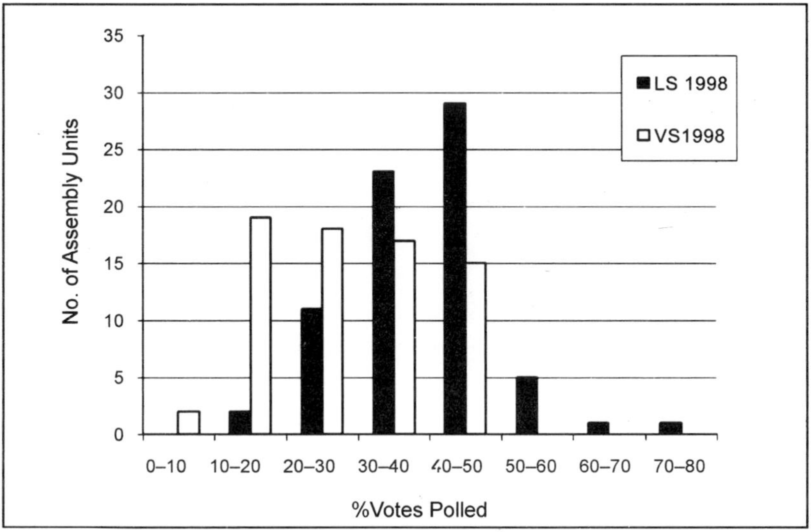

support to the party. Areas of very low support mainly included central part of Alwar and whole of Bharatpur constituency except the eastern segments. Mandawa and Khandela also recorded very low support for the party. Areas of low support included northern part of Alwar, eastern part of Bharatpur, western part of Bayana, whole of Sawai Madhopur except Gangapur and Karauli, central part of Jhunjhunu and segments lying in southern part of Sikar constituencies. The party made a strong showing in the urban and semi urban areas in general but failed to maintain its hold in the urban areas of Alwar and Bharatpur.

Assembly Elections 1998

BJP faced a severe debacle in the region in Assembly elections 1998. Following its rule of eight years in the State, a strong anti-incumbency wave shrunk its vote share to 28.91 per cent and its success to a bare handful of eight seats.

The average per seat vote share of the party was 28.53 per cent, 10.65 per cent less than the preceding Lok Sabha elections. The vote percentage in individual constituencies varied between 4.04 per cent in Nagar to 48.69 per cent in Hawa Mahal. The decline in the level of support for the party in Hawa Mahal is notable as it had polled above

Figure 6.15

Spatial Variation in Intensity of Support for BJP in North East Rajasthan (Lok Sabha, 1998 and Assembly Elections 1998)

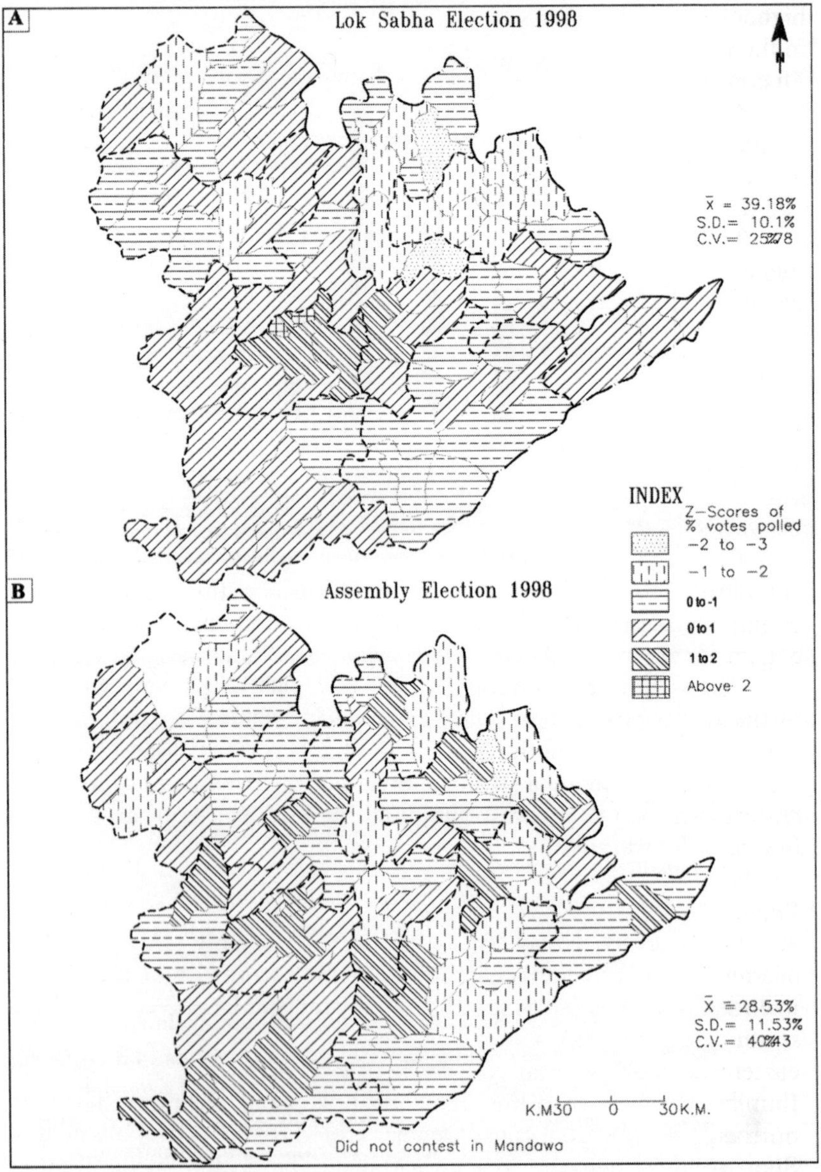

70 per cent in the area in the other three elections. The standard deviation of inter constituency distribution of votes was 11.53 and coefficient of variation was 40.43 per cent which was 14.65 per cent higher than Lok Sabha elections (Table 6.6). This indicates relatively higher degree of disparity in spatial distribution of support for the party in the region during these elections. The party polled above average in 36 constituencies, i.e. 50.70 per cent of the seats contested by it.

Amongst this adverse swing, the party candidates won in Kotputli, Mandawar, Ramgarh, Bari, Dholpur, Bamanwas, Bassi and Hawa Mahal. The party recorded a victory in Kotputli for the first time (Figure 6.9B).

The striking difference in the level of support for the party in the two levels of elections is evident in Figure 6.14. There was a clear shift of the frequency distribution towards the lower end of the scale.

The proportion of Assembly units in which the vote share of the party was below 30 per cent increased to 54.92 per cent (39) as compared to 18.05 per cent in the Lok Sabha elections. In two constituencies it polled below 10 per cent votes; in 19 constituencies between 10 to 20 per cent; in 18 constituencies between 20 to 30 per cent; in 17 constituencies between 30 to 40 per cent; and in 15 constituencies between 40 to 50 per cent votes (Table 6.10).

On the whole the south western region comprising Assembly constituencies of Tonk district; central part comprising constituencies of Jaipur district and some areas in the western part in Sikar district extended substantial support to the party (Figure 6.13B).

The areal pattern of intensity of support for the party as depicted by the Z-score values in Figure 6.15B reveals that areas of high to very high support for the party were the south western, central and north western parts constituencies of Tonk, Jaipur and Sikar districts. In the eastern part of the study area, pockets of above average support were few and scattered including eastern part of Bharatpur, eastern and southern part of Dausa districts, Mandawar, Bansur, Ramgarh, Rajgarh and Dholpur constituencies. In Jhunjhunu, Alwar, Bharatpur and Sawai Madhopur districts the support for the party was below average in majority of the constituencies. Areas of very low support included northern, eastern part and Thanagazi constituency of Alwar, north eastern and southern part of Bharatpur, major part of Karauli, eastern part of Sawai Madhopur and western part of Dausa districts; Jhunjhunu and Dhod constituencies. The party received low support in northern and southern part of Jhunjhunu, some areas in eastern part of Sikar district, Uniara in Tonk, southern part of Sawai Madhopur, eastern part of Karauli, eastern and western part of Dholpur, south western part of Bharatpur, northern and central part of Alwar districts and Dudu, Kotputli and Jamwa Ramgarh in Jaipur district. In Nagar, the support for the party was extremely low.

It is evident from the foregoing discussion that except Tonk and Jaipur, the constituent Assembly units of the remaining districts exhibit high variation in their level of support for BJP. The party fared well in urban and semi urban areas of Sikar, Jaipur, Tonk, Bharatpur and Dholpur. In Alwar, Sawai Madhopur, Jhunjhunu and Dausa it could not make an impressive appeal in urban areas too.

A comparative study of Figure 6.15A and B indicates that there was substantial difference in the areal pattern of support for the party at the two levels of electoral contest. There were areas like eastern part of Jhunjhunu, some areas in Dholpur, Alwar and Dausa districts which exhibited striking contrast in their support for BJP during the two elections. On the contrary, in Tonk (along with Kekri) and Jaipur districts the performance of the party was consistent to some extent. Nevertheless the vote share of the party declined in these areas too.

7 Vote Trends and Support Stability

In this chapter vote trends and nature of stability of support for INC and BJP have been examined in detail. Since the Lok Sabha elections held in the year 1996 have not been included in this study, the elections under consideration have been paired into two distinct groups for the purpose of analysis instead of analysing the trends for all the four elections together. The elections have been paired as under:

1. Lok Sabha 1991 and Assembly Elections 1993
2. Lok Sabha 1998 and Assembly Elections 1998

Attempt has been made to delineate the areas which exhibit differential voter preferences at the two levels of electoral contest; to identify the nature of temporal variation of party support in these areas; and to demarcate the strong and weak, stable and unstable areas of support for each party in each set of elections.

Vote Trends and Support Surfaces for INC

Various categories of vote trends and support surfaces have already been explained in the preceding Chapter 6. An analysis of Assembly unitwise vote trends and pattern of support stability for INC for both pairs of elections indicates strong moorings of the party in the region. In both sets of elections, the floor support for the party was above 30 per cent in nearly 60 per cent of the Assembly units. During Lok Sabha 1991 and Assembly elections 1993, the level of party support was constant or growing in 69.44 per cent Assembly units. In 22 Assembly units the party support suffered a decline out of which in 12 Assembly units the floor support was above 30 per cent.

55.56 per cent (40) Assembly units exhibited significant variation in their party preferences which was manifest as growth or decline in party vote share. Out of these 34.72 per cent (25) units exhibited striking variations in their support for INC over the two elections, large enough to be coded as 'unstable support surfaces'.

In 1998 elections, 72.22 per cent (52) Assembly units provided a constant or growing support to INC. It suffered a decline in votes in 20 Assembly units, out of which its floor support was above 30 per cent in seven Assembly units.

In 73.61 per cent (53) Assembly units the party's vote share fluctuated large enough to be termed as 'growth' or 'decline'. Out of these, in 36 Assembly units the fluctuation was high enough to be classified as 'unstable'. There was a marked increase in the extent of 'unstable surface' (in terms of proportion of Assembly units) in 1998 elections as compared to Lok Sabha 1991 and Assembly elections 1993. This may be attributed to the swing in favour of the party during Assembly elections 1998. The stable and strong surface of the party expanded and comprised of 22 Assembly units as compared to 17 in 1991–93. The weak surface shrunk to one Assembly unit from six in 1991–93. This underlines the relatively stronger standing of the party in 1998 elections vis-à-vis 1991–93 elections.

Lok Sabha 1991 and Assembly Elections 1993

Table 7.1 summarizes the vote trends of INC at various levels of floor support during Lok Sabha 1991 and Assembly elections 1993.

Table 7.1 *Vote Trends for INC at Various Floor Support Levels (Lok Sabha 1991 and Assembly Elections 1993)*

Floor Support	*Number of Constituencies*			*f*	*%f*
	Constant support	*Growth*	*Decline*		
0 to 10%		1	1	2	2.78
10 to20%	1	3	1	5	6.94
20 to 30%	6	9	8	23	31.94
30 to 40%	13	4	8	25	34.72
40 to 50%	10	1	4	15	20.83
50 to 60%	2			2	2.78
N	32	18	22	72	
% Total	44.44	25.00	30.56		

Note: f indicates no. of Assembly units at various floor support levels
% f indicates relative frequency at various floor support levels
% Total indicates proportion of total Assembly units considered (72 for INC)

INC acquired a constant support in 44.44 per cent (32) Assembly units out of which in 25 Assembly units the floor support was more than 30 per cent and in 12 Assembly units , it was above 40 per cent. The party recorded a growth in support, indicating larger vote share in Assembly elections, in 18 Assembly units. A constant electoral support at high floor levels and growth in electoral support in areas of low floor support indicates an improvement in party performance.

The party's vote share declined in 30.56 per cent (22) Assembly units. In 12 Assembly units the decline was at high floor levels above 30 per cent which bespeaks of its competitive status despite the decline.

Figure 7.1 A illustrates the spatial pattern of vote trends of INC during Lok Sabha 1991 and Assembly elections 1993. The support for the party recorded a growth in majority of Assembly units of Alwar and Bharatpur districts, southern and western parts of Sawai Madhopur district, Khetri, Lachhmangarh in Sikar and Dholpur. The level of support remained constant in Tonk, south eastern and central part of Jaipur, eastern part of Sawai Madhopur, Dholpur (except Dholpur unit) and southern part of Bharatpur districts. The support remained constant in major part of Jhunjhunu and scattered parts of Sikar also. The support for the party declined in central part of the study area comprising of south western and central part of Jaipur district, entire Dausa district except Sikrai, Jaipur district, north eastern and south-eastern part of Sawai Madhopur, central and eastern parts of Sikar district, Pilani, Gudha, Rajgarh and Nagar.

The proportion of Assembly units comprising various support surfaces for INC in 1991–93 have been shown in Table 7.2.

Table 7.2 *Classification of Assembly Units on the Basis of Stability of Support for INC and BJP (1991–93, 1998–98)*

Support	*INC*		*BJP*	
	A	*B*	*A*	*B*
Stable	47 (65.28)	36 (50)	43 (60.56)	32 (45.07)
(a) Strong	17 (23.61)	22 (30.56)	22 (30.98)	9 (12.68)
(b) Weak	6 (8.33)	1 (1.39)	2 (2.81)	7 (9.86)
(c) Marginal	24 (33.33)	13 (18.05)	19 (26.76)	16 (22.54)
Unstable	25 (34.72)	36 (50)	28 (39.44)	39 (54.93)

Note: A – Lok Sabha 1991 and Assembly Elections1993
B – Lok Sabha 1998 and Assembly Elections 1998

Figures in parentheses indicate proportion of total number of Assembly units considered for a party in an election (71 for BJP and 72 for INC).

The party had a stable support in 65.28 per cent (47) Assembly units. Nearly 34.72 per cent (25) Assembly units exhibited unstable support for the party. The party received a consistent strong support in 17 and marginal support in one third of the Assembly units. Its performance was weak in 68.33 per cent Assembly units. A detailed

Table 7.3 *Support Surfaces for INC (LS 1991 – VS 1993)*

Strong Areas			*Weak Areas*			*Marginal Areas*	*Vulnerable Areas*
a	*b*	*c*	*a*	*b*	*c*		
Kekri (SC)	*Phulera	*Lachhmangarh (SC)	Behror	Nagar	Khairthal (SC)	Kumher	**Kaman**
Bassi	*Lalsot (ST)			Rajgarh (ST)	Sawai Madhopur	Bansur	**Tizara**
Fatehpur	*Todabhim (ST)				Alwar	Bharatpur	**Ramgarh**
Toda Rai Singh	*Neem-ka-Thana					Kathumar (SC)	**Jaipur Rural**
						Bari	Amber
Bairath						Sanganer	**Dholpur**
*Sri Madhopur						Bayana	Pilani
*Niwai (SC)						Rajakhera	Mandawar
*Jhunjhunu						Banipark	Hindaun
*Uniara						Nawalgarh	Dudu (SC)
*Mandawa						Gangapur	**Nadbai**
*Sikrai (ST)						Tonk	Sapotra (ST)
*Danta Ramgarh						Thanagazi	Bandikui
						Weir (SC)	Dhod

Cont'd...

...Cont'd

		Surajgarh (SC)	**Kotputli**
		Chomu	Khandar
		Johari Bazaar	Khetri
		Karauli	**Khandela**
		Malpura	Bamanwas
		Phagi (SC)	Dausa (SC)
		Hawa Mahal	Jamwa Ramgarh
		Gudha	Mahuwa
		Rupbas (SC)	**Sikar**
		Lachmangarh	Kishan Pole
			Deeg

Note: *Assembly units in which the party won in both elections.
Names in bold indicate Assembly units where fluctuation was more than 20 per cent

Figure 7.1

Spatial Pattern of Vote Trends and Stability of Support for INC in North East Rajasthan (Lok Sabha 1991 and Assembly Elections 1993)

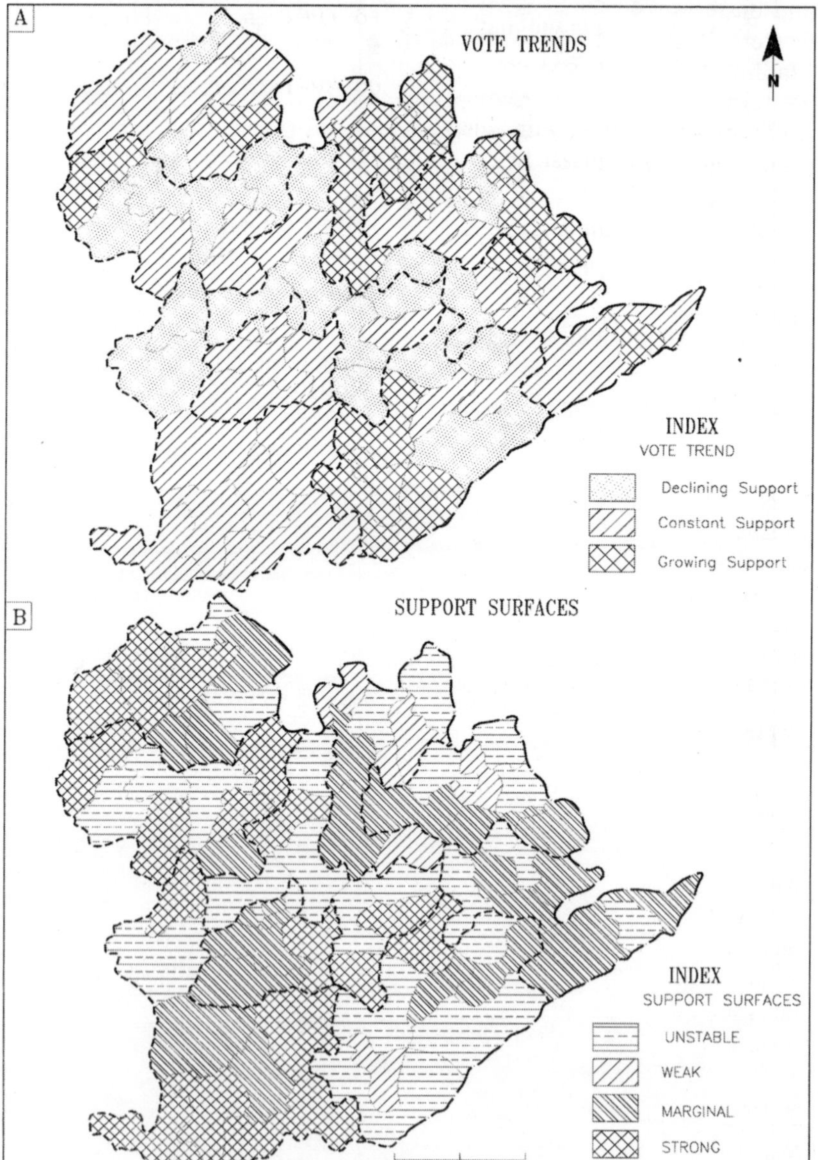

classification of Assembly units comprising various support surfaces has been given in Table 7.3.

As Figure 7.1 B reveals INC enjoyed a strong support in southern and eastern parts of Tonk district, substantial area in Sikar district, western Jhunjhunu and scattered pockets of Dausa, Jaipur and Sawai Madhopur districts. The party received marginal support in north western and central part of Tonk, eastern parts of Jhunjhunu, southern urbanized areas of Jaipur, central part of Alwar, southern parts of Bharatpur, eastern parts of Sawai Madhopur and parts of Dholpur districts. Areas of weak support were mainly located in Alwar district along with Nagar and Sawai Madhopur. Areas of unstable support included northern part of Alwar, north-eastern Bharatpur, western and southern Sawai Madhopur, central parts of Sikar and Jaipur districts along with some parts of Jhunjhunu and Dausa districts.

Among the strong areas, INC won the majority in both the elections in Sri Madhopur, Jhunjhunu, Mandawa, Danta Ramgarh, Neem-ka-Thana, Lachhmangarh (SC), Uniara, Niwai, Phulera, Lalsot, Sikrai and Todabhim.

Lok Sabha 1998 and Assembly Elections 1998

In Lok Sabha 1998 and Assembly elections 1998, the vote trends for INC at various levels of floor support indicated substantial hike in the voter appeal of the party as compared to the former pair of elections. There was a decline in the number of Assembly units where INC received constant support or suffered a decline in support, whereas there was a marked rise in the number of Assembly units recording growth (Table 7.4).

Table 7.4 *Vote Trends for INC at Various Floor Support Levels (Lok Sabha 1998 and Assembly Elections 1998)*

Floor Support	*Number of Constituencies*				
	Constant Support	*Growth*	*Decline*	*f*	*%f*
0 to 10%		1		1	1.39
10 to20%		8	5	13	18.06
20 to 30%	2	5	8	15	20.83
30 to 40%	5	11	5	21	29.17
40 to 50%	6	5	2	13	18.06
50 to 60%	6	3		9	12.50
N	19	33	20	72	
% Total	26.39	45.83	27.78		

Note: f indicates no. of Assembly units at various floor support levels
% f indicates relative frequency at various floor support levels
% Total indicates proportion of total Assembly units considered in an election (72 for INC)

In 26.39 per cent (19) Assembly units the party received constant support out of which in 17 Assembly units the level of floor support was higher than 30 per cent. In 45.83 per cent (33) Assembly units the vote share of the party registered a growth. The party support declined in 27.78 per cent (20) Assembly units, although the floor support level was higher than 30 per cent in seven Assembly units. Thus the voter appeal of the party improved remarkably during Assembly elections 1998 which earned the party a sweeping success on 54 seats. Total 53 (73.61%) Assembly units exhibited significant fluctuation in support for INC in terms of growth or decline. This underlines variation in voter preferences at different levels of electoral contests.

The Assembly unitwise vote trends for INC have been mapped in Figure 7.2A. The party support was constant or growing in the western part of the study area whereas the party lost support in most of the Assembly units located in the eastern part of the study area, particularly the south eastern region. The areas of growth in support included entire Jhunjhunu and major part of Sikar district, the urbanized south eastern part of Jaipur district along with Chomu and Phagi, Niwai, eastern part of Dholpur district and some scattered parts in eastern Bharatpur, northern part of Alwar, Dausa and Todabhim of Karauli districts. Constant support was recorded in eastern part of Sikar, south western and central part of Jaipur, south western and central part of Tonk, southern part of Sawai Madhopur and scattered parts in east of Bharatpur and Alwar districts. Eastern and northern part of Jaipur, northern part of Sawai Madhopur, Karauli, western Dholpur, central part of Alwar and scattered parts in Dausa, Bharatpur and Tonk were areas of declining support for INC. It is interesting to note that the party support recorded a growth in five of the six urban Assembly units. In majority of the reserved Assembly unit too, the party support either registered a growth or remained constant. Hindaun, Sapotra, Bamanwas and Dudu were exception to this trend.

In terms of stability of support there was an expansion in the 'unstable' support surface. There was a drop of 11 Assembly units (15.28%) in the 'stable support surface' vis-à-vis 1991–93.

The strong surface included 22 (30.56%) Assembly units and the marginal support surface comprised of 13 (18.05%) Assembly units. Bansur was the only area where party's position was weak (Table 7.2). A detailed classification of Assembly units into various support surfaces has been made in Table 7.5.

As Figure 7.2B clearly indicates that the western part comprising of Jhunjhunu, Sikar, Tonk (except Dudu and Uniara), Jaipur (except Kotputli and Bassi) and southern part of Sawai Madhopur districts was

Figure 7.2

Spatial Pattern of Vote Trends and Stability of Support for INC in North East Rajasthan (Lok Sabha 1998 and Assembly Elections 1998)

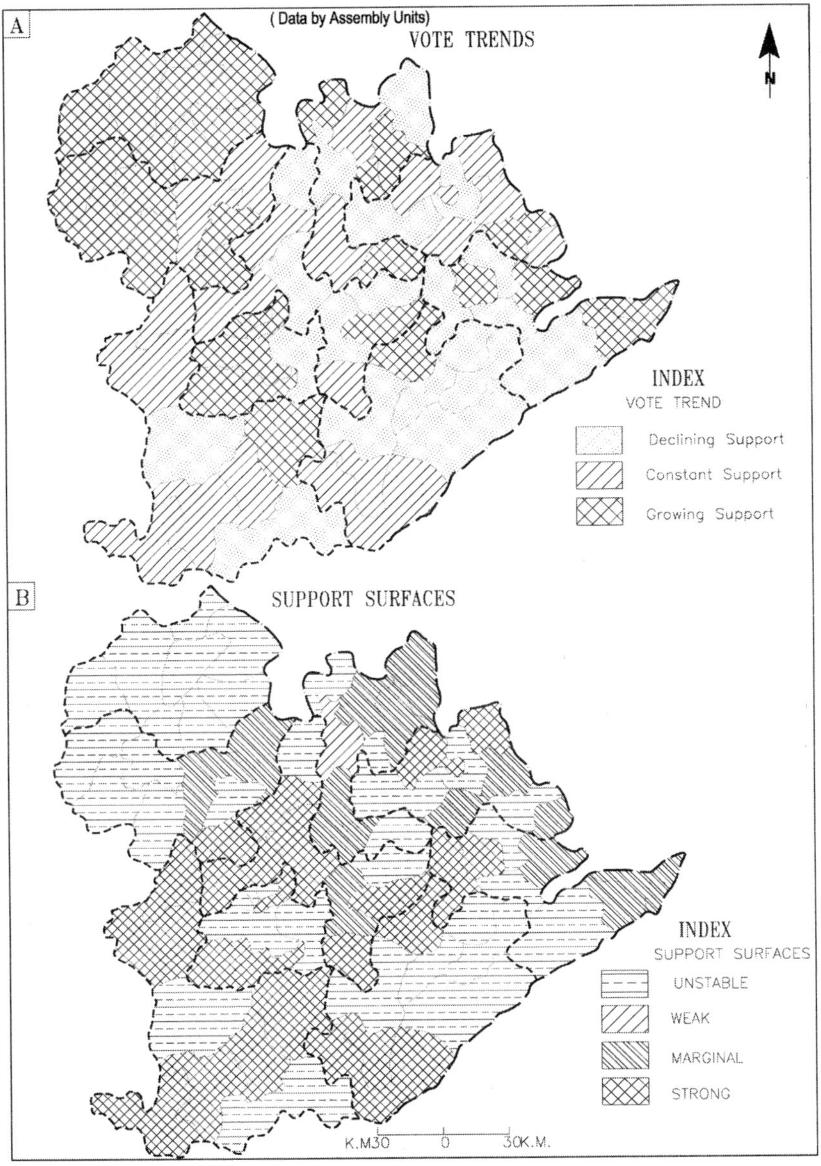

predominantly a region of either strong and stable support or unstable but growing support for the party. Thus the performance of the party was quite impressive in this region. Similar pattern also existed in northern part of Alwar, eastern part of Bharatpur and Dholpur districts, Todabhim, Lalsot, Sikrai, Rajgarh, Mahuwa and Weir. The unstable areas of the eastern part of the study region including northern Sawai Madhopur and major part of Karauli districts; Bari, central part of Alwar district; Nagar, Nadbai, Bayana and Bandikui exhibited an opposite trend where the party lost support during the Assembly elections. Bassi, Kotputli, Dudu and Uniara were also included in this category.

Among the Assembly units classified as 'strong' areas for the party, it won Johari Bazaar, Jaipur Rural and Ramgarh in the Assembly elections. In the remaining Assembly units, it won in both the elections.

Vote Trends and Support Surfaces for BJP

An analysis of vote trends and extent of various kinds of support surfaces for BJP in the two pairs of elections reveals a drastic change in the party's standing in the region in this period. The party had an appreciable standing in the region during 1991–93 but in 1998 elections its performance was dismal. During 1991–93, the floor support of party's votes was above 30 per cent in 60.56 per cent (43) of the Assembly units. The party support remained constant or registered a growth in 45.07 (32) Assembly units. In 54.93 per cent Assembly units, the vote share of the party suffered a decline which underlines the widespread impairment in party's voter appeal in Assembly elections 1993. The support for the party was unstable in 39.44 per cent (28) Assembly units.

In 1998 elections, the proportion of Assembly units in which the floor support for the party was above 30 per cent stooped down to 19.72 per cent. In less than a third of the total Assembly units, it received constant and growing support. In 69.01 per cent (49) Assembly units, the party faced a decline in vote share out of which in 35 Assembly units the floor support was below 30 per cent. The unstable support area comprised of 54.93 per cent (39) Assembly units. The stable support area shrunk to 45.07 per cent and there was a decline of 18.3 per cent in the proportion of Assembly units where the party was 'strong'. Proportion of Assembly units which comprised 'weak' support area for the party increased by 7.05 per cent. Thus BJP, after eight years of continuous rule in the State, was a victim of voters' wrath which adversely affected its showing in Lok Sabha as well as Assembly elections held in 1998.

Table 7.5 *Support Surfaces for INC (LS 1998 – VS 1998)*

Strong Areas			*Weak Areas*			*Marginal Areas*	*Vulnerable Areas*		
a	*b*	*c*	*a*	*b*	*c*				
*Sawai Madhopur	*Jamwa Ramgarh	Johari Bazaar		Bansur		Mandawar	**Surajgarh**	**Gangapur**	Rajgarh (ST)
*Kaman		Jaipur Rural				Khairthal (SC)	**Gudha**	**Bassi**	Kishanpole
Ramgarh	*Mahuwa	*Chomu				Tizara	**Jhunjhunu**	**Kotputli**	Sanganer
*Khandar (SC)		*Weir (SC)				Thanagazi	**Pilani**	Bayana	Sri Madhopur
*Kekri (SC)		*Todabhim (ST)				Kathumar (SC)	**Mandawa**	**Bamanwas**	**Uniara**
*Toda Rai Singh		*Phagi (SC)				Dholpur	**Fatehpur**	**Lachhmangarh (SC)**	Kumher
*Dudu (SC)		*Sikrai (ST)				Rupbas (SC)	**Dhod**	Hawa Mahal	Banipark
*Lalsot (ST)		*Niwai (SC)				Deeg	**Nawalgarh**	Bari	Bandikui
*Phulera						Neem-ka-Thana	**Malpura**	Lachhmangarh	**Sikar**
*Bairath						Raja Khera	**Nagar**	**Sapotra**	**Danta Ramgarh**
*Amber						Khandela	Nadbai	**Alwar**	**Behror**
*Tonk						Bharatpur	Khetri	Karauli	Hindaun (SC)
						Dausa			

Note: *Assembly units in which the party won in both elections.
Names in bold indicate Assembly units where fluctuation was more than 20 per cent

Lok Sabha 1991 and Assembly Elections 1993

There was considerable fluctuation in electoral support for BJP in the region during Lok Sabha 1991 and Assembly elections 1993. The support for the party remained constant in nearly one-third (33.80%) Assembly units, whereas in 47 (66.20 per cent) of them the fluctuation in vote share of the party over the two elections was large enough to be termed as 'growth' or 'decline'. There was a growth in 11.27 per cent (8) Assembly units whereas there was a decline in 54.93 per cent (39) Assembly units (Table 7.6). This indicates substantial variation in electoral support for BJP in Assembly elections vis-à-vis Lok Sabha ones, which was on the negative side in major part of the study region.

The level of support for the party was constant above the floor support level of 30 per cent in 20 (28.17 per cent) Assembly units. Seven (9.86%) Assembly units at floor support level above 30 per cent recorded a growth in vote share and 16 (22.54%) Assembly units retained a floor support of 30 per cent despite a decline.

Table 7.6 *Vote Trends for BJP at Various Floor Support Levels (Lok Sabha 1991 and Assembly Elections 1993)*

Floor Support	*Number of Constituencies*				
	Constant Support	*Growth*	*Decline*	*f*	*%f*
0 to 10%	—	—	3	3	4.23
10 to20%	1	—	8	9	12.68
20 to 30%	3	1	12	16	22.54
30 to 40%	7	4	10	21	29.58
40 to 50%	8	3	5	16	22.54
Above 50	5	—	1	6	8.45
N	24	8	39	71	
% Total	33.80	11.27	54.93		

Note: f indicates no. of Assembly units at various floor support levels
% f indicates relative frequency at various floor support levels
% Total indicates proportion of total Assembly units considered for an election (71 for BJP)

Figure 7.3(A) clearly illustrates vote trends for BJP in various parts of the study region. The areas of growing support were few and widely scattered over parts of Sikar, Tonk, Dausa, Sawai Madhopur and Bharatpur districts. The party support was constant in Kekri, southern and urban areas of Jaipur, central and north eastern Tonk, parts of Sikar district, Mandawa, Khandar, Hindaun, Khairthal and

Figure 7.3

Spatial Pattern of Vote Trends and Stability of Support for BJP in North East Rajasthan (Lok Sabha 1991 and Assembly Elections 1993)

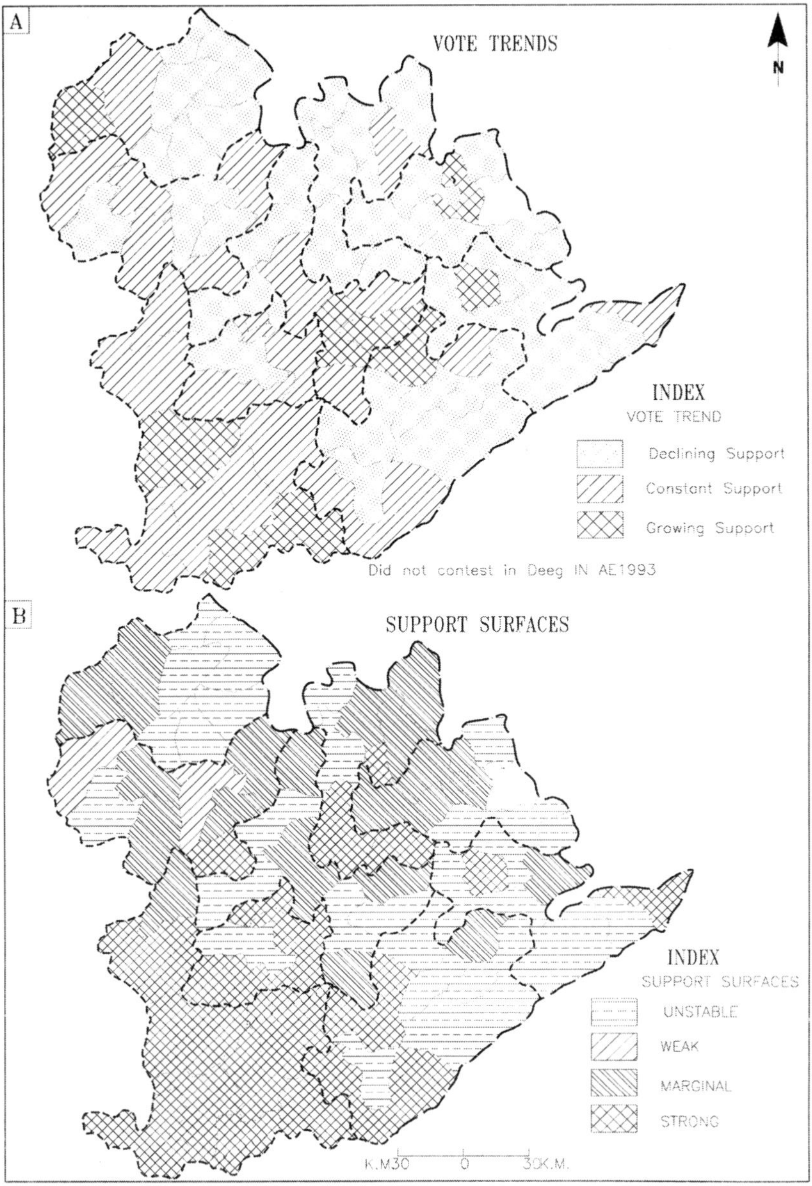

Raja Khera. In the northern and eastern part of the study area comprising of majority of the Assembly units of Jhunjhunu, Alwar, Bharatpur, Dholpur and Sawai Madhopur districts along with northern and central part of Jaipur district there was widespread decline in support for the party.

The party received a stable support in 60.56 per cent (43) Assembly units, of which its support was 'strong' in 22, 'marginal' in 19 and 'weak' in 2 Assembly units (Table 7.2). A detailed classification of the Assembly units into various support surfaces for BJP has been given in Table 7.7.

Predominantly southern part of the study area comprising of Tonk district, southern part of Jaipur district and western part of Sawai Madhopur district provided strong stable support to BJP. In the northern part of the study area, it acquired strong support in very few areas including southern part of Alwar, Weir and Rajakhera. Except Bharatpur, the party had a strong base in all urban Assembly units. The party received a marginal support in eastern part of Alwar, western part of Bharatpur, major part of Sikar and scattered pockets in Jaipur, Dausa and Sawai Madhopur districts. Unstable support surface included eastern Jhunjhunu, north western Alwar, major part of Dausa and Bharatpur, western Dholpur, eastern Sawai Madhopur and central parts of Jaipur districts (Figure 7.3B). It is noteworthy that except some parts in Dausa district, the direction of fluctuation in the unstable areas was largely negative.

The party held a weak standing in Lachhmangarh and Khandela in Sikar district. Except Niwai, Bamanwas and Uniara, BJP claimed the majority in both the elections in the Assembly units classified as 'strong' surfaces.

Lok Sabha 1998 and Assembly Elections 1998

In Lok Sabha and Assembly elections of 1998, the electoral support for BJP was constant in only 21.13 per cent (15) Assembly units. It recorded a growth in 9.86 per cent (7) Assembly units whereas in 68.01 per cent (49) Assembly units it suffered a decline. This indicates widespread decline in support base of the party during Assembly elections of 1998 (Table 7.8).

As illustrated by Figure 7.4A the areas of growth in support for the party were located in north eastern part of the study area comprising of Assembly units of Alwar district, Kumher and Mahuwa. The party recorded a growth in Bamanwas also. The areas of constant support were mainly located in Tonk, Sikar, central part of Jaipur and Alwar districts. The party suffered a decline in Jhunjhunu, western, southern and central

Table 7.7 *Support Surfaces for BJP (LS 1991 – VS 1993)*

Strong Areas			*Weak Areas*			*Marginal Areas*		*Vulnerable Areas*		
a	*b*	*c*	*a*	*b*	*c*					
*Rajakhera	*Thanagazi	Uniara	Lachhmangarh (SC)	Khandela		Bandikui	Khairthal	**Kaman**	Jhunjhunu	Amber
Niwai (SC)	*Alwar	*Weir				Mandawa	Phulera	**Nadbai**	Sikrai (ST)	Sapotra (ST)
*Tonk	*Rajgarh (ST)	*Malpura				Mandawar	Nagar	**Bansur**	Nawalgarh	
*Chomu	Bamanwas					Kotputli	Fatehpur	Pilani	**Gangapur**	
*Dudu	*Jaipur Rural					Hindaun (SC)	Danta Ramgarh	Karauli	Bari	
*Toda Rai Singh	*Banipark					Lachhmangarh	Jamwa Ramgarh	**Behror**	**Kumher**	
*Khandar						Lalsot		**Gudha**	**Sanganer**	
*Phagi(SC)						Rupbas (SC)		**Mahuwa**	Bharatpur	
*Kekri						Ramgarh		**Sawai Madhopur**	Todabhim	
*Bassi						Tizara		**Kathumar (SC)**	Bairath	
*Johari Bazaar						Neem-ka-Thana		**Bayana**	**Dausa**	
*Kishanpole						Sikar		Dhod	Dholpur	
*Hawa Mahal						Sri Madhopur		Surajgarh	Khetri	

Note: *Assembly units in which the party won in both elections
Niwai was won by INC in both elections
Names in bold indicate Assembly units where fluctuation was more than 20 per cent

Sikar, southern Sawai Madhopur, Karauli, Dholpur, entire Dausa except Mahuwa and major parts of Jaipur and Bharatpur districts.

Table 7.8 *Vote Trends for BJP at Various Floor Support Levels (Lok Sabha 1998 and Assembly Elections 1998)*

Floor Support	*Number of Constituencies*			*f*	*%f*
	Constant support	*Growth*	*Decline*		
0 to 10%	—	—	2	2	2.82
10 to20%	1	1	18	20	25.35
20 to 30%	2	3	15	20	21.13
30 to 40%	7	3	10	20	14.08
40 to 50%	5	—	4	9	5.63
Above 50					
N	15	7	49		
% Total	21.13	9.86	69.01		

Note: f indicates no. of Assembly units at various floor support levels
% f indicates relative frequency at various floor support levels
% Total indicates proportion of total Assembly units contested in an election

The stable support surface of the party comprised of 32 (45.07 per cent) Assembly units. It held a strong support in nine Assembly units, a marginal support in sixteen Assembly units and weak support in seven Assembly units (Table 7.2).

The unstable support surface comprised of 54.93 per cent (39) Assembly units. As evident from Figure 7.4B and Table 7.9, the strong area included Assembly units of south western part of Tonk district, some parts of Jaipur city, Phulera, Lalsot and Dholpur. Marginal support surface included Assembly units of Sikar, central part of Jaipur, northern part of Sawai Madhopur, central part of Bharatpur, south eastern part of Alwar districts, Lachhmangarh, Sikrai, Niwai and Phagi. The party support was weak in Assembly unties of central part of Alwar, northern part of Bharatpur district and Khandela. The unstable support surface, comprising major part of the study area, included whole of Jhunjhunu and Karauli districts, south eastern and north western Tonk, southern and eastern Sawai Madhopur, major part of Dholpur and Dausa, southern Bharatpur and northern part of Alwar districts, Dhod and Neem-ka-Thana. The adverse wave affected the traditional stronghold of the party, urban Assembly units of Jaipur too and it lost substantially in Banipark and Kishanpole. Bassi, Dudu, Jamwa Ramgarh and Kotputli were also included in unstable area. A comparative examination of Figure 7.4A and B reveals that in majority of the unstable areas, the fluctuation in support was on the negative side.

Figure 7.4

Spatial Pattern of Vote Trends and Stability of Support for BJP in North East Rajasthan (Lok Sabha 1998 and Assembly Elections 1998)

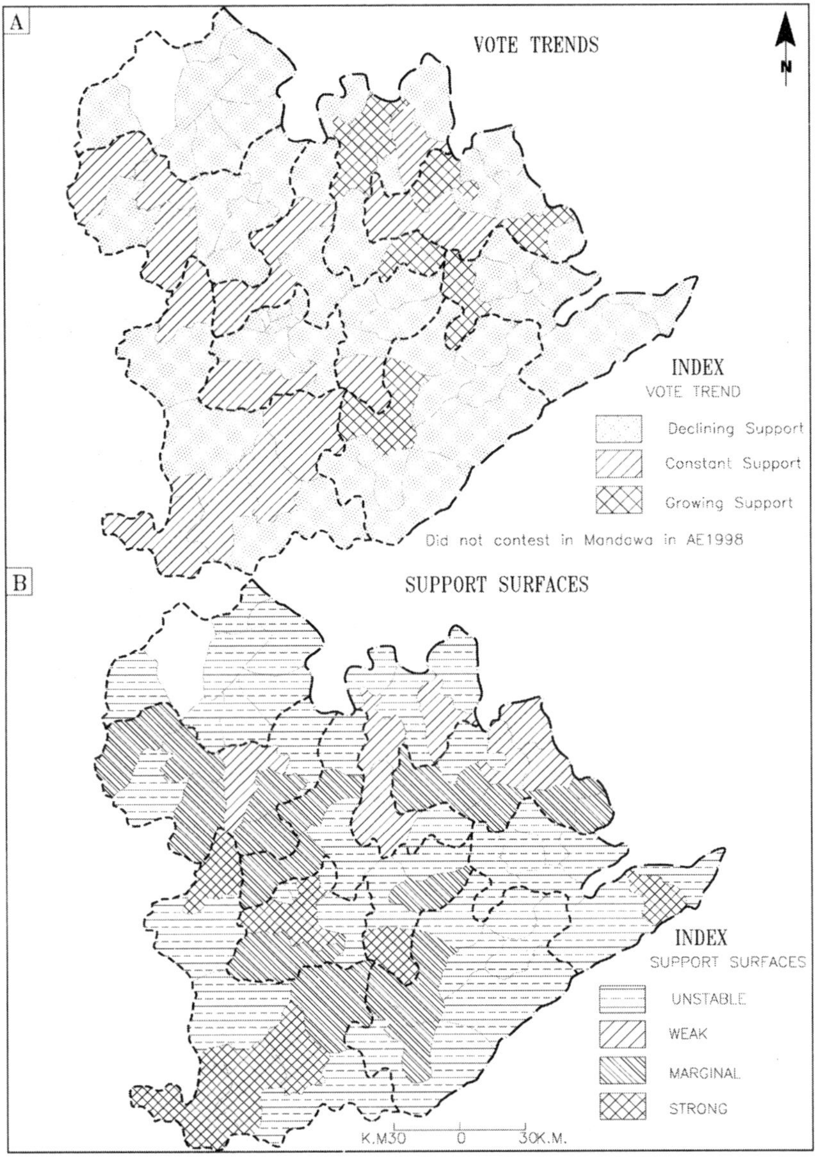

Table 7.9 *Support Surfaces for BJP (LS 1998 – VS 1998)*

Strong Areas			*Weak Areas*			*Marginal Areas*		*Vulnerable Areas*		
a	*b*	*c*	*a*	*b*	*c*					
Tonk	*Dholpur		Khairthal (SC)	Nagar	Bansur	Lachhmangarh	Sri Madhopur	**Nadbai**	**Nawalgarh**	Gudha
Phulera	Sanganer			Deeg		Kathumar (SC)	Amber	**Dhod**	Weir(SC)	Uniara
Lalsot (ST)	Johari Bazaar			Kaman		Sawai Madhopur	Bamanwas	**Gangapur**	**Jamwa Ramgarh**	Ramgarh
Toda Rai Singh	*Hawa Mahal			Thanagazi		Chomu	Sikrai (ST)	**Jhunjhunu**	**Karauli**	Rupbas
Kekri(SC)				Khandela		Bharatpur	Phagi (SC)	**Todabhim (ST)**	**Khetri**	Mahuwa
						Danta Ramgarh	Bairath	**Hindaun**	**Neem-ka-Thana**	Surajgarh (SC)
						Kumher	Sikar	**Sapotra**	**Pilani**	**Kishanpole**
						Niwai (SC)		**Tizara**	Khandar (SC)	**Jaipur Rural**
						Lachhmangarh (SC)		**Bayana**	Dudu(SC) Mandawar	Fatehpur
								Dausa	**Bari**	**Banipark**
								Alwar	Bandikui	Malpura
								Behror	Rajakhera	Bassi
								Rajgarh (ST)	Kotputli	

Note: *Assembly units in which the party won in both elections
Names in bold indicate Assembly units where fluctuation was more than 20 per cent

Among the 'strong' areas, BJP won both the elections of Lok Sabha and Assembly in Dholpur and Hawa Mahal. In Sanganer and Johari Bazaar it won in Lok Sabha elections whereas in the remaining areas it lost to INC.

Contextual Explanation of Party Votes

The following section examines the relationship between the electoral performance of the two parties, i.e. INC and BJP and the various socio-economic contexts.

Contextual Explanation of Electoral Performance of INC

As an essentially aggregative party, the Congress party derives varying degree of electoral support from all sections of society. Owing to this 'umbrella' character of the party, one cannot expect strong or consistent relationship between electoral performance of the Congress and the various socio-economic contexts. The nature and magnitude of association between the electoral performance of the Congress party and the various socio-economic contexts has changed from election to election. This fluctuating nature of ecological relationship is essentially a function of the changes in socio-political climate prevailing at the time when the elections are held.

Urban Developmental Context

Regression of the Assembly unitwise vote percentage of INC on the factor scores of the Urban Developmental Context for the two sets of elections yielded the following results:

Election	*Regression Equation*	*R*	R^2
LS 1991	$Y = 37.58 - 1.175 X_1$	–0.096	0.009
VS 1993	$Y = 36.64 - 3.235^{**}X^1$	–0.302	0.091
LS 1998	$Y = 38.38 - 1.330 X_1$	–0.102	0.010
VS 1998	$Y = 41.537 + 2.689^{*}X_1$	0.203	0.041

Note: * Significant at 0.05 level
** Significant at 0.01 level
Y stands for vote share of INC per Assembly unit and X for Urban Developmental Context

The relationship between Urban Developmental Context and Congress votes was negative in three of the four elections which suggest a relatively weaker support for the party in more urbanized areas of the study region. Assembly elections 1998 were an exception when the association was positive, although moderate. This reversal in the trend may be understood in the wake of the strong swing in favour of the party in Assembly elections 1998 which earned it substantial support in the urbanized areas too. The explanatory strength of the context has varied between 0.9 per cent in 1991 to 9.1 per cent in 1993. During both the Lok Sabha elections, the influence of the context on spatial pattern of support for the party was negligible whereas during the Assembly elections, it was moderately significant.

Social Backwardness Context

The regression of vote share of INC on factor scores of Social Backwardness Context yielded the following results for the two sets of elections:

Election	*Regression Equation*	*R*	R^2
LS 1991	$Y = 37.58 + 3.085^{**}X_2$	0.251	0.063
VS 1993	$Y = 36.64 + 0.561\ X_2$	0.052	0.003
LS 1998	$Y = 38.38 + 7.827^{**}X_2$	0.599	0.359
VS 1998	$Y = 41.537 + 0.878\ X_2$	0.066	0.004

Note: ** Significant at 0.01 level
Y stands for vote share of INC per Assembly unit and X for Social Backwardness Context

There has been a consistent positive relationship between the Social Backwardness Context and electoral support for the Congress party. This underlines a relatively stronger performance of the party in the areas where the proportion of weaker sections of population is higher. In both the Lok Sabha elections, the relationship was stronger vis-à-vis the Assembly elections. The level of explanation offered by this context varied between 0.3 per cent in 1993 to 35.9 per cent in Lok Sabha elections 1998. During Lok Sabha elections 1991, the backward classes were more in favour of Janata Dal in wake of the Mandal issue. Nonetheless, a moderate positive association obtained between the context and the distribution of party votes (significant at 0.01 level). During Lok Sabha elections 1998, the context accounted for a significant 35.9 per cent of the vote variance of the party, owing to the return of this traditional vote bank of the party in its favour. It is notable that this context did not exercise any significant influence on the voting pattern of the party during both the Assembly elections.

Gender Context

By regressing the vote share of the INC on factor scores of the Gender Context, the following equations were obtained:

Election	Regression Equation	R	R^2
LS 1991	$Y = 37.58 + 6.840^{**}X_3$	+0.557	0.310
VS 1993	$Y = 36.64 + 1.802\ X_3$	+0.168	0.028
LS 1998	$Y = 38.38 -0.374^{**}X_3$	–0.029	0.001
VS 1998	$Y = 41.54 + 3.921^{**}X_3$	+0.296	0.088

Note: ** Significant at 0.01 level
Y stands for vote share of INC per Assembly unit and X for Gender Context

The relationship between the vote share of the INC and the Gender Context has been quite inconsistent. In 1991, 1993 and Assembly elections 1998, the relationship was positive whereas in Lok Sabha elections 1998, it was negative. In Lok Sabha 1991 and Assembly elections 1998 the association between the two was considerably strong (significant at 0.01 level). The strong positive correlation of 0.56 in 1991 indicates strong support for the party in areas scoring high on gender context. Contrastingly, in Lok Sabha elections 1998, the party performance was relatively weak in such areas. The variation in party votes explained by the gender context varied from 0.1 per cent in Lok Sabha elections 1998 to 31 per cent in Lok Sabha elections 1991. Among the Assembly elections, the influence of the context was significant in 1998 elections when it accounted for 8.8 per cent of variation in electoral support for the party.

Overall Explanation of Voting Pattern of INC

Regression of the vote percentage of INC on the factor scores of all the three contexts together, for all the four elections, yielded the following results:

Table 7.10 *R^2 Values of Multiple Regression of Electoral Performance of INC on the Three Individual Contexts and Combined Context of All Three Taken Together*

Elections	X_1	X_2	X_3	X_{1-3}
LS 1991	0.009	0.063	0.310	0.382
VS 1993	0.091	0.003	0.028	0.122
LS 1998	0.010	0.359	0.001	0.370
VS 1998	0.041	0.004	0.088	0.133

In both the Lok Sabha elections, the various socio-economic contexts together explained significant proportion of the vote variance of Congress, which was 38.2 per cent and 37 per cent in 1991 and 1998 respectively. The influence of the contexts was markedly lower during the Assembly elections. The combined explanatory strength of the three contexts was 12.2 per cent in 1993 and 13.3 per cent in Assembly elections 1998. The results conform to our hypothesis that secular forces exercise greater influence on voter preferences in elections for the Lok Sabha vis-à-vis the Assembly ones.

The actual complexion of the influence of individual contexts has varied from election to election. None of the contexts has exercised a consistent influence in determining the voting levels in favour of the INC. In Lok Sabha elections 1991, Gender Context exercised a decisive influence in determining the vote share of the party. Social Backwardness Context was also significant but the influence of Urban Developmental Context was negligible. In the consecutive Assembly elections, Urban Developmental Context explained 9.1 per cent of the vote variance of the party while the influence of the remaining two contexts was of very low order. In Lok Sabha election 1998, Social Backwardness context was most important amongst the three contexts, whereas the remaining two contexts were insignificant. The situation reversed in Assembly elections 1998 when Urban Developmental context and Gender Context were important although the explanation offered by them was not of very high order.

The varying complexion of the relationship between the INC votes and various contexts can be attributed to the aggregative nature of the Congress party, which draws support from all sections of the society, although the actual complexion of this support varies from one election to the next.

Contextual Explanation of Electoral Performance of BJP

It is expected that a party with well defined ideology and restricted mass base would bear more clearly defined relationships with the socio-economic contexts. BJP is often considered to possess its base among the upper sections of the society particularly in urban areas. It is also often termed as the 'Hindu Chauvinist' party. This image has usually alienated the minorities and weaker sections of the society from the party. In 1991, the Ram Janmabhoomi issue further buttressed this image. The event drew the sentiments of the females, aged and higher sections of the society, especially the Hindus in favour of the party. The party resorted to a moderate approach during the 1998 elections and made several efforts to shed its Hindu cover and to woo the minorities as well as the backward classes.

Urban Developmental Context

By regressing the Assembly unitwise percentage vote share of BJP on the factor scores of Urban Developmental Context, the following equations were obtained:

Election	*Regression Equation*	*R*	R^2
LS 1991	$Y = 43.397 + 5.510^{**}X_1$	0.547	0.29
VS 1993	$Y = 34.901 + 4.941^{**}X_1$	0.348	0.120
LS 1998	$Y = 39.178 + 5.748^{**}X_1$	0.569	0.324
VS 1998	$Y = 28.499 + 3.082^{**}X_1$	0.269	0.072

Note: ** Significant at 0.01 level
Y stands for vote share of BJP per Assembly unit and X for Urban Developmental Context

The results corroborate our contention that BJP derives high support in the urbanized areas of the study region. The relationship between the party votes and the urban developmental context was fairly strong as well as positive (significant at 0.01 level) in all the elections. In the Lok Sabha elections, the party enjoyed high level of support in the urban and semi-urban areas of the region which is indicated by the high positive correlations of above 0.5 in both the elections. The relationship was relatively less pronounced during Assembly elections. The explanatory strength of this context was highest in Lok Sabha elections 1998 when it accounted for 32.4 per cent of vote variance of the party. The influence of this factor was lowest in Assembly elections 1998 when the explanation offered by the context declined to 7.2 per cent. This drop in support for the party in urban areas can be attributed to the widespread anti-incumbency wave against the party in these elections. Nevertheless, at both levels of electoral contest, BJP commands a fairly strong base in the urbanized areas.

Social Backwardness Context

Regression of vote percentage of BJP on the factor scores of Social Backwardness Context yielded the following results:

Election	*Regression Equation*	*R*	R^2
LS 1991	$Y = 43.397 + 2.511^{**}X_2$	0.249	0.62
VS 1993	$Y = 34.901 + 5.812^{**}X_2$	0.409	0.166
LS 1998	$Y = 39.178 + 1.772^{**}X_2$	0.175	0.031
VS 1998	$Y = 28.499 + 3.450^{**}X_2$	0.300	0.090

Note: ** Significant at 0.01 level
Y stands for vote share of BJP per Assembly unit and X for Social Backwardness Context

It is interesting to note that the relationship between vote percentage of BJP and Social Backwardness Context was significant and positive in all the four elections (significant at 5 per cent level or above). The relationship was stronger during the Assembly elections vis-à-vis the Lok Sabha ones. The vote variance of the party accounted for by this context varied between 3.1 per cent in Lok Sabha 1998 to 16.6 per cent in Assembly elections 1993. The higher explanatory strength of the context during Assembly elections as compared to the Lok Sabha ones indicates a relatively higher support for the party in the areas scoring high on this factor during Assembly elections.

Gender Context

Following regression equations were obtained by regressing the vote share of BJP on the factor scores of Gender Context:

Election	*Regression Equation*	*R*	R^2
LS 1991	$Y = 43.397 - 1.252 X_3$	–0.124	0.015
VS 1993	$Y = 34.901 + 1.082 X_3$	0.076	0.005
LS 1998	$Y = 39.178 + 1.887^{*} X_3$	0.187	0.035
VS 1998	$Y = 28.499 + 2.576^{**} X_3$	0.224	0.050

Note: * Significant at 0.05 level. ** Significant at 0.01 level.
Y stands for vote share of BJP per Assembly unit and X for Gender Context

The relationship between vote percentage of BJP and the Gender Context was negative in 1991 and positive in the remaining three elections. But the association between the two was significant only in the 1998 elections. Although no consistent trend was observable in the relationship between spatial distribution of BJP support and Gender Context at the two levels of electoral contest, but a gradual increase in the explanatory power of the factor as well as magnitude of the correlation coefficient indicates a gradual strengthening of the party in areas scoring high on this factor. The level of explanation offered by this factor varied from a minimum of 0.5 per cent in 1993 to 5 per cent in Assembly elections 1998.

Overall Explanation of Voting Pattern of BJP

'R^2' values obtained by Regression of votes polled by BJP in the two pairs of elections with the individual contexts and all the three contexts taken together are as under:

Table 7.11 *R^2 Values of Multiple Regression of Electoral Performance of BJP on the Three Individual Contexts and Combined Context of All Three Taken Together*

Election	X_1	X_2	X_3	X_{1-3}
LS 1991	0.29	0.062	0.015	0.377
VS 1993	0.120	0.166	0.005	0.293
LS 1998	0.324	0.031	0.035	0.390
VS 1998	0.072	0.090	0.050	0.213

The combined explanatory strength of the three contexts was higher in both the Lok Sabha elections as compared to the Assembly elections. Thus, in case of BJP also, the socio-economic factors have exerted a greater influence in determining the spatial pattern of electoral support of the party during Lok Sabha elections vis-à-vis the Assembly ones. In the Lok Sabha elections the combined explanatory strength of the three contexts was 37.7 per cent in 1991 and 39 per cent in 1998. The variation accounted for by these contexts although relatively lower than Lok Sabha, was fairly high during the Assembly elections also being 29.3 per cent in 1993 and 21.3 per cent in 1998.

An examination of the relative influence of individual contexts reveals that during Lok Sabha elections Urban Developmental context has been very significant in determining vote levels of the party. The party enjoys a substantial support in more urbanized areas during Lok Sabha contests. During Assembly elections, Social Backwardness Context has been more important as compared to the Urban Development Context. Thus, the support for the party becomes more evenly spread among various sections of the society as well as less restricted to the urbanized areas, during Assembly elections. Closer identification of candidates with the electorate, personal liking and disliking and local caste equations may be the underlying cause behind the increased support for the party in areas with higher proportion of socially backward classes among voters.

The Gender Context was significant only during 1998 elections. A comparison of the R^2 values for INC and BJP reveal that the combined explanatory strength of the three contexts was on par for both the parties during Lok Sabha Elections. But during Assembly elections, the combined 'R^2' values for BJP were much higher than INC. This indicates that BJP commands a more clearly identifiable socio-economic base than INC. Thus, our hypothesis that 'the areal pattern of support in socio-economic terms is more clearly defined for parties whose ideologies, programmes and appeals to particular sections of the community are more sharply drawn', which is BJP in this case, is upheld.

A comparison of 'R^2' values of individual contexts, for various election years, for both the parties underlines the difference in the socio-economic base of the two parties. BJP receives a consistent greater support in the urbanized areas, especially during Lok Sabha elections and an increased support in areas with higher proportion of socially backward classes in Assembly elections. Contrastingly, INC exhibits striking variations in the nature of spatial spread of its support base during various elections.

8 Findings and Analysis

Limitation of the Study

The discussions encompassing identification and ecological analysis of spatial patterns of various aspects of political phenomena including election results in nine Lok Sabha and 72 Assembly constituencies of north east Rajasthan reveal some important facts about the electoral behaviour. Before summarizing the major findings of this work it is worthwhile to mention some of the limitations this work suffers from and provide due explanations for the same.

The entire course of this research work was centred around

1. seeking maximum possible explanations (in terms of geographical influences) to the spatial patterns of voting behaviour; and
2. covering maximum possible aspects of voting behaviour within the scope of the study.

Nevertheless, the work does suffer from certain limitations imposed primarily by non availability of relevant data. The study in no way seeks to suggest that our selected set of socio-economic variables is the sole or even the most important determinants of party performance. After an extensive review of the findings of the previous researches in this field in Indian context, the hypotheses were conceived and tested with respect to the study area. The socio-economic variables were selected in line with the hypotheses. Attempt has been made to measure just how far the selected variables 'account for' variations in electoral performances. Voting behaviour is a highly complex reality and even a comprehensive and perfect set of socio-economic measures would leave much to be explained, simply because political life is not merely derivative but enjoys its own autonomy. A host of political variables such as political mobilization, party electoral campaigns, voter perceptions, the roles of various associational groups and so on, are of vital importance in determining the electoral outcomes but the same could not be incorporated in the analysis due to lack of susceptibility to generalization and meaningful measurement.

Caution is called for in interpreting the findings if the ecological fallacy is to be avoided. The findings speak only of the political behaviour of areas of given characteristics, not that of individuals or even of sections of the community within such areas. The study was restricted in scope to examine the voting behaviour in relation to levels of socio-economic development, gender and class composition of the population of electoral areas. The scholar fully acknowledges the paramount importance of factors such as caste affiliations, religion and patron client relationships in guiding the voter choices but the same could not be incorporated in the study due to non availability of data. Nevertheless, influence of these factors was examined to some extent while investigating the contemporary issues at the time of respective elections.

The correlations obtained while measuring the associations between the electoral variables and socio-economic variables were not very strong in terms of magnitude. But small values of 'R' should not be misinterpreted so as to infer that the relationships are not significant. It should be remembered that the significance of correlation coefficient depends on the sample size. Even small values of 'R' are significant when number of observations is large. For N=72, an absolute value of 'R' greater than or equal to 0.236 (2/%N) is significant at 5 per cent level of significance. Therefore keeping in mind the large number of observations, the small values of 'R' should not be considered meaningless.

Summary of the Findings

On the basis of exhaustive examination of the research problem to the maximum possible extent within the limitations of this study we arrive at the following findings:

Non Uniformity of Representation in Lok Sabha and State Assembly

High degree of non-uniformity exists among the Lok Sabha and Assembly constituencies with respect to their geographical extent which follows the variations in the distribution of population in the region. Disparities in the population size in various parts of the study area can, to a large extent, be explained in terms of diversities in topographic characteristics, climate and level of development of the area which is turn explain the disparate geographical extent of the electoral areas. The Lok Sabha constituencies and their Assembly segments located in the plain, fertile and relatively more developed

Eastern Plains in the northern, central and eastern part of the study area are smaller in size and those situated in the region of undulating, dissected topography and relatively less developed southern part of the study area are larger. Consequently, Assembly constituencies of Alwar, Bharatpur, Dausa and Jaipur districts are relatively small in terms of area whereas constituencies lying in Sawai Madhopur, Tonk and Karauli districts are relatively large in the region. Smallest constituencies include those comprising the major urban centres and adjoining semi urban areas.

The spatial organization of constituencies is based on the guiding principle of 'uniformity of representation' but in practice it no longer stands true. On the one hand no revision of boundaries of Lok Sabha and Assembly constituencies had been made from 1976 to 2008 and on the other hand the growth of population had taken place at a fast but differential rates in various constituencies, wide disparities had emerged among the electoral districts with respect to sizes of both electorate and population. Thus the mass of population represented in the Lok Sabha or State Assembly by an elected member became far from being homogeneous. Disparities also existed in the size of population practically eligible to exercise its franchise which is a direct function of the age structure of population in the region. The spatial variations in inter constituency electorate size can to a large extent be attributed to topography, nature of economy, level of urbanization and spacing of urban centres in the region. Higher concentration of electorate occurs in regions having closely spaced urban centres, having high population density and high ratio of electorate to total population whereas lower concentration was observed in lesser populated areas, predominantly those having uneven topography and rural economy resulting in low population density and low electorate-population ratio. The absolute size of electorate is relatively large in Assembly constituencies located in Jaipur, Sikar and parts of Jhunjhunu district. Tonk, Alwar, Bharatpur and Karauli districts are areas where the electorate size is relatively small. Over the four elections, Sawai Madhopur, Dausa and Dholpur districts and the region comprising Jaipur city and surrounding areas have recorded substantial increase in their electorate size. Consequent upon natural addition to the electorate by way of more people attaining the required age and revision of electoral rolls, moderate changes have occurred in the size of registered voters in majority of Assembly units with time. The changes have been more pronounced in relatively more urbanized areas where immigration of population, owing to better living conditions and larger employment opportunities, has contributed significantly. In Bharatpur district, the electorate size of all the Assembly units (except Bharatpur) has been strikingly low in all the elections. On the extreme end are the urban Assembly units of Jaipur, where the electorate size has been far greater as compared to the remaining part of the study region, in all the elections.

Excluding the urban Assembly units with extremely high density of electorate, density of electorate in the region varied from 50 to 300 persons per sq. km. Low density areas included the Assembly units located in south western, southern and western part of the study area whereas moderate and high densities occurred in northern, central and north eastern parts.

Poll Participation

The study focussed on two main aspects of electoral participation in the study area – the identification and ecological analysis of spatial patterns of voter turnout in the region and comparison of spatial patterns of voter participation at the two levels of electoral contest, i.e. for the State Assembly and the Lok Sabha.

The extent of voter participation in the region is certainly not very satisfactory. More than one-third of the eligible and registered voters fail to exercise their franchise during each election. Whereas less than a half of the electorate cast their vote in 1991, the effective voter turnout was around 60 per cent in the other three elections, with minor variations.

Nevertheless, the results pointed towards a positive trend as the voter turnout in the area registered an increase in both Lok Sabha and Assembly elections, between 1991 and 1998. The level of electoral participation in the study area was higher and more evenly distributed during Assembly elections than the Lok Sabha ones. Part of the explanation for such differential levels of voting may lie in the fact that in State level elections, the electorate feels far more personally involved in the election process than the Lok Sabha elections. The complexion and policies of the ruling party in the State legislature directly influence the voter. Thus the voter feels more obliged to exercise his right to choose his government in the State level elections. Higher degree of identification of the candidate among the voters, local level caste or community affiliations or conflicts, personal likes and dislikes also draw larger number of electorate to the polling booths during Assembly elections. Moreover, the reactions of the voter to the local issues, practices and performance of the incumbent State government which have influenced his day to day life also find expression in the elections to the State Assembly. The Union government in New Delhi, in comparison, is a distant entity.

The spatial pattern of electoral participation was strikingly different at the two levels of elections. The study area could be delineated into well-defined regions of high and low turnout during Lok Sabha elections, whereas during Assembly elections it was marked by a scattered pattern. Various Assembly units exhibit marked variation in the rate of voter turnout at different levels of elections. During Lok Sabha elections, the rate of voter turnout was fairly high in northern part of the study area, including Assembly units of Jhunjhunu, Sikar, Alwar, Bharatpur and Dausa whereas it was quite low in the southern part of the study area including Assembly segments of all the reserved constituencies, i.e. Tonk, Sawai Madhopur and Bayana.

During Assembly elections, south western part of Tonk district, Dholpur district, Bayana, Bassi, Phulera and Sawai Madhopur record substantial increase in turnout. Increased turnout in areas which are part of reserved constituencies in Lok Sabha elections and turn into general seats in Assembly elections underlines the class bias in voting decision of electorate. The Assembly segments of Dausa Lok Sabha constituency exhibit a contrasting behaviour, wherein the level of turnout is higher during Lok Sabha elections vis-à-vis the Assembly ones. The urban Assembly segments invariably poll low at both levels of electoral contest.

The voter turnout in the study area was positively associated with polling booth accessibility. Although the relationship was not very significant in 1991 and 1993, but for both elections held in 1998 results were significant. Ratio of polling booths accounted for 11 per cent of the variation in voter turnout in Lok Sabha elections 1998. Proportion of small villages explained 7 per cent and 15 per cent of the total variation in voter turnout in Assembly and Lok Sabha elections 1998 respectively. The influence of degree of polling booth accessibility was greater in Lok Sabha elections than the Assembly ones.

The bivalent analysis of voter turnout with margins of victory as a measure of degree of party competition revealed a close positive relationship between the two in the region. The results were not very encouraging for 1991; were relatively better in 1993 but a clear, close, positive correspondence obtained between level of voter participation and closeness of party competition in 1998 elections.

The selected socio-economic variables were found to exercise a decisive influence in determining the level of voter participation in the region. In 1991, the selected set of variables explained 21 per cent of the total variation in voter turnout which increased to nearly 50 per cent in Assembly elections 1998. The socio-economic attributes of the study area exert a greater influence in determining the spatial patterns of voter turnout during Assembly elections vis-à-vis the Lok Sabha ones, as indicated by higher R^2 values for Assembly elections. The spatial patterns of voter participation are more clearly defined in socio-economic terms during Assembly elections as compared to the Lok Sabha elections.

The results obtained by stepwise regression, bivariate and partial correlation coefficients of voter turnout and the selected socio-economic variables, may be summarized as under:

- The rate of electoral participation has been relatively high in rural areas having higher concentration of agricultural workers and agricultural labourers. A consistent positive relationship between proportion of agricultural workers and voter turnout indicates higher degree of political awareness in rural areas. The rate of participation in agricultural class was higher in Assembly elections as compared to the Lok Sabha ones.
- Contrastingly, the rate of electoral participation was relatively lower in the urban, densely populated areas with higher proportion of population engaged in other services. During Lok Sabha elections, the urban areas manifested a fluctuating behaviour but during Assembly elections the rate of electoral participation has been conspicuously low.
- The rate of voter participation was relatively low in areas where the concentration of Scheduled Caste (SC)/Scheduled Tribe (ST) population was high.

Lok Sabha elections 1998 exhibited a somewhat different socio-economic complexion of voter turnout and significant positive associations obtained between voter turnout and sex-ratio, proportion of working population and literacy rate, the attributes quite insignificant in the other three elections. This indicates that there was an increased turnout in areas of higher concentration of female electorate and literate population. Lok Sabha elections 1998, following the downfall of Vajpayee government were held amidst an air of political and economic instability and there was widespread dissent among the masses because of soaring prices of daily utility commodities especially edible oil and onion, along with discontent in the State against the misgovernance of Shekhawat government. These factors may have led to increased turnout among segments of population hitherto indifferent to franchise.

The analysis of spatial pattern of voting turnout points towards some issues of grave concern. There is a growing apathy among the urban voters towards the electoral process, 'since the impression has been gaining ground that the elections make little difference to the actual nature and complexion of governments' (Dikshit and Sharma, 1983). The entrenched capitalist interests have to a great extent succeeded in organizing society and its control mechanism in its own best interests so that the political process of elections has become of only minor importance in the distribution of real power (Miliband, 1969). Besides, since political parties like competing business houses invariably converge in terms of their policy proposals (Downs, 1957), changes in government are seldom followed by any spectacular policy shifts. This indifference of urban, educated, enlightened section of the society from the election process is certainly not conducive for a healthy growth and functioning of a democracy. This may result in a decline in turnout in the rural areas too since 'there is good deal of evidence to show that changes in the pattern of participation in rural areas are often preceded by such changes in urban areas' (Dikshit and Sharma, 1983).

The low rates of participation in reserved constituencies, particularly during Lok Sabha elections and increased turnout in the same areas with change in nature of the constituency during Assembly elections indicates abstention on part of general class of voters to vote for a SC/ST candidate rather than a low turnout among reserved category of voters themselves. The Assembly seats reserved for SC/ST candidates also registered a marked rise during the Assembly elections in general. These trends underline the paramount importance of caste and class considerations in political decision-making of voters and portend the deep-seated social cleavages prevailing in the region.

In the multiparty political system, very often the party obtaining little more than 40 per cent share of total votes polled acquires majority. In a situation where only a segment of the total population is eligible to cast its vote and less than two-thirds of the electorate actually go to the poll booth at the time of election; moreover the candidate acquiring less than a half of the total effective votes is held victorious. Does the representative thus elected truly represent the choice of the majority? Under these circumstances, the democracy, in true sense, as a government 'by all the people' has remained unrealized.

Party Performance

The political scene in the study area is more or less bipolar during both levels of elections and the real contest is mainly between Congress (INC) and Bhartiya Janata Party (BJP) in major parts of the study area. These two parties together bag nearly three-fourths of the total votes polled in the region except for minor fluctuations in some areas consequent upon emergence of a third force which are, more often than not, defectors or former party candidates contesting as independents. During the elections studied, it was a two party contest in majority of the constituencies in both the Lok Sabha elections. In Assembly elections, the contest was multi-cornered in a few regions especially in south western Sikar and parts of Alwar and Bharatpur districts where other parties like BSP, RJD, CPI, CPM, JP, JD and often independents have posed a tough contest before the two parties and have also achieved localized success. The communist parties are conspicuously influential in south western Sikar especially Dhod and in north eastern part of the study area comprising Behror, Bansur, Khairthal, Kaman, Nagar, and Lachhmangarh. The contest has often been three cornered and small parties like BSP, RJD, JP, and JD have taken lead.

A comparison of spatial patterns of party victories clearly underlined that the party preferences of the electorate undergo marked shifts from election to election. The electorate of the study area is highly moved and influenced by the prevailing issues. Performance of the seating candidate and personality of the candidate also influence his choice to a great extent. Performance of Congress in Dausa during Lok Sabha elections speaks of the popularity enjoyed by Late Rajesh Pilot in the area and so is true about the sweeping success of Late Shish Ram Ola in Jhunjhunu in Lok Sabha elections 1998. Substantial seats won by independents especially during Assembly elections and appreciable standing of Mahendra Kumari in Alwar in Lok Sabha election 1998 clearly manifest the decisive influence of personality and popularity of the candidates on voter preferences. The influence of Mandir and Mandal issue and consequent alienation of minorities and backward classes from INC translated into losses to the party in 1991 whereas the wrath of the voters against the misgovernance in the eight years of BJP rule in the State expressed itself in the rout of BJP in Assembly elections 1998.

A comparison of spatial patterns of performance of Congress and BJP during the four election years revealed that the electoral support for both the parties has lacked territorial consistency. The territorial distribution of electoral support for both the parties was more clearly defined during Lok Sabha elections whereas during the Assembly elections it was more scattered. Substantial changes in the electoral preferences were observed in some areas, between Lok Sabha and successive Assembly election. This may be accounted for by the fact that in case of the recruitment of representatives for the State legislature caste affiliation and other local, regional interests and conflicts play a more pronounced role in influencing voters' choices. This often leads to considerable differences in the patterns of voting even between such constituencies whose socio-economic-political characteristics are similar.

The degree and variability of distribution of electoral support for each party is different at the two levels of election. In both sets of elections, the average per seat vote share of BJP was higher and more evenly spread, as compared to INC, in Lok Sabha elections. During the Assembly elections, the average vote share of the party declined, variability increased and the number of seats won also reduced. Contrastingly, Congress improved upon its performance in Assembly elections as compared to the Lok Sabha ones, which was reflected in higher per Assembly unit average vote share, more even distribution of support and increased number of Assembly units where the party gained majority. Except for elections when there was a wave against or in favour of a particular party, as was the case in 1991 (against INC in the first phase of poll) and Assembly elections 1998 (against BJP), the two parties stood on par in terms of their vote share in Assembly 1993 and Lok Sabha elections 1998.

The electoral support for INC did not undergo any drastic changes during the four elections, both in terms of overall strength and uniformity of distribution. Contrastingly, the support for BJP underwent substantial fluctuations during this period. This indicates that whereas Congress has held a stable support base in the region, the support of BJP has been prone to voter's changing hues. The electoral support for BJP exhibited marked territorial concentration during Assembly elections whereas it was more evenly spread during Lok Sabha elections.

The analysis of vote trends further confirmed the territorial inconsistency in level of support for both the parties between the two levels of electoral contest. The vote trends of the Congress reaffirmed that it received relatively higher support in Assembly elections as compared to Lok Sabha elections. The extent of unstable support surfaces, 34.72 per cent Assembly units in 1991–93 and 50 per cent Assembly units in 1998 elections underlines the fluctuations in electoral preferences between Lok Sabha and Assembly elections. The performance of the party was better in 1998 Lok Sabha and Assembly elections as compared to 1991 and 1993 elections. The core areas of INC support which have consistently rendered strong support to the party, have been southern and north eastern part of Tonk district, Kekri, central part of Jaipur district comprising Chomu, Phulera and Bairath Assembly units, Bandikui and Lalsot in Dausa district and Todabhim. In the remaining part of the north east Rajasthan the support for the party had been subjected to fluctuations from election to election.

BJP had an appreciable standing in the region in 1991–93 but suffered substantial loss in territorial extent of its support base during

1998 elections particularly during Assembly elections 1998. In 1991–93 elections the electoral support for the party suffered a decline in 54.93 per cent Assembly units and during 1998 elections the proportion of these Assembly units increased to 69.01 per cent. This clearly reveals that the level of electoral support for the party tends to be lower in the Assembly elections vis-à-vis the Lok Sabha elections. The extent of unstable support surface, 39.44 per cent and 54.93 per cent in 1991–93 and 1998 elections respectively, points towards the high degree of fluctuation in voter preferences for the party at the two levels of electoral contest. The core areas of BJP support included south western part of Tonk district, Kekri, urban segments of Jaipur district, eastern part of Dholpur district and northern part of Sawai Madhopur district.

Both INC and BJP have a fairly, identifiable socio-economic base in the region. During Lok Sabha elections, more than one-third, 38.2 per cent in 1991 and 37 per cent in 1998, of the variation in spatial distribution of support for INC was accounted for by the selected socio-economic determinants. Similarly, the selected variables explained 37.7 per cent and 39 per cent of the vote variance of BJP during Lok Sabha elections 1991 and 1998 respectively. The influence of these variables was not of similar strength during the Assembly elections and for both the parties the combined explanatory strength of the three contexts was significantly lower during Assembly elections as compared to the preceding Lok Sabha elections. During both the Assembly elections the spatial distribution of support for BJP was more clearly defined in socio-economic terms (higher R^2 values) than the Congress which connotes that the political support base of Congress is more evenly spread among various sections of the society whereas that of BJP is relatively more confined to particular sections of the society during Assembly elections. The regression of factor scores of individual contexts on Congress votes reveals that the nature and strength of relationship of electoral performance of Congress with individual contexts varies from election to election. The negative relationship of Congress vote with Urban Developmental context in three of the four elections indicates relatively weak performance of the party in more urbanized and developed areas particularly during Assembly elections. In Assembly elections 1998 there was a reversal in this trend and Congress received high degree of support in urban areas too.

Weak positive relationship obtained between Social Backwardness context and INC vote. The relationship was of very low order and insignificant during the Assembly elections. Only in Assembly elections 1998 INC received widespread support in SC/ST majority areas.

The nature and strength of association between INC vote and Gender context has also changed from election to election. This context was explained 31 per cent of the vote variance of the party in Lok Sabha elections 1991. In three of the four elections, the relationship between Gender context and INC vote was positive. The absence of consistent relationship between electoral performance of the Congress and various socio-economic contexts implies that the complexion of the socio-economic support base of the party keeps changing from election to election. This may be explained as being due to umbrella character of the party. The Congress has essentially been an aggregative party, which derives support from all sections of society through in varying degrees depending upon the socio-political climate at the time of elections.

BJP commands a more consistent and clearly identifiable support base in the region which is manifested in the relatively strong and consistent relationships between party's vote share and individual contexts. The party holds a strong base in the more urbanized and developed areas of the region and invariably derives strong support in these areas at both levels of contest. Amidst the widespread disenchantment towards the party in Assembly elections 1998 the party still made an appreciable standing in the urban and semi urban areas. The relationship between Urban Developmental context and BJP vote was relatively stronger during Lok Sabha elections.

The association between Social Backwardness context and BJP vote share was significant and positive in all elections, although it was not of a very high order. The support for the party increased in socially backward majority areas during Assembly elections.

The party gradually improved its performance in areas with high concentration of female population. The relationship of party votes with Gender context was stronger in 1998 elections as compared to 1991–93.

Thus BJP has a more consistent support base in socio-economic terms, contrary to INC. Nevertheless, the degree of support among various sections of the society does fluctuate between different levels of elections.

Relatively lower R^2 values of combined ecological context for Assembly elections indicate that the electoral support for BJP is relatively more evenly spread among various sections of the society during Assembly elections vis-à-vis the Lok Sabha ones.

Thus the surmise that secular forces exercise a greater influence in determining the electoral preferences in Lok Sabha elections than the Assembly ones is upheld. Our analysis also validates the hypothesis that the areal pattern of electoral support is more clearly defined in socio-economic terms for parties whose ideologies, programmes and appeals to particular sections of community are more sharply drawn.

We arrive at the thumb rule that electorates apply quite different sets of consideration in exercising franchise in elections to the State Assembly vis-à-vis the Lok Sabha contests.

Bibliography

Adhikari, Sudeepta (1997). *Political Geography*, Rawat Publications, Jaipur and New Delhi.

Agnew, J.A. (1990). 'From Political Methodology to Geographical Social Theory? A Critical Review of Electoral Geography, 1960–87', in R.J. Johnston, F.M. Shelley and P.J. Taylor (eds), *Developments in Electoral Geography*, Routledge, London, pp. 15–21.

Ahmad, B. (1970). 'Caste and Electoral Politics', *Asian Survey*, 10 (11), pp. 979–92.

—— (1971). 'Political Stratification and the Indian Electorate', *Economic and Political Weekly*, Annual Number 6 (3, 4 and 5), pp. 251–58.

Ahmad, H. (1966). 'Election Data Analysis as a Tool of Research in Political Geography', *Pakistan Geographical Review*, 21, pp. 34–40.

Alford, R.R. (1963). 'The Role of Social Class in American Voting Behaviour', *Western Political Quarterly*, 16, pp. 180–99.

Amani, K.Z. (1970). 'Election in Haryana: A Study in Electoral Geography', *The Geographer*, 17, pp. 27–40.

—— (1972). 'Voting Patterns in Indian Election: Uttar Pradesh – A Case Study', *Geographical Review of India*, 34, pp. 122–33.

—— (1973). 'Electoral Geography and Indian Elections', *Geographical Review of India*, 35, pp. 355–64.

—— (1974). 'Questions Raised by the Map of 1974 Indian Elections', *Professional Geographer*, 26, pp. 207–09.

Bansal, Sudhir (1992). *Spatial Patterns of Voting Behaviour between Parliamentary and Assembly Elections in Rajasthan (1980–85). A Comparative Analysis*, Ph.D. Thesis, Department of Geography, University of Rajasthan, Jaipur.

Barnett, M.J. (1973). 'Aggregate Models of British Voting Behaviour', *Political Studies*, 21, pp. 121–34.

Baxter, L. (1969). *District Voting Trends in India: A Research Tool*, Columbia University Press, New York.

Bhalla, L.R. (2001). *Geography of Rajasthan*, Kuldeep Publications, Ajmer.

Bhalla, R.P. (1973). *Elections in India (1950–72)*, S. Chand, Delhi.

Bhambhri, C.P. (1991). *Elections 1991: An Analysis*, B.R. Publishing Corporation, Delhi.

Bhatkal, R.G. (1967). *Political Alternatives in India*, Popular, Bombay.

Bhunia, S.B. (1968). 'Social and Economic Context of Indian Elections', *Economic Studies*, 8 (11–12), pp. 644–77.

Birdsall, S.S. (1969). 'Preliminary Analysis of the 1968 Wallace Vote in the South East', *Southeastern Geographer*, 9, pp. 55–66.

Blair, H.W. (1979). *Voting, Caste, Community, Society: Explorations in Aggregate Data Analysis in India and Bangladesh*, Young Asia Publications, New Delhi.

Brass, P.R. (1969). *Factional Politics in an Indian State: The Congress Party in Uttar Pradesh*, University of California Press, Berkeley.

—— (1975). 'Ethnic Cleavages in Punjab Party System, 1952–1972', in Barnett et al. (eds), *Electoral Politics in Indian States*, Manohar Book Service, New Delhi, pp. 7–69.

—— (1978). 'Indian Election Studies', *South Asia*, 1 (2), pp. 90–108.

Brunn, S.D., W.L. Hoffman and G.H. Ramsa (1969). 'The Defeat of Youngstown School Levy: A Study in Urban Political Geography', *Southeastern Geographer*, 9, pp. 69–79.

Busteed, M.A. (1975). *Geography and Voting Behaviour*, Oxford University Press, London.

Campbell, A. et al. (1954). *The Voter Decides*, Row Peterson, Evanston.

Census of India (1991), Series 21, Rajasthan, District of Ajmer, Alwar, Bharatpur, Dholpur, Jaipur, Jhunjhunu, Sawai Madhopur, Sikar, Tonk, Directorate of Census Operations, Rajasthan.

Centre for the Study of Developing Societies (1967). *Party Systems and Election Studies*, Allied Publishers, Bombay.

Chandidas, R. (1971). 'Fluctuating Voter Loyalties: Budhlada Assembly Constituency in 1969', *Economic and Political Weekly*, 6 March, p. 592.

—— (1972). 'Poll Participation Slump', *Economic and Political Weekly*, 15 July, pp. 1359–68.

Chandidas, R. et al. (eds) (1968). *India Votes: A Source Book on Indian Elections*, Popular, Bombay.

Chandra, K. (2004). *Why Ethnic Parties Succeed: Patronage and Ethnic Head Counts In India*, Cambridge University Press, Cambridge.

Chibber, P.K. (1999). *Democracy without Associations: Transformations of the Party System and Social Cleavages in India*, Vistaar, New Delhi.

Chowdhary, N.K. (1994). *Assembly Elections, 1993*, Shipra Publications, Delhi.

Conford, J. (1970). 'Aggregate Election Data and British Party Alignments, 1885–1910', in E. Allaedt and S. Rokkan (eds), *Mass Politics*, The Free Press, New York, pp. 106–07.

Cox, K.R. (1968a). 'Suburbia and Voting Behaviour in the London Metropolitan Area', *Annals of the Association of American Geographers*, 58, pp. 111–27.

—— (1968b). 'A Spatial Interactional Model for Political Geography', *East Lakes Geographer*, 4, pp. 58–76.

—— (1969a). 'The Voting Decision in a Spatial Context', *Progress in Geography*, 1, pp. 81–117.

—— (1969b). 'The Spatial Structuring of Information Flow and Partisan Attitudes', in M. Doggan and S. Rokkan (eds), *Quantitative Ecological Analysis in Social Sciences*, MIT Press, Cambridge (Mass.), pp. 157–85.

—— (1971). 'The Spatial Components of Urban Voting Response Surfaces', *Economic Geography*, 47, pp. 27–35.

Crisler, Robert M. (1952). 'Voting Habits in United States', *Geographical Review*, 42, pp. 300–01.

Dahl, R.A. (1966). *Who Governs*, Yale University Press, New Haven and London.

Das Gupta, B. and W.H. Morris-Jones (1969). 'India's Political Arenas: Interim Report on an Ecological Perspective', *Asian Survey*, 9 (6), pp. 399–424.

—— (1975). *Patterns and Trends in Indian Politics: An Ecological Analysis of Aggregate Data on Society and Elections*, Allied Publishers, Delhi, p. 100.

Dean, V.K. (1949). 'Geographical Aspects of Newfoundland Referendum', *Annals of the Association of American Geographers*, 39, pp. 70–77.

Dikshit, H.H. and S.K. Giri (1983). 'Changing Spatial Pattern of the Parliamentary Constituencies in India from 1951–1976', *Geographical Review of India*, 45, pp. 83–95.

—— (1984). 'Concept and Purpose of Electoral Geography', *Transactions of the Institute of Indian Geographers*, 6, pp. 85–88.

Dikshit, R.D. (1971a). 'Geography and Federalism', *Annals of Association of American Geographers*, 61, pp. 97–115.

—— (1971b). 'Military Interpretation of Federal Constitutions: A Critique', *Journal of Politics*, 33, pp. 180–89.

—— (1971c). 'The Failure of Federalism in Central Africa: A Politico-geographical Postmortem', *The Professional Geographer*, 23, pp. 224–29.

—— (1975). *The Political Geography of Federalism: An Inquiry into Origins and Stability*, Macmillan, London and Delhi and John Wiley, New York.

—— (1977). 'The Retreat from Political Geography', *Area*, 9, pp. 234–39.

—— (1979). 'Political Geography', in Moonis Raza (ed.), *A Survey of Research in Geography 1969–1972*, Allied Publishers, New Delhi.

—— (1980). 'On the Place of Electoral Geography in Political Geography', *Transactions of the Institute of Indian Geographers*, 2, pp. 23–28.

—— (1995). 'Geography of Elections: An Introduction to Theory and Practice', in R.D. Dikshit (ed.), *Geography of Elections: The Indian Context*, Rawat Publications, Jaipur and New Delhi, p. 36.

Dikshit, R.D. (ed.) (1995). *Geography of Elections: The Indian Context*, Rawat Publications, Jaipur and New Delhi.

Dikshit, R.D. and J.C. Sharma (1980). 'The 1980 Assembly Elections in Punjab: An Enquiry into Bases of Political Party Support', *Annals of the National Association of Geographers of India*, 2 (1), pp. 36–48.

—— (1981). 'A Solution to the Unit of Analysis Problem in the Electoral Geography of India', *The National Geographical Journal of India*, 27, pp. 14–20.

—— (1982). 'Electoral Performance of the Congress Party in Punjab (1952–1977): An Ecological Analysis', *Transactions of the Institute of Indian Geographers*, 4, pp. 1–15.

—— (1983). 'Trends and Patterns in Voter Turnout in Punjab, 1967–1980: An Ecological Analysis', *The National Geographical Journal of India*, 29, pp. 18–29.

Dikshit, R.D. and S. Singh (1993), 'Friends and Neighbours Influence in Indian Elections: A Case Study of Rural Voting in the Sonepat Parliamentary Constituency (Haryana) 1989', *Asian Profile*, 21, pp. 483–93.

Dikshit, R.D. and Vinod Sharma (1993). 'Voting Preferences in State vis-à-vis National Elections Under a Federal System: A Case Study of Haryana', *Transactions of the Institute of Indian Geographers*, 15 (1), pp. 51–70.

Dikshit, S.K. (1988). 'Spatial Analysis of Electoral Participation in Haryana', *Geographical Review of India*, 50 (2), pp. 1–7.

—— (1993). *Electoral Geography of India with Special Reference to Sixth and Seventh Lok Sabha Elections*, Vishwavidhyalaya Prakashan, Varanasi.

Dixit, Srikant (2004). 'Geographical Determinants of Voting Behaviour in Indian Context', *Geographical Review of India*, 66 (2), pp. 115–21.

Easton, D. (1965). *A Systems Analysis of Political Life*, John Wiley, New York.

Elkins, D.J. (1975). *Electoral Participation in a South Indian Context*, Vikas Publishing House, New Delhi.

Fisher, M. and J.V. Bondurant (1956). *The Indian Experience with Democratic Elections*, University of California, Berkeley.

Goguel, F. (1951). *Geographie des Elections Francaise de 1970 a 1951*, Armand Colin, Paris.

Golledge, R.G., L.A. Brown and F. Williamson (1972). 'Behavioural Approaches in Geography: An Overview', *Australian Geographer*, 12, pp. 59–79.

Gosnell, Harold F. and Norman N. Gill (1935). 'An Analysis of the Presidential Vote in Chicago', *American Political Science Review*, 29, pp. 967–84.

Goyal, O.P. (1969). 'Politics, Caste and Voting Behaviour', *Political Science Review*, 8 (2), pp. 237–44.

Graham, B.D. (1967). 'A Report on Some Trends in Indian Elections: The Case of Uttar Pradesh', *Journal of Commonwealth Political Studies*, 5, pp. 179–99.

Gudgin, G. and P.J. Taylor (1974). 'Electoral Bias and the Distribution of Party Voters', *Transactions of the Institute of British Geographers*, 63, pp. 53–73.

—— (1978). *Seats, Votes and the Spatial Organisation of Election*, Pion, London.

Gupta, R.D. (1985). *Spatial Patterns of Voting Behaviour in the General Assembly Elections in Rajasthan (1967–1980)*, Ph.D. Thesis, Department of Geography, University of Rajasthan, Jaipur.

Handbook for Returning Officers, Election Commission of India, accessed online at www.eci.gov.in.

Haring, Lloyd (1959). 'An Analysis of Spatial Aspects of Voting Behaviour in Tennessee', Unpublished Ph.D. Thesis, University of Iowa.

Hussain, M. and A.M. Mir (1984). 'The Assembly Election in Jammu & Kashmir: A Study in Spatial Voting Behaviour in 1983', *National Geographical Journal of India*, 30, pp. 53–62.

Jalan, Seema (2006a). 'Electoral Performance of Political Parties in a Federal System: A Comparative Study of Indian National Congress and Bhartiya Janata Party in North East Rajasthan', *The Geographer*, 53 (1), pp. 20–35.

—— (2006b). 'Voting Preferences in Lok Sabha vis-à-vis Assembly Elections: A Case Study of Indian National Congress in North East Rajasthan (1991–1993 and 1998)', *Transactions of the Institute of Indian Geographers*, 28 (2), pp. 27–38

—— (2009). 'Status of Electoral Geography and Potential Areas of Research in India', *The Geographer*, 56 (2), July.

Jalan, Seema and R.D. Gurjar (2002). 'Spatial Patterns of Electoral Participation in Lok Sabha and Assembly Elections in North East Rajasthan, India (1991–1993 and 1998)', *Studies in Geography*, 20, pp. 1–20.

Johnston, R.J. (1972). 'Spatial Elements in Voting Patterns at the 1968 Christchurch City Council Elections', *Political Science*, 24 (1), pp. 49–61.

—— (1974). 'Social Distance, Proximity and Social Contact', *Geografiska Annaler*, 566, pp. 57–67.

—— (1976a). 'Parliamentary Seat Redistribution: More Opinions on the Theme', *Area*, 8, pp. 30–34.

—— (1976b). 'Spatial Structure, Plurality System and Electoral Bias', *Canadian Geographer*, 20, pp. 310–28.

—— (1977a). 'Principal Components Analysis and Factor Analysis in Geographical Research: Some Problems and Issues', *South African Geographical Journal*, 59, pp. 30–44.

—— (1977b). 'The Electoral Geography of an Election Campaign', *Scottish Geographical Magazine*, 93, pp. 98–108.

—— (1978). *Multivariate Statistical Methods in Geography: A Primer on the General Linear Model*, Longman, London.

—— (1979). *Political, Electoral and Spatial Systems: An Essay in Political Geography*, Clarendon Press, Oxford.

—— (1987). *Money and Votes*, Croom Helm Ltd., New York.

Johnston, R.J., F.M. Shelley and P.J. Taylor (1990). *Developments in Electoral Geography*, Routledge, London.

Kasperson, R.E. and J.V. Minghi (eds) (1969). *The Structure of Political Geography*, Aldine, Chicago.

Kay, S.A. (1991). *Introduction to the Analysis of Political Data*, Prentice Hall, New Jersey.

Key, V.O. (1968). *The Responsible Electorate*, Belknap Press of Harvard University Press, Cambridge, Mass.

Khan, R. (1969). 'Charminar: Communal Parties and Electoral Behavior in Hyderabad City', *Political Science Review*, 8 (1), pp. 569–90.

—— (1971). 'Muslim Leadership and Electoral Politics in Hyderabad: A Pattern of Minority Articulation', *Economic and Political Weekly*, 6 (15), pp. 783–94.

Khan, R., B.A.P. Sharma and K.R. Acharya (1975). *Electoral Politics in Andhra Pradesh: An Interpretation of Multivariate Factors in Political Behavior of Voters in Two Selected Constituencies*, Monograph, Osmania University, Hyderabad.

King, Gary (1997). *A Solution to the Ecological Inference Problem: Reconstructing Individual Behaviour from Aggregate Data*, Princeton University Press, Princeton.

Kondo, N. (2007). 'Election Studies in India', *Discussion Paper No. 98*, Institute of Developing Economies, JETRO, Japan.

Kothari, R. (1970). *Caste in Indian Politics*, Orient Longman, New Delhi.

Kothari, R. (ed.) (1967). 'Party Systems and Election Studies', *Occasional Papers of the Centre for Developing Society No. 1*, Allied Publishers, Bombay.

Krehbiel, E. (1916). 'Geographical Influences in British Elections', *Geographical Review*, 2, pp. 419–32.

Krishna, M.P. (1967). *Elections, Candidates and Voters*, Sterling, New Delhi.

Lalwani, M. (1999). 'Elections and Macro Policy Signals: Political Budget Cycle Hypothesis', *Economic and Political Weekly*, 11 September.

Lewis, P.F. (1965). 'Impact of Negro Migration on the Electoral Geography of Flint, Michigan, 1932–62: A Cartographic Analysis', *Annals of the Association of American Geographers*, 55, pp. 1–25.

Lewis, P.W. and G.E. Skipworth (1966). 'Some Geographical and Statistical Aspects of the Distribution of Votes in Recent General Elections', University of Hull, Department of Geography, Miscellaneous Series, No. 32.

Lipset, S.M. (1960). *Political Man*, Garden City, Doubleday, p. 187.

—— (1967). *Party System and Voter Alignments: Cross-National Perspectives*, The Free Press, New York.

Manual of Election Law, accessed online at www.eci.gov.in.

McPhail, I.R. (1971). 'Recent Trends in Electoral Geography', *Proceedings of the Sixth New Zealand Geography Conference*, Christchurch, 1, pp. 7–12.

Milbrath, L.W. (1965). *Political Participation*, Rand McNally, Chicago, p. 142.

Mishra, S.N. et al. (1982). *The Tribal Voting Behaviour: A Case Study of Bihar Tribes*, Concept Publishing Company, New Delhi.

Mishra, V.C. (1976). *Geography of Rajasthan*, National Books Trust, New Delhi.

Narain, I. and M. Sharma (1969). 'Election Politics in India: Notes Towards Empirical Theory', *Asian Survey*, 9 (3), pp. 202–20.

Narain, I. et al. (1978). *Election Studies in India: An Evaluation*, Allied Publishers, New Delhi.

Narain, Iqbal (1971a). 'Democratic Interlude for Nation Building: 5th Lok Sabha Elections', *Economic and Political Weekly*, 6, pp. 38–47.

—— (1971b). *Fifth Lok Sabha Election in Rajasthan: Constituency Profiles*, Mimeographed, Department of Political Science, University of Rajasthan, Jaipur.

Narain, R. (1970). *Voting Behaviour in Uttar Pradesh*, Monograph, University of Lucknow, Lucknow.

Newton, K. (1976). *Second City Politics: Democratic Processes and Decision-Making in Birmingham*, Oxford University Press, London.

Norris, Robert E. and L.L. Haring (1980). *Political Geography*, A Bell and Howell Company, Columbus.

Pal, S. (1972). *Indian Elections Since Independence*, Election Archives, New Delhi.

Palmer, N.D. (1976). *Elections and Political Development: The South Asian Experience*, Vikas Publishing House, Delhi.

Pattabhiram, M. (ed.) (1967). *General Elections in India: An Exhaustive Study of Main Political Trends*, Allied Publishers, New Delhi.

Paullin, C.O. (1932). *Atlas of the Historical Geography of the United States*, American Geographical Society, New York.

Pomper, G.M. (1976). *Voter's Choice*, Light and Life Publishers, New Delhi.

Prasad, R.C. (1975). *The Mature Electorate*, Ashish, New Delhi.

Prescott, J.R.V. (1959). 'The Functions and Methods of Electoral Geography', *Annals of Associations of American Geographers*, 49, pp. 296–304.

—— (1969). 'Electoral Studies Political Geography', in R.F. Kasperson and J.V. Minghi (eds), *The Structure of Political Geography*, Aldine Press, Chicago, pp. 376–83.

—— (1972). *Political Geography*, Methuen & Co., London.

Reynolds, D.R. (1969a). 'A "Friends and Neighbours" Voting Model as a Spatial Interactional Model for Electoral Geography', in K.R. Cox and R.G. Golledge (eds), *Behavioural Problems in Geography*, Northwestern University Press, Evanston, pp. 81–100.

—— (1969b). 'A Spatial Model for Analyzing Voting Behaviour', *Acta Sociologica*, 12, pp. 122–30.

—— (1974). 'Spatial Contagion in Political Influence Processes', in K.R. Cox, D.R. Reynolds and S. Rokkan (eds), *Locational Approaches to Power and Conflict*, Halsted Press, New York, pp. 233–74.

—— (1990). 'Towards Electoral Geography as the Politics of Place', in R.D. Dikshit (ed.), *Geography of Elections: The Indian Context*, Rawat Publications, Jaipur and New Delhi, pp. 484–93.

Rice, Stuart A. (1928). *Quantitative Methods in Politics*, Alfred A. Knopf, New York.

Roberts, M.C. and K.W. Rummage (1965). 'The Spatial Variations in Urban Left-Wing Voting in England and Wales, 1951', *Annals of the Association of American Geographers*, 55, pp. 161–78.

Robinson, W.S. (1950). 'Ecological Correlation and the Behaviour of Individuals', *American Sociological Review*, 15, pp. 351–57.

Rogerson, P.A. (2001). *Statistical Methods for Geography*, Sage Publications, London.

Rowley, G. (1969). 'Electoral Behaviour: A Note on Certain Recent Developments in Electoral Geography', *Professional Geographer*, 21 (6), pp. 398–400.

Roy, Meenu (1992). *The Battle of the Ballot*, Classic Publishing House, Jaipur.

—— (1999). *Elections 1998: A Continuity in Coalition*, National Publishing House, Jaipur and New Delhi.

—— (2000). *Electoral Politics in India: Election Process and Outcomes, Voting Behaviour and Current Trends*, Deep and Deep Publications Pvt. Ltd., New Delhi.

Sauer, O.O. (1918). 'Geography and the Gerrymander', *American Political Science Review*, 12, pp. 403–26.

Sharma, J.C. (1980). 'The Geography of Political Choice in Punjab (1952–1977): An Ecological Analysis of Patterns and Trends of Electoral Behaviour Based on Aggregate Data for Elections to the State Assembly', Unpublished Ph.D. Thesis, Punjabi University, Patiala.

—— (1982). 'The Indian Context and Geographical Study of Voting Behaviour', *Indian Geographical Studies*, 19, pp. 9–16.

—— (2003). 'Gerrymandering and Drawing of Assembly and Parliamentary Constituencies in India: A Case of Himachal Pradesh', *The National Geographical Journal of India*, 49 (4), pp. 9–16.

Sharma, J.C. and Ramesh Chand (2004). 'Levels of Consistency in Electoral Patterns in Assembly Elections of Himachal Pradesh (1977–1998)', *Geographical Review of India*, 66 (4), pp. 361–70.

Sharma, Kuldeep (1990). *Congress-I in Rajasthan Assembly Election (1977–80–85)*, Ph.D. Thesis, University of Rajasthan, Jaipur.

Sheth, D.L. (1970). 'Political Development of Indian Electorate', *Economic and Political Weekly*, 5, pp. 137–48.

Sheth, P.N. (1973). 'Indian Electoral Behaviour: Patterns of Continuity and Change', *Indian Journal of Political Science*, 34 (2), pp. 199–210.

Shukla, V.N. revised by Mahendra P. Singh (2001). *Constitution of India*, Eastern Book Company, Lucknow.

Siegfried, A. (1913). *Tableau Politique de la France de 1'Oueste*, A. Colin, Paris.

—— (1949). *Geographic Electorale de I'Ardeche Sous la IIIe Republique*, A. Colin, Paris.

Singh, C.P. (1978). 'Sixth General Election: A Geographical Analysis', Unpublished UGC Report, Delhi.

—— (1980). *The Seventh Parliamentary Election in India: A Geographical Analysis*, ICSSR Project Report, New Delhi.

—— (1981a). 'Geography and Electoral Studies', *Transactions of the Institute of Indian Geographers*, 3 (1), pp. 81–87.

—— (1981b). 'Indian Electoral Geography: Some Methodological Aspects', *Annals of the National Association of Geographers*, 1, pp. 105–08.

—— (2000). 'A Century of Constituency Delimitation in India', *Political Geography*, 19, pp. 517–32.Singh, R.L. (1971). *India: A Regional Geography*, NGSI, Varanasi.

Singh, R.P. (1981). *Electoral Politics in Manipur*, Concept Publishing Company, New Delhi.

Sinha, K. (1985). 'Measuring Party Competition: A New Approach', *Geographical Review of India*, 47, pp. 1–6.

Sinha, M. (1977). *Electoral Geography of India with Reference to Parliamentary Elections of 1971*, D. Phil. Thesis, Department of Geography, Allahabad University.

Sirsikar, V.M. (1962). 'The Study of Voting Behaviour in India: Limitations and Problems', *Political Science Review*, 2 (1), pp. 54–59.

—— (1965). *Politicai Behaviour in India*, Manaktalas, Bombay.

Smith, Howard R. and John F. Hart (1955). 'The American Tariff Map', *Geographical Review*, 45, pp. 327–46.

Soja, E.W. (1974). 'A Paradigm for the Geographical Analysis of Political System', in K.R. Cox, D.R. Reynolds and S. Rokkan (eds), *Locational Approaches to Power and Conflict*, Halsted Press, New York, pp. 43–72.

Srivastava, M. (1982). *Electoral Geography of an Indian State, Uttar Pradesh*, Atul Dissertations, Allahabad.

Statistical Reports of Lok Sabha Elections 1991 and 1998, Election Department, Rajasthan, Jaipur.

Statistical Reports of Vidhan Sabha Elections 1993 and 1998, Election Department, Rajasthan, Jaipur.

Sukhwal, B.L. (1971). *India: A Political Geography*, Allied Publishers, New Delhi.

Taylor, P.J. (1989). *Rethinking Electoral Geography*, Longman Scientific and Technical, London.

—— (1973). 'Some Implication of the Spatial Organization of Elections', *Transactions of the Institute of British Geographers*, 60, pp. 121–36.

—— (1977). *Quantitative Methods in Geography: An Introduction to Spatial Analysis* , Houghton Mifflin, Boston.

Taylor, P.J. and R.J. Johnston (eds) (1979). *Geography of Elections*, Penguin, Harmondsworth.

Thrift, N. (1983). 'On the Determination of Social Action in Space and Time', *Environment and Planning D: Society and Space*, 1, pp. 23–58.

Tripathy, P.P. and K.S. Padhy (1994). *Voting Behaviour of Tribals in India*, Saujanya Books, New Delhi.

Varma, S.P. and C.P. Bhambhri (eds) (1967). *Elections and Political Consciousness in India*, Meenakshi Prakashan, Meerut.

Varma, S.P. and Iqbal Narain (1968). *Fourth General Election in India*, Orient Longman, New Delhi.

—— (1973). *Voting Behaviour in a Changing Society*, National Publishers, New Delhi.

Weiner, Myron and J.O. Field (eds) (1974). *Studies in Electoral Politics in Indian States: The Communist Parties of West Bengal*, Vol. I, Manohar Book Service, New Delhi.

—— (1975a). *Studies in Electoral Politics in Indian States: Three Disadvantaged Sectors*, Vol. II, Manohar Book Service, New Delhi.

—— (1975b). *Studies in Electoral Politics in Indian States: Party Systems and Cleavages*, Vol. IV, Manohar Book Service, New Delhi.

—— (1977). *Studies in Electoral Politics in Indian States: The Impact of Modernization*, Vol. III, Manohar Book Service, New Delhi.

Weiner, Myron and J.O. Field (1975). 'How Tribal Constituencies in India Vote', in *Studies in Electoral Politics in Indian States: Three Disadvantaged Sectors*, Vol. II, Manohar Book Service, New Delhi.

—— (1977). 'India Urban Constituencies', in *Studies in Electoral Political in Indian States: The Impact of Modernization*, Vol. III, Manohar Book Service, New Delhi.

Weiner, W. and R. Kothari (eds) (1963). *Indian Voting Behaviour*, Mukhopadhyay, Calcutta.

Wheare, K.C. (1963). *Federal Government*, 4th edition, Oxford University Press, London.

Wright, J.K. (1932). 'Voting Habits in the United States: A Note on two Maps', *Geographical Review*, 22, pp. 666–72.

Websites

www.ceoraj.nic.in
www.eci.gov.in
www.rajelect.nic.in

Index